Dependent Industrialization
in Latin America

Rhys Owen Jenkins

The Praeger Special Studies program—utilizing the most modern and efficient book production techniques and a selective worldwide distribution network—makes available to the academic, government, and business communities significant, timely research in U.S. and international economic, social, and political development.

Dependent Industrialization in Latin America
The Automotive Industry in Argentina, Chile, and Mexico

PRAEGER SPECIAL STUDIES IN INTERNATIONAL ECONOMICS AND DEVELOPMENT

Praeger Publishers   New York   Washington   London

Library of Congress Cataloging in Publication Data

Jenkins, Rhys Owen, 1948-
    Dependent industrialization in Latin America.

    (Praeger special studies in international economics and
development)
    Includes bibliographical references and index.
    1. Automobile industry and trade—Argentine Republic.
2. Automobile industry and trade—Chile.   3. Automobile
industry and trade—Mexico.   4. International business enterprises.   I. Title.
HD9710.L32J45   338.4'7'6292098   76-25352
ISBN 0-275-23220-4

PRAEGER PUBLISHERS
111 Fourth Avenue, New York, N.Y. 10003, U.S.A.

Published in the United States of America in 1977
by Praeger Publishers, Inc.

To Ruth

Cuando sonó la trompeta, estuvo
todo preparado en la Tierra
y Jehová repartío el mundo
a Coca-Cola, Anaconda,
Ford Motor y otros entidades

When the trumpet sounds
All will have been made ready on earth
And Jehovah will divide the world
Among Coca-Cola, Anaconda,
Ford Motors and the others.

Pablo Neruda, <u>Canto General</u>

PREFACE

This study arose from a general concern with the problems of imperialism and underdevelopment, particularly as they affected Latin America. Many writers have contributed to our understanding of the operations of contemporary imperialism in Latin America at a theoretical level, but considerable empirical work still needs to be done to fill in the details of the mechanisms of imperialism. One fruitful approach to advance knowledge in this direction is the study of individual industries. The industry selected here, motor vehicles, is only one of many. Hopefully, in the future, similar studies will be undertaken.

The fieldwork on which this study is based was carried out during two separate visits to Latin America, the first of nine months in 1971-72, financed by the United Kingdom Social Science Research Council, and the second of three months in 1974, financed by the University of East Anglia. I am indebted to all the individuals and organizations, too numerous to mention, who assisted me during my visits to Latin America—officials of automotive companies, trade associations, and government agencies, as well as individual researchers. I am also grateful to Brian Van Arkadie, Charles Cooper, Chris Edwards, David Felix, D. G. Rhys, and Constantine Vaitsos, who read and commented on all or part of earlier versions of this study. My greatest intellectual debt is to Robin Murray, who supervised the doctoral thesis on which this study is based and who, despite many disagreements, provided me with the stimulus to complete the work. I am also indebted to the comrades of the Conference of Socialist Economists who first stimulated my interest in the theory of imperialism. Finally, I would like to thank the staff of the Institute of Development Studies at the University of Sussex library where much of this work was written.

CONTENTS

LIST OF TABLES AND FIGURES

LIST OF ABBREVIATIONS

ACARA	Asociación de Concesionarios de Automotores de la República Argentina
ACCIA	Asociación Chilena de Importadores de Automoviles
ADEFA	Asociación de Fabricas de Automotores (Argentina)
AMIA	Asociación Mexicana de la Industria Automotriz
ANDA	Asociación Mexicana de Distribuidores de Automóviles
ANFAVEA	Asociacão Nacional dos Fabricantes de Vehiculos Automotores
BCRA	Banco Central de la Republica Argentina
CAFA	Camara Argentina de Fabricantes de Automotores
CESO	Centro de Estudios Socio-Economicas de la Universidad de Chile
CFIA	Comisión para el Fomento de la Industria Automotriz (Chile)
CIF	Cost, insurance, and freight
CIFARA	Camara Industrial de Fabricantes de Autopiezas de la Republica Argentina
CKD	Completely knocked down (vehicles)
CONADE	Consejo Nacional de Desarrollo (Argentina)
CORFO	Corporación de Fomento (Chile)
DIRINCO	Dirección de Industria y Comercio (Chile)
ECLA	Economic Commission for Latin America
EEC	European Economic Community
FLACSO	Facultad Latinoamericana de Ciencias Sociales
FOB	Free on board
GEIA	Grupo Ejecutivo de la Industria Automovilistica (Brazil)
GDP	Gross domestic product
GNP	Gross national product
IASF	Industria Automotriz Santa Fe (Argentina)
ICHA	Instituto Chileno del Acero
IKA	Industrias Kaiser Argentina
ILDIS	Instituto Latinoamericano de Investigaciones Sociales
IME	Industrias Mecanicas del Estad
LAFTA	Latin American Free Trade Area
MITI	Ministry for International Trade and Industry (Japan)
NEDO	National Economic Development Office (United Kingdom)
ODEPLAN	Oficina de Planificación Nacional (Chile)
OECD	Organization for Economic Cooperation and Development
SKD	Semiknocked down (vehicles)
SMMT	Society of Motor Manufacturers and Traders
SOMEX	Sociedad Mexicana de Crédito Industrial
UDC	Underdeveloped country
UNCTAD	United Nations Conference on Trade and Development
UNIDO	United Nations Industrial Development Organization

Dependent Industrialization in Latin America

1

INTRODUCTION

The underdevelopment of Latin America can only be understood if the continent is seen in relation to the international economy of which it is an integral part and has been since the Conquest. This is not to assert that the external relationships are the determining factor in the development of the region, but rather that they form a conditioning situation that "determines the limits and possibilities of action and behaviour of men."[1] Because the internal dynamics of the Latin American economy has taken different forms in response to changes in the structure of the world economy, development and underdevelopment cannot be seen as two stages in a single growth path common to all societies. They are two sides of the same coin, part of a single system whose dynamics can only be explained in terms of their interaction. This broad perspective, which has been used by Latin American economists, sociologists, and political scientists to analyze the continent's underdevelopment, provides the framework within which this study is written. It is an attempt to see the way in which external relationships have manifested themselves in a specific instance over a short period of time, and the effect that this has had on the internal dynamics of the economy.

THE CONTEXT OF THE STUDY

The earliest form in which the link to the world economy established itself in Latin America was through the plunder of the conquistadores, which supplied a basis for primary accumulation in Europe during the early phase of capitalist development. The first two or so centuries of colonization saw the development of a series of mining cores and the export of gold and silver to Spain

1

that acted as an intermediary between Latin America and the rest of Europe.[2] The postindependence period of the nineteenth century saw the consolidation of what has become known in Economic Commission for Latin America (ECLA) terminology as "desarrollo hacia afuera," loosely translated as "foreign-oriented development." This traditional form of external dependence was characterized by monoexport for the world market from a primary producing enclave showing little integration with the local economy. Although regional differences existed within Latin America that affected the pattern of development in a number of ways, for example, in the impetus given to local manufacturing activities and the extent of local infrastructure development, the basic elements of the system remained the same. Internal expansion was dependent on the world market for the particular country's exports. In the event of a crisis, such as that of the early 1930s, or a gradual deterioration of the terms of trade, as occurred from about 1950, the dynamism of the economy was seriously impaired.

The first real break with this pattern of development came in the 1930s when a number of factors came together to initiate the so-called "desarrollo hacia adentro" (inward-oriented development). The world economic depression that led to a sharp fall in Latin American exports and to an adverse movement in the terms of trade, reducing the continent's capacity to import by more than 30 percent between 1930 and 1934,[3] was the major factor behind this change. In the most advanced Latin American countries* this provided a stimulus to a process of industrialization that had begun during the period of "desarrollo hacia afuera" and to a breakdown of the old oligarchic system of domination, already under pressure. Thus, although appearing as a sharp break with the past, the crisis of the 1930s only accentuated trends already evident both at the level of the international economy (the reversal of the upward trend in the import coefficient of the industrialized countries and the deterioration of primary product prices) and internally in Latin America (industrialization and the changing balance between different classes).[5]

After World War II the strategy of import-substituting industrialization was given a theoretical underpinning by ECLA, which saw it as a means of lessening the dependence of the Latin American

---

*Argentina, Brazil, Chile, Colombia, Mexico, and Uruguay, which began their industrialization at the end of the nineteenth century or in the early twentieth century. The need to distinguish these countries from those that did not begin their industrialization until after World War II has been emphasized by V. Bambirra.[4]

countries on the world economy through a reduction in the import coefficient. Only in the 1960s did it become evident that this very policy had led to the creation of "the new dependence."[6] This involved the penetration of the Latin American industrial structure by foreign capital and technology, either through direct investment or licensing agreements, and corresponded to a new phase in the integration of the world economy based on the operations of the multinational corporation.

The new forms of external dependence have a number of characteristic features. First, import substitution tends to take place in finished consumer goods, so that there has been a shift in the composition of Latin American imports away from such products toward capital goods, raw materials, and intermediate inputs. In 1968, imports of consumer goods for Latin America as a whole were only 16.2 percent of total imports (compared with 20.7 percent in 1955) and were less than 10 percent in Argentina, Brazil, and Colombia, while intermediates and raw materials came to 45.8 percent and capital goods were 37.5 percent of all imports.[7] This means an increased rigidity in imports that becomes very difficult to reduce when exports decline because they are now essential for the maintenance of capacity utilization and employment and for the expansion of productive capacity and the creation of new employment. Thus, although quantitatively (in terms of the import coefficient) dependence on foreign trade has been reduced, qualitatively (in terms of the structure of imports and hence the effect on internal growth) it has increased. As a result, it has been necessary to preserve a traditional export sector as a source of foreign exchange, especially in view of the limited development of manufactured exports.*

A second feature is the growing importance of foreign indebtedness in Latin America. Payments related to the presence of foreign capital (both private and public) are absorbing an increasing share of the continent's export earnings. This has risen from just over 20 percent in the early 1950s to more than 40 percent of total current income in the late 1960s.[9] Thus, as well as finding import requirements becoming increasingly rigid with the industrialization of the postwar period, the capacity to import has been compressed by having a growing burden of financial payments imposed upon it.

The latest phase in Latin America's relationship to the world economy has also been characterized by the increased importance of direct foreign investment in manufacturing industry, as opposed

---

*Exports of manufacturers, although increasing, accounted for only 7.5 percent of the region's total exports in 1968.[8]

to the traditional areas where it was located, mainly in the extractive industries and public utilities. The proportion of total U.S. investment in Latin America in the manufacturing sector increased from 6.3 percent in 1929 to 16.5 percent in 1950 to 20.3 percent in 1961, reaching a record level of 36.3 percent in 1971.[10] In the most industrialized countries of the region, Argentina, Brazil, and Mexico, a much higher proportion of U.S. investment was in the manufacturing sector, and in 1971 it was more than 60 percent of total U.S. investment in each of these countries.[11] U.S. investment accounted for only 49.1 percent of the total direct foreign investment in Latin America in 1950 and 59 percent of the total in 1969,[12] so that this trend is not necessarily representative. Nevertheless, what evidence exists suggests that the share of European investment in manufacturing is also increasing. In the case of British investments in Latin America, manufacturing increased its share from 56.3 percent in 1962 to 68 percent in 1968.[13]

This trend is reflected in the growing participation of foreign capital and technology in the manufacturing sector, which has aroused considerable concern in Latin America. The increasing involvement of foreign technology is indicated by the rapid growth of technical assistance and royalty payments in recent years. It has been estimated that payments for technology grew at an annual average rate of 27 percent in Argentina (1965-70), 21 percent in Brazil (1965-69), and 15 percent in Mexico (1953-68).[14] The use of foreign technology is even more extensive than the penetration of foreign capital. For example, in Chile, one study of 281 large firms found that while 43 percent of the firms had some foreign shareholding, a further 17 percent with no foreign capital paid royalties.[15]

The growth of foreign investment has tended to attract more attention than foreign technology because of the displacement of national firms that it has involved.

> The inflow of private foreign capital in the form of direct investment or in association with national enterprises, while constituting a contribution of capital and often of technical know-how, represents excessively stiff competition for national investors, who have gradually been displaced from those industrial activities that offer the best financial prospects. Thus the initial capital contribution usually severely limits the ultimate possibility of capital formation by national entrepreneurs.[16]

There is considerable evidence of the extent of penetration of Latin American manufacturing by foreign capital in the 1960s. In 1964, foreign firms in Argentina accounted for 28 percent of indus-

trial output,[17] while in Brazil, four years earlier, foreign capital
controlled an estimated 31 percent of industry.[18] Not surprisingly,
considering its proximity to the dominant world capitalist power,
the most heavily penetrated of the major Latin American economies
is Mexico, where, by 1970, according to one estimate, multinational
corporations accounted for 34.9 percent of industrial production.[19]
In Chile, foreign companies accounted for 20.3 percent of the total
share capital of all manufacturing Sociedades Anonimas in the year
before the Unidad Popular government came to power.[20] Thus, it
appears that between one fifth and one third of industry in a number
of Latin American countries is in the hands of foreign capital.
R. Vernon estimates that, for the continent as a whole, about one
sixth of manufacturing sales is accounted for by U.S. subsidiaries,[21]
to which must be added European and Japanese investment, suggesting
that the share of all foreign firms would be around 25 to 30 percent.
     The tendency for foreign firms to increase their participation
in Latin American manufacturing is the local manifestation of the
internationalization of capital that has occurred during the past two
decades. In Chile, during the late 1960s, foreign firms increased
their participation in the total share capital from 16.6 percent in
1966 to 20.3 percent in 1969, while in Mexico one study found that
foreign firms increased their share of production from 19.6 percent
in 1962 to 27.6 percent in 1970.[22] Although no data are available
on changes in foreign participation for industry as a whole, the
share of foreign firms in the sales of Argentina's largest 100 firms
increased from less than half in 1956 to two thirds in 1971, at the
same time as increasing concentration raised the share of the largest
hundred in total production.
     The process of denationalization can take three forms. One
form is the direct takeover of locally owned firms by foreign groups.
As Table 1.1 indicates, the proportion of new subsidiaries formed
by acquisitions of existing firms has increased sharply, particularly
since the late 1950s. This trend is particularly marked in the most
advanced countries of the region where there is a considerable
nucleus of preexisting locally owned industry. Some writers have
gone so far as to compile lists of firms taken over by foreign enterprises in Argentina and Brazil during the 1960s.[23] These amount
to more than 50 acquisitions in each case and do not pretend to be
exhaustive. They are particularly concentrated in advanced technology sectors, such as the automotive industry, chemicals, pharmaceuticals, and machinery and metallurgical products.
     The second form taken by denationalization is that of a competi-
tive struggle that drives local firms out of a particular industry.
Over time there tends to be increasing concentration in most of the
newly established import-substituting industries that takes the form

TABLE 1.1

Number of New Manufacturing Subsidiaries of
U.S. Multinational Corporations in Latin America

	Pre-1946	1946-57	1958-67
Latin America			
Total	206	340	750
Acquisitions	47	97	331
Argentina			
Total	45	34	79
Acquisitions	11	13	42
Mexico			
Total	46	90	216
Acquisitions	9	31	116

Source: J. W. Vaupel and J. P. Curhan, The Making of Multinational Enterprise: A Sourcebook of Tables Based on a Study of
187 Major U.S. Manufacturing Companies (Cambridge: Harvard
University Graduate School of Business Administration, 1969),
p. 256.

of the displacement of nationally owned firms by the multinational
corporations with their superior financial, technological, or managerial resources. This phenomenon of denationalization within a sector
has not been studied in any great detail, but appears to have occurred
in the pharmaceuticals industry, and, as will be discussed later, in
the automotive industry to some extent.[24]

Finally, the location of foreign investment in the fastest growing
sectors of industry means that the natural process of differential
growth rates alone leads to an increasing penetration by foreign
capital. There is ample empirical evidence of such a concentration
of foreign investment, which also, incidentally, suggests that global
figures for the share of foreign subsidiaries in the manufacturing
sector tend to underestimate their strategic significance. As
Table 1.2 shows, foreign firms account for more than half of the
invested capital or output in a number of industries in each of the
major Latin American economies. Despite the different universe
taken in the studies represented, the table shows the same sectors
turning up time and time again: rubber, transport equipment,
tobacco, and pharmaceuticals.

The tendency for foreign subsidiaries to be large firms also
adds to their strategic significance. Thus, typically, the share of
foreign capital in the output of the larger firms in a particular

TABLE 1.2

Industries in Which the Participation of Foreign Subsidiaries Is Greater than 50 Percent

Argentina	Brazil	Chile	Mexico	Venezuela
Rubber	Rubber	Tobacco	Rubber	Rubber
Pharmaceuticals	Chemicals	Rubber	Tobacco	Electrical equipment
Vehicles and parts	Machinery	Transport equipment	Pharmaceuticals	Transport equipment
Tractors	Electrical products		Nonelectrical machinery	
"Frigorificos"	Pharmaceuticals		Electrical machinery	
	Vehicles and parts		Transport equipment	
	Other (including tobacco)			

Sources: Argentina: Share of value of production for all industry, 1964, from Consejo Nacional de Desarrollo (CONADE), La Concentración en la Industria Argentina en 1964 (Buenos Aires, 1969), pp. 71–78. Brazil: Share of assets of 500 largest manufacturing firms, late 1960s, from F. Fajnzylber, Sistema Industrial y Exportación de Manufacturas, ECLA (E/CN.12/), 1970, Table 2.7. Chile: Share of assets of all manufacturing limited companies, 1968–69, from G. Gassic, "Concentración, Entrelazamiento y Desnacionalización en la Industria Manufacturera," unpublished (Documento de Trabajo, CESO), 1971, Table 38. Mexico: Share of production for all industry, 1970, from F. Fajnzylber and T. Martínez Tarrago, Las Empresas Transnacionales, Expansión a Nivel Mundial y Proyección en la Industria Mexicana (Versión Preliminar) (Mexico, 1975), p. 256. Venezuela: Share of paid-up capital of all firms employing more than 100 persons, 1966, from CORDIPLAN, II Encuesta Industrial (Caracas, 1968).

7

country is higher than its share of the output of all firms. In Argentina, for example, whereas in 1963 it was estimated that foreign firms accounted for 22.8 percent of industrial production,[25] a few years later it was found that within the group of the largest 50 firms in the country their share was 51 percent.[26] Similarly, in Mexico, the share of production accounted for by foreign firms rose from 26.7 percent for a group of 938 firms to 47 percent for the largest 100.[27]

These, then, are the characteristic features of what has come to be known as the "new dependence." In the last few years, a number of global studies of the extent of foreign capital penetration in various Latin American economies have given empirical substance to what were previously little more than vague generalizations, concerning, for example, the domination of dynamic sectors of the economy by foreign capital.[28] There has also been a vast literature of a theoretical nature on the economic, sociological, and political aspects of dependence that has refined further the general concepts and analytical framework used. The main criticism of the theory is that it has remained at a high level of generality and abstraction. Those empirical studies that have been undertaken within its framework, at least as far as economic studies are concerned, have confined themselves to analyzing what has been described above as the characteristic feature of dependence, that is, its phenomenal form. What are missing are concrete studies of the mechanisms involved in the new relationship between Latin America and the world economy, and a working through of the implications of these mechanisms for the development of the region.[29]

THE INDUSTRY AS A FOCUS FOR STUDY

This study is an attempt to make more specific those mechanisms that integrate Latin America with the world economy and the way in which the region has been conditioned by the development and expansion of the advanced industrialized countries. The choice of an industry as the field for study requires some explanation, however. One may contrast it with two alternatives, either the study of the economy as a whole or the study of the individual firm. A number of global studies of Latin American economies have already been undertaken, but, as was suggested in the previous section, these have failed to go beyond a fairly descriptive analysis of the main features of dependence. This is a consequence of imposing an artificial framework, that of the nation-state, on the analysis of what is essentially an international phenomenon. This is to say that dependence is not a bilateral relationship between, say

Mexico and the developed world, but a much more complicated multi-lateral relationship within a single world system. The second problem of such an approach is that it loses the variety of mechanisms involved in the relationship by looking at global aggregates. These mechanisms are, at least in part, specific to individual industries and can only be examined in detail through a number of industry studies.30

The other alternative is to look at the operations of the individual firm. As has been pointed out by C. Palloix, this, too, is an inappropriate level at which to analyze the process of internationalization (and hence dependence, which is an aspect of this process), the reason being that it confines key factors, such as the market, to the theoretical level as explanations that are not themselves explained.31 This is particularly obvious in the work of Vernon, who explains the development of multinational enterprises in terms of exogenous factors, such as the protection of markets and the search for raw materials.32 The individual firm is no more an appropriate focus for the analysis of internationalization than it is for the study of concentration within a particular economy. In the chapters that follow, it will be argued that the process of competition within an industry is an essential factor in explaining the features of the "new dependence."

The advantage of an industry study is that it gives a well-defined field for analysis at the international level that can be articulated with the periphery, avoiding both the extremes of generality of a global study and of specificity of a firm study. It brings out the way in which multinational corporations are established and consolidated and makes it possible to study the operations of the international oligopoly. Factors normally exogenous, such as competition between firms, concentration, and denationalization, can be considered as endogenous. Such an approach is able to go beyond the examination of forms (patterns of investment in the case of country studies or organizational setups in the case of firm studies) to look at dynamic processes.

At the same time, one must recognize the limitations and dangers inherent in choosing the industry as the focus of study. J. Schumpeter, in discussing capitalist development, summarizes the problem:

> Since we are dealing with an organic process, analysis
> of what happens in any particular part of it—say, in an
> individual concern or industry—may indeed clarify
> details of mechanisms but is inconclusive beyond that.
> Every piece of business strategy acquires its true signi-
> ficance only against the background of that process and
> within the situation created by it.33

In discussing the automotive industry in the following chapters, it must always be borne in mind that it is part of the global process of dependent industrial development that has been sketched out in the preceding pages. As Schumpeter adds later, "the problem that is usually being visualized is how capitalism administers existing structures whereas the relevant problem is how it creates and destroys them. As long as this is not recognized, the investigator does a meaningless job."[34]

THE CHOICE OF A SPECIFIC INDUSTRY

A number of factors led to the choice of automobiles as the industry to be studied. In the first place, it is a quantitatively important sector in terms of the proportion of industrial value added that it generates, both in the advanced industrial countries and in those Latin American countries where it has been developed to the fullest extent, namely, Argentina, Brazil, and Mexico.* The importance of the industry as far as foreign investment is concerned is even more pronounced. The transport equipment sector, of which the automotive industry is the major component, accounted for 20.6 percent of the total sales of U.S. manufacturing affiliates in Latin America in 1966.[36] In Argentina almost 20 percent of the foreign investment approved by the government between 1958 and 1969 was in the transport equipment industry.[37] In Chile the same sector accounted for almost 10 percent of the total funds received from abroad by subsidiaries and affiliates of multinational corporations between 1961 and 1969,[38] and in Mexico it represented 16 percent of gross fixed investment by foreign firms in the industrial sector.[39]

Another indicator of the importance of the automotive industry from the point of view of the multinational corporation is the share of the industry in the total payments made by the various countries for foreign technology. In Argentina the automotive industry accounted for 37 percent of all royalty payments in 1970.[40] The proportion was even higher in Brazil where the terminal industry alone paid 46.3 percent and, together with the parts industry, 55.3 percent of the total in the late 1960s.[41] In Mexico and Chile the fact that a significant proportion of the parts used in the automotive industry is still imported makes royalty payments less important

---

*In Argentina and Brazil the industry accounts for about 12 percent of industrial production, and in Mexico for over 6 percent. See Chapter 3. In Britain the industry accounted for about 7.5 percent of the gross output of manufacturing in 1963.[35]

TABLE 1.3

Ranking of Automotive Manufacturers Among
Largest Firms, 1970

United States	General Motors (1)	Ford (3)	Chrysler (8)
United Kingdom	British Leyland (8)	Ford (12)	Vauxhall (59)
France	Renault (1)	Peugeot (14)	Citroen (17)
West Germany	Volkswagen (1)	Daimler-Benz (4)	Opel (19)
Japan	Toyota (3)	Nissan (8)	Honda (17)
Argentina	Fiat (2)	Ford (6)	General Motors (10)
Brazil	Volkswagen (2)	General Motors (6)	Ford (8)
Mexico	Automex (12)	Ford (13)	DINA (17)

Source: United States, United Kingdom, France, West Germany, and Japan
from the London Times Index of Leading Companies; Argentina from Mercado;
Brazil from Quem e Quem na Economica Brasileira, August 1973; and Mexico
from Ceceña, Anexo 1.

as a means of transferring funds. In Mexico the automotive industry
accounted for almost 12 percent of total royalty payments in 1968,[42]
while in Chile they are extremely low.

The automotive industry has exhibited a substantial internationalization of capital during the postwar period that has been
reflected in a rapid growth of both manufacturing and assembly
operations in Latin America since the mid-1950s. It seems particularly suitable, therefore, as an industry in which to study the relationship of the region to the world economy and its consequences.

Another reason for choosing this particular industry is that it
is dominated at the international level by a relatively small number
of large firms. In each country where they operate, the automotive
manufacturers are among the largest firms, both in the developed
world and in the more advanced Latin American countries. (See
Table 1.3.) This not only serves to underline the importance of the
industry in each of these countries but also makes it easier to cope
with the analysis. Since ten companies account for 82 percent of
the world's vehicle output, it makes it possible to build up a picture
of the industry as a whole from individual company data in a way
that would not be possible with an industry having a large number
of firms.

A final reason for choosing the automotive industry is that it
represents a well-defined sector with a particular product or a
limited number of products. Therefore, it does not pose the same
practical problems as would an industry with a much more diversified
output, such as chemicals. Moreover, the fact that for all the major
companies in the industry vehicle production is their main or only
activity means that certain problems are avoided (at least to some

extent) in the use of company data. The small number of firms and products is also the main reason for limiting the study to the terminal industry, and only considering the parts and components industry in passing in relation to it, since the parts industry is highly diversified both in terms of the firms that comprise it and the products that it produces.

NOTES

1. T. Dos Santos, "The Crisis of Development Theory and the Problem of Dependence in Latin America," in Underdevelopment and Development: The Third World Today, ed. H. Bernstein (New York: Penguin, 1973), p. 77.

2. S. J. and B. H. Stein, The Colonial Heritage of Latin America: Essays in Economic Dependence in Perspective (New York: Oxford University Press, 1970), pp. 3-27.

3. Economic Commission for Latin America (ECLA), Economic Survey of Latin America, 1949 (E/CN. 12/164/Rev. 1), 1951, Table 28.

4. V. Bambirra, "Integración Monopólica Mundial e Industrialización: Sus Contra–dicciones," Sociedad y Desarrollo 1 (1972): 53-55.

5. See C. Furtado, Economic Development of Latin America: A Survey from Colonial Times to the Cuban Revolution, trans. S. Macedo (C.U.P., 1970), pp. 39-42, for the changes in the international economy; F. Cardoso and E. Faletto, Dependencia y Desarrollo en América Latina: Ensayo de Interpretación Sociológica (Mexico City: Siglo XXI, 3rd ed., 1971), pp. 54-101; and A. Bianchi, "Introducción: Notas sobre la Teoría del Desarrollo Económico Latinoamericano," in Ensayos de Interpretación Económica, ed. A. Bianchi (Santiago: Editorial Universitaria, 1969), pp. 17-31, on industrialization before 1930.

6. T. Dos Santos, El Nuevo Carácter de la Dependencia (Santiago: Centro de Estudios Socio-económicos, 1968).

7. ECLA, Economic Survey of Latin America, 1970 (E/CN. 12/868/Rev. 1), 1971, Table 71.

8. ECLA, Economic Survey, 1970, op. cit., Table 69.

9. O. Caputo and R. Pizarro, Imperialismo, Dependencia y Relaciones Económicas Internacionales (Santiago: Centro de Estudios socio-económicas, 1970), Table II-6. See also A. G. Frank, "Invisible Foreign Services or National Economic Development," in Latin America: Underdevelopment or Revolution, Essays on the Development of Underdevelopment and the Immediate Enemy (New York: Monthly Review Press, 1969), pp. 181-91.

10. ECLA, External Financing in Latin America
(E/CN. 12/649/Rev. 1), 1965, Table 15; and U.S., Department of
Commerce, Survey of Current Business (various issues).

11. U.S., Department of Commerce, Survey of Current
Business 53 (1972).

12. ECLA, Economic Survey of Latin America, 1971
(E/CN. 12/935/Rev. 1), 1972, Table 8.

13. Board of Trade Journal (various issues).

14. United Nations, Conference on Trade and Development
(UNCTAD), Major Issues Arising from the Transfer of Technology
to Developing Countries (TD/B/AC. 11/10), 1972, Table III-3.

15. E. Acevedo and H. Vérgara, "Concentración y Capital
Extranjera en la Industria Chilena," Economía y Administración,
no. 15 (1970), Table 12.

16. "Industrial Development in Latin America," EBLA 14
(1969).

17. Cuadernos de Cicso, El Poder Económico en la Argentina
(Buenos Aires: Cicso, n.d.), Table 9.

18. Ruben Medina, Desnacionalização: Crime Contra o
Brasil? (Sao Paulo: Editôra Saga, 1970).

19. F. Fajnzylber and T. Martinez Tarrago, Las Empresas
Transnacionales, Expansión a Nivel Mundial y Proyección en la
Industria Mexicana, mimeographed (Versión Preliminar)(México,
Centro de Investigacion y Docencia Economica, 1975), p. 258.

20. L. Pacheco, "La Inversión Extranjera y las Corporaciones
Internacionales en el Desarrollo Industrial Chileno," in Proceso a la
Industrialización Chilena, CEPLAN (Santiago: Ediciones Nueva
Universidad, 1972), Table 2.

21. R. Vernon, Sovereignty at Bay, the Multinational Spread
of U.S. Engerprises (New York: Penguin, 1973), p. 34.

22. B. Sepulveda and A. Chumacero, La Inversión Extranjera
en México (Mexico City: Fondo de Cultura Económica, 1973), Table
14. It is not clear why the estimate for 1970 is lower than that
previously quoted.

23. E. Galeano, "The Denationalization of Brazilian Industry,"
Monthly Review 22 (1969): 11-30; and Rogelio Garcia Lupo, Contra
la Ocupación Extranjera, 3rd ed. (Buenos Aires: Editorial Centro,
1971), pp. 177-78.

24. See Furtado, op. cit., on the pharmaceuticals industry,
p. 176.

25. Consejo Nacional de Desarollo (CONADE), La Concentración en la Industria Argentina en 1964 (Buenos Aires, 1969),
pp. 71-78.

26. G. Martorell, Las Inversiones Extranjeras en la Argentina
(Buenos Aires: Editorial Galerna, 1969), Chap. 6.

27. Ricardo Cinta G., "Burgesía Nacional y Desarrollo," in El Perfil de México en 1980, vol. 3, Instituto de Investigaciones Sociales, Universidad Nacional Autónoma de México (Mexico City: Siglo XXI, 1972), Table 10.

28. In addition to the studies already quoted, see F. Gasparian, "The Internationalization of the Brazilian Economy," mimeographed, on Brazil; L. Pacheco, "La Inversión Extranjera en la Industria Chilena" (Diss., University of Chile, 1970), on Chile; J. A. Mayobre, Las Inversiones Extranjeras en Venezuela (Caracas: Monte Avila Editores, 1970), on Venezuela; and J. L. Ceceña, México en la Órbita Imperial (Mexico City: Ediciones "El Caballito," 1970), on Mexico.

29. For a similar criticism, see P. O'Brien, "A Critique of Latin American Theories of Dependency," in Beyond the Sociology of Development, ed. I. Oxaal, T. Barnett, D. Booth (London: Routledge Kegan Paul, 1975), pp. 7-27.

30. See, for example, Vaitsos' findings on the use of different mechanisms for transferring profits abroad in different industries. C. V. Vaitsos, Transfer of Resources and Preservation of Monopoly Rents, Economic Development Report No. 168 (Cambridge: Harvard University, Development Advisory Service, 1970).

31. C. Palloix, Note de Recherche sur le Proces d'Internationalisation, mimeographed (Grenoble, 1972), p. 11.

32. See the comments of Palloix in R. Vernon, "Future of the Multinational Enterprise," in C. P. Kindleberger, The International Corporation: A Symposium (Cambridge, Mass: MIT Press, 1970); Palloix, op. cit., pp. 8-9.

33. J. Schumpeter, Capitalism, Socialism and Democracy, 4th ed. (London: Allen & Unwin, 1954), pp. 83-84.

34. Ibid.

35. See National Economic Development Office, Motor Manufacturing E.D.C., The Effect of Government Policy on the Motor Industry (M.M.S.O., 1968), p. 6.

36. H. K. May, The Effects of U.S. and Other Foreign Investment in Latin America (New York: Council for Latin America, 1970), Table 5.

37. S. M. MacDonnell and M. R. Lascano, La Industria Automotriz, Aspectos Económicas y Fiscales (Buenos Aires: Departmento de Estudios, Division Planes, 1974), p. 1.

38. UNCTAD, Major Issues Arising from the Transfer of Technology: A Case Study of Chile (TD/B/AC.11/20), 1974, Table 15.

39. Sepulveda and Chumacero, op. cit., Tables 12 and 13.

40. B. C. Raddavero, "Análisis de la Transferencia de la Tecnología Externa a la Industria Argentina," Economica 18 (1972): 367-88.

41. ECLA, <u>The Transfer of Technology in the Industrial Development of Brazil: General Aspects of the Problem</u> (E/CN. 12/937), 1974, Table 6.

42. UNCTAD, <u>Major Issues in Transfer of Technology to Developing Countries: Addendum</u> (TD/B/AC 11/10/Add. 1), 1972, p. 30.

2

THE INTERNATIONAL
AUTOMOTIVE INDUSTRY

In this chapter the development of the automotive industry is traced back to the early twentieth century. The opening section analyzes the growth of a mass production industry in a few centers, namely, the United States and Western Europe, up to World War II. In the following sections the changes observed in the industry in the postwar period, at both the national and international levels, are described and explained. This later period, which is of central interest from the point of view of this thesis, it will be argued, has been characterized by the emergence of a world industry dominated by a few international firms. It is no longer possible to analyze the development of the automotive industry in a particular country without taking this fact into account. An understanding of the growth and structure of the Latin American automotive industry hinges on the nature of oligopolistic competition at the international level.

THE AUTOMOTIVE INDUSTRY BEFORE
WORLD WAR II

In the early stages of the industry's development, its technology was fairly simple, scales of production low, and capital requirements small. In the United States, car producers were, in the main, assemblers that bought most of their parts and components from outside suppliers. Even in Britain, where the supplier industry was less well developed, "it was not difficult to enter the industry. A knowledge of general engineering techniques and a modest amount of capital were all that were required."[1] In the United States it has been estimated that there were 181 companies in the industry during the early 1900s,[2] while in Britain, 198 different makes of

16

cars had been put on the market up to 1913, of which over 100 quickly disappeared.[3] This period corresponds to the initial phase in the introduction of a new product as described in the product cycle theory, characterized in the literature by high unit costs, labor-intensive production processes, and short runs.[4]

The major technological innovation that changed this was the introduction of mass production by Henry Ford, coinciding as it did with the changeover from wood to metal bodies around 1910 in the United States.[5] Europe, with its smaller, less standardized markets, was slower than the United States in adopting these techniques. Mass production methods did not begin to be introduced until the 1920s and then not on such an impressive scale as on the other side of the Atlantic. In the mid-1930s, large pressed items were first used, increasing scale requirements considerably.

The consequences of the assembly line were felt throughout the world automotive industry. Between 1909 and 1921, Ford increased his output from 12,000 to almost 2 million cars a year and his share of the U.S. market from 10 to 55 percent.[6] In the five-year period following the introduction of the conveyor belt, he was able to make a 50 percent saving in the production costs of the Model T. In order to achieve this expansion, the price of the Model T was cut to less than one third of its initial level over a period of several years. At the same time, for the American automotive industry as a whole, the capital-labor ratio index rose sharply from 58.5 in 1909 to 93.6 in 1919 (1929 = 100).[7] In Britain, too, similar trends became evident from the mid-1920s onward, although not on such a spectacular scale. The Society of Motor Manufacturers and Traders (SMMT) index of prices, however, fell from 100 in 1924 to 52 ten years later.[8]

As a result, the interwar period saw a considerable increase in concentration in both the United States and Western Europe. The number of firms in the industry fell from the early 1920s in both Britain and the United States. In the latter it declined from 108 in 1923, to 44 in 1927, to 35 in 1931, and to only 12 in 1941,[9] and General Motors, Ford, and Chrysler accounted for 75 percent of the market by 1929, increasing in 1930 to 90 percent. In Britain the number fell from 88 in 1922 to 31 in 1929 and 22 by 1938.[10] Three firms (Morris, Austin, and Singer) accounted for 75 percent of output in 1929 and in 1938 six firms produced 90 percent of the total. Similar trends appeared in the other two major producing countries, France and Germany. Here the industry was even more fragmented than in Britain during the early 1920s, with 150 firms in France (1921) and more than 200 in Germany (1925). Significant levels of concentration were attained by the late 1920s in France, where three firms made 68 percent of sales in 1928, and the late

1930s in Germany where by 1937 three firms produced 74 percent of all cars.[11]

Undoubtedly, the main factor behind the increased concentration of the interwar period was the new technology of mass production. The comments of G. Maxcy and A. Silberston in their classic study of the British automotive industry sum up this process neatly and apply with equal force to the other major producing countries:

The factor that sealed the fate of the smaller concerns was the growth of mass production techniques on the part of companies such as Morris and Austin which had succeeded in producing models that were successful with the public. . . . [and further] The concentration of some 75 percent of car production in the hands of these manufacturers and the elimination of many small producers during the 1920s had been brought about by the competitive pressure exerted by a few rapidly expanding companies benefiting from the economies of scale that accompanied the introduction of elementary mass-production techniques.[12]

A secondary factor leading to intensified competition in the European automotive industry was the entry of subsidiaries of Ford and General Motors into the British and German industries during the 1920s.[13] In the United States a change in the nature of the car market to become primarily a replacement market from the mid-1920s onward led to a slowdown in the rate of growth of the industry and intensified competition for market shares. (Peak output was attained in 1929 and was not surpassed until after World War II.)

Thus, the rise in concentration during the interwar years can be explained in terms of the classic mechanism of competition with increasing returns. Economies of scale and technical progress combine to give the largest and fastest growing firms a cost advantage, which enables them to expand further and faster than their competitors. The introduction of mass production considerably increased the scale at which costs were minimized and this, reinforced by the other factors tending to increase competition, created the concentration movement observed.

The development of the industry in the major producing countries was reflected internationally in several ways. The earlier introduction of mass production techniques in the United States meant that the U.S. firms enjoyed a considerable competitive advantage over the European producers in the years immediately after World War I. This led the European countries to adopt tariffs and other measures to protect their infant automotive industries against U.S. competition. This created an international structure, with the United States, Britain, France, Germany, and Italy dominating as exporters while at the same time enjoying virtually isolated domestic markets. International trade in vehicles, therefore, was almost exclusively directed toward the less industrialized countries.[14]

The same factors that led to increased concentration within national boundaries also caused firms to look for new markets. The preferred form of expansion was through exports, although some assembly plants were set up during this period. In 1929, the U.S. companies exported 536,000 vehicles, to which can be added a further 200,000 or more assembled abroad. In the same year the foreign sales of the four main European producing countries came to only 122,000, all through exports.[15] This brings out both the dominance of exports vis-a-vis foreign assembly operations and of the United States vis-a-vis Europe. The introduction of mass production in Europe improved the continent's competitive position and increased its share of world exports from 15 percent in 1929 to 40 percent by 1938. This did not represent a significant intensification of competition at the international level, however. Britain, for example, only exported 15 percent of its car output in 1938, and 75 percent of this was to areas where the United Kingdom enjoyed tariff preferences.[16]

CONCENTRATION IN THE POSTWAR PERIOD

Since World War II there have been further increases in concentration in each of the major car-producing countries. In the United States the independents, those companies other than the Big Three (General Motors, Ford, and Chrysler), managed to obtain about 22 percent of the total market in the early postwar years. This was made possible by the shortage of both new and used cars in this period, following several years with virtually no production. With the return to normal market conditions in 1953, however, their share fell sharply to only 7.6 percent.* This led to a spate of mergers, first between Kaiser-Frazer and Willys-Overland in 1953, followed a year later by the Nash-Hudson and the Studebaker-Packard mergers.[18] In 1963, Studebaker-Packard stopped production in the United States, and, in 1970, Kaiser-Willys, which had stopped

---

*In the immediate postwar years, secondhand cars were selling at above the list price for new cars, and as late as 1952 car dealers were selling new cars at list prices and making a profit on their used car resales, all of which indicate abnormal market conditions.[17]

producing cars during the 1950s, sold its remaining jeep operations to American Motors (the outcome of the Nash-Hudson merger), the only surviving independent.

The same process has been evident throughout Europe and has intensified considerably since 1960. A number of small European producers either have gone out of business or have been taken over by their larger competitors. Concentration seems to be tending toward a situation in which each major producing country has one nationally owned firm dominating the market, competing against a number of smaller foreign subsidiaries.

This process has reached its logical conclusion in the United Kingdom, where British Leyland is now the only major locally owned automotive manufacturer and competes against the subsidiaries of the U.S. Big Three, Ford, Vauxhall, and Chrysler. The formation of a major British company dates back to the early 1950s when the merger of Austin and Morris created the British Motor Corporation, but it is only since 1960 that virtually all the independent British companies, that is, those that are not American subsidiaries, have been brought under one roof. In 1960, the four leading producers accounted for 82.7 percent of British car production, and now four firms dominate the entire industry, with only a few thousand units produced by specialists, such as Rolls Royce and Aston Martin.

The early 1960s saw a number of mergers and takeovers (see Figure 2.1). Jaguar took over Daimler and Guy in 1960 and 1961, respectively. In 1960, too, Leyland made its first venture into the passenger car field by taking over Standard-Triumph International, and in the following year it merged with ACV, its major rival in heavy trucks. In 1966, the industry was further consolidated through the BMC-Jaguar merger and the takeover of Rover, which had previously absorbed Alvis, by Leyland. Finally, in 1968, British Motor Holdings (the product of the BMC-Jaguar merger) and Leyland merged, with considerable government encouragement, to form the British Leyland Motor Corporation. These mergers were not sufficient, however, to create a viable British automotive company, and, in 1975, the government was forced to intervene directly by taking a shareholding in the firm.

At the same time, the U.S. companies were tightening their hold on the British automotive industry. General Motors had held all Vauxhall's shares since the 1920s. In 1960, Ford bought out the 45 percent of British Ford's shares held by minority shareholders in order to "obtain greater operational flexibility and enable us better to co-ordinate our European and American manufacturing facilities and integrate further our product lines and operations on a world-wide basis."[19] In retrospect it can be seen that this was an important step in the internationalization of the automotive industry.

FIGURE 2.1

The Formation of British Leyland, 1960-68

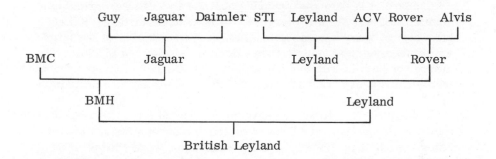

Source: Compiled by the author.

Four years later Chrysler gained a foothold in the British
market through buying up 30 percent of Rootes' shares. Since then,
it has increased its participation, first to give it overall control
(despite initial resistance from the British government) and eventually
almost complete ownership.

France had already achieved a high degree of concentration by
1960, with 96.1 percent of passenger car output being accounted for
by four firms, so that concentration during the 1960s and early 1970s
was not as marked as in Britain. It did, however, see the elimination of Facel-Vega in 1964 and the disappearance of Panhard as an
independent make, so that, in 1973, Renault, Citroen, Peugeot, and
Simca accounted for all French car production save some 4,000 units.
More significant, however, were the changes in ownership of Simca
and Citroen during this period. Chrysler had already obtained a
minority holding in Simca in 1958; in 1963, it achieved majority
control and since then has increased its share further. Citroen has
experienced a series of difficulties as an independent company, and,
in 1968, Fiat obtained a 15 percent share in the company, but General
de Gaulle vetoed the Italian company's attempt to gain control. Although Fiat was able to increase its holding to 49 percent during the
early 1970s, it subsequently divested itself of its holding. In 1974,
heavy losses by Citroen led to a government-sponsored takeover of
its car operations by Peugeot and a merger of its commercial
vehicle subsidiary, Berliet, with Renault's Saviem. These moves,
together with the close cooperation between Peugeot and Renault,
which have a number of jointly owned factories producing parts and

components, suggest that the French car industry is moving toward a situation in which there is one major national firm as in Britain.

The 1950s and 1960s also saw a dramatic reduction in the number of French commercial vehicle producers, with firms such as Chenard et Walker disappearing completely. There were also a number of takeovers and mergers, such as those involving Salmson and Saviem, Delahaye and Hotchkiss, and the takeover of the largest French commercial vehicle firm, Berliet, by Citroen in 1967. The merger of Berliet with Saviem reduced the number of firms producing medium and heavy trucks to two, the other being Unic, a subsidiary of Fiat.

In 1960, four firms in Germany accounted for 86.9 percent of total car production, and here again there has been further concentration, so that by 1973 these same companies were producing 94.0 percent of German output. The main stimulus to concentration has been Volkswagen's failure to expand its range from the Beetle on which it has relied for so long. This has led the company to collect other German firms in an attempt to diversify its product line. In 1964, it bought a half share in Auto Union, which had previously been completely owned by Daimler-Benz, and, in 1966, took full ownership of the company. In 1969, NSU, which had been responsible for the development of the Wankel engine, was taken over. Volkswagen also has a joint company with Porsche. With Borgward's failure in 1961 and BMW's takeover of Hans Glas in 1967, there remain three German companies, Volkswagen, Daimler-Benz, and BMW, competing against the subsidiaries of General Motors and Ford.

A similar increase in concentration has occurred in the commercial vehicle industry in Germany. In 1969, Daimler-Benz strengthened its position as the market leader by buying Hanomag and Henschel from Rheinstal. MAN's merger with Bussing, the decision of Krupp to abandon commercial vehicle production, and the failure of International Harvester in its attempt to enter the German market in the mid-1960s has left only three major truck-producing groups in Germany: Daimler-Benz, MAN, and Magirus Deutz, which merged with Fiat in early 1975.

Fiat dominated the Italian market in 1960, having taken over Autobianchi three years earlier, with 86.5 percent of total production. The four leading firms—Fiat, Alfa Romeo, Lancia, and Innocenti—accounted for 99.8 percent of Italian output. Although Fiat attempted to consolidate its position by taking over Lancia and Ferrari in 1969, increased competition from the state-owned Alfa Romeo reduced its market share slightly to 84.2 percent in 1973. Its only competitors in the domestic market (apart from imports) are Alfa Romeo and Innocenti, which was taken over by British Leyland in 1972. In commercial vehicles the position of Fiat is even more dominant. Together with its subsidiaries OM and Autobianchi, the company controls more than 99 percent of all Italian production.

To a greater or lesser extent, increased concentration has characterized the automotive industries of all the major car-producing countries of Western Europe during the 1960s. Although Sweden is not a major producing country, the same has been true there. At the beginning of the decade there were three firms producing vehicles in the country: Volvo, Saab, and Scania Vabis. In 1968, the truck firm Scania Vabis and the car firm Saab merged, so that Sweden now has two diversified groups producing both passenger cars and commercial vehicles.

The Japanese automotive industry expanded spectacularly during the 1960s. In the late 1960s and early 1970s there were signs that the growth of the domestic market was slowing down and the industry was becoming increasingly dependent on exports for its dynamism. In 1961, the then leading firms of Nissan, Toyota, Toyo-Kogyo, and Fugi Heavy Industries accounted for 82 percent of Japanese car production. By 1971, the four largest firms, which now included Mitsubishi in place of Fuji, produced 93.8 percent of Japan's cars. This concentration has taken place since the mid-1960s, smaller firms being absorbed by Toyota and Nissan, which, by 1970, were accounting for 70 percent of the home market and 90 percent of Japanese exports.

The government, through the Ministry for International Trade and Industry (MITI), has played a leading role in promoting concentration in the Japanese automotive industry. The first step was the takeover of Prince Motors by Nissan in 1966, although two years previously the Mitsubishi companies (Mitsubishi Japan and Shin Mitsubishi) had come together to form one group. Attempts to form a Mitsubishi-Isuzu-Fuji group failed, and, in 1968, Fuji joined Nissan. The Toyota group includes both Hino and Daihatsu Motors, and it seems likely that Suzuki will also join it in the near future. A major change occurred in the industry in the early 1970s with the liberalization of the Japanese foreign investment code, and, in 1971, Chrysler was permitted to take a 35 percent shareholding in Mitsubishi, the fourth largest Japanese automotive company. It was followed by General Motors with a similar arrangement with Isuzu, but the projected Ford-Toyo-Kogyo deal fell through. This means that apart from the Big Two, there are now only two Japanese producers, Honda and Toyo-Kogyo, without foreign participation. (For further details on the Japanese automotive industry, see Chapter 9.)

THE INTERNATIONALIZATION OF THE
AUTOMOTIVE INDUSTRY

The term "internationalization" in this context is used to describe the increasingly worldwide nature of the automotive industry in the postwar period, in contrast to its largely national structure during the interwar years. This is reflected not only in the considerable expansion of trade in motor vehicles but also in the interpenetration of the markets of the leading producing countries, a feature notably absent before. It is also reflected in the growth of foreign assembly operations by the major multinational companies and by the increasing number of links between these firms.[20]

Table 2.1 indicates the considerable growth that has taken place in international trade in cars over the last two decades.[21] In the 1950s, prior to the formation of the European Economic Community (EEC), the European car producers continued to enjoy substantial tariff protection, as they had since World War I. The British and French tariffs stood at 30 percent; the Italian at 35 to 45 percent, depending on the type of car; and the German at 17 to 21 percent. During this period, exports expanded rapidly between 1953 and 1959, when they trebled, mainly as a result of the boom in U.S. car imports, which increased from a negligible 25,000 in 1954 to a peak of 614,000 in 1959.[22] In the next two years, world exports stagnated as a result of the contraction in U.S. imports following the introduction of the compacts, but the 1961-64 period saw a renewed growth of trade, probably due to the trade-creating

TABLE 2.1

Car Exports by Leading Countries, 1950-70
(thousands of units)

1950	720	1958	1,765	1966	3,269
1951	839	1959	2,178	1967	3,226
1952	703	1960	2,264	1968	4,304
1953	746	1961	2,008	1969	4,811
1954	943	1962	2,487	1970	5,361
1955	1,162	1963	2,893	1971	6,608
1956	1,175	1964	3,124	1972	6,633
1957	1,434	1965	3,150		

Sources: Society of Motor Manufacturers and Traders (SMMT) 1950-58; National Economic Development Office Data Book, Motor Industry Statistics, 1959-70 (London: Her Majesty's Stationery Office, 1971), and author's compilation.

TABLE 2.2

Imported Passenger Cars as Percent of Total
New Car Registrations

	1958	1973
West Germany	10.4	25.8
France	1.4	20.9
Italy	4.2	28.0
Britain	2.5	27.4
United States	9.3	17.9

Sources: 1958: E. Mahler, L'Industrie Automobile ct ses
Perspectives d'avenir dans le Nouvel Equilibre Europeen et Mondial
(Lausanne: L'ere Nouvelle, 1966); 1973: Economist Intelligence
Unit, Motor Business (various issues, 1974).

effects of the formation of the Common Market. By 1965, the EEC's
common external tariff was 22 percent and internal tariffs had been
reduced to about 30 percent of their initial level, while intra-EEC
trade in cars had increased 378 percent since 1958.[23] The final
period of rapid growth from 1967 onward was associated with a
reduction of the British tariff to 22 percent in 1968 and the Kennedy
Round, which subsequently halved tariffs to 11 percent in both Britain
and the EEC.

Exports grew at a faster rate than production, so that the
vehicle exports of the eight leading countries increased as a share
of world output from 10.1 percent in 1950 to 17.9 percent in 1960,
reaching 26.2 percent by 1970.

A particular feature of the growth of trade in cars has been
the increasing interpenetration of markets among the leading producing
countries, breaking with the prewar pattern of exports to less industrialized countries from a heavily protected home base, which
persisted into the 1950s. This, of course, has been particularly
marked among the Common Market countries. Between 1958 and
1970, the market share of French cars in West Germany increased
from 1.9 to 13.8 percent, while correspondingly in France, German
cars were up from 0.9 to 10.9 percent and Italian cars from 0.2 to
6.3 percent. In Italy the market penetration of German cars rose
from 1.3 to 16.1 percent and that of the French from 0.7 to 10.9
percent.

The same pattern emerges if one looks at the share of all
imports in new registrations for the major producing countries,
as shown in Table 2.2. As can be seen from the table, imports

have increased their share markedly, so that in 1973 between 18 and 28 percent of the cars sold in the major producing countries (apart from Japan) were foreign made. Even without membership in the EEC, British imports of cars reached almost 20 percent of total sales in 1971, with imports from the Common Market trebling between 1965 and 1970. The less spectacular increase in U.S. imports may be explained by the fact that the United States always has been a relatively low tariff market for cars and because of the sharp increase in imports in the years immediately preceding 1958 from only 1.6 percent of the market in 1956. The figure for West Germany also gives a misleading impression of the growth in market penetration by imports, since the 1958 figure was almost double the 1957 level of 5.3 percent.

Another aspect of the internationalization of the motor industry is the growth of the overseas assembly and manufacturing operations of the major companies.[24] The number of assembly contracts in operation increased from 170 in 1960 to 430 at the end of 1968, and the number of countries with assembly operations increased from 42 to 70 over the same period.[25] Table 2.3 indicates the considerable extent of overseas operations by the major car-producing countries.

The spread of the multinational automotive companies is reflected not only in their manufacturing and assembly operations but also in the extension of their sales networks.[26] Indeed, for the major European and Japanese companies, exports are as, if not more, important than overseas production (see Table 2.4), although, for the U.S. companies, the reverse is true.

TABLE 2.3

Number of Assembly Contracts by
Country of Origin, 1969

	Number	Countries
United States (including subsidiaries)	133	43
France	77	39
West Germany	56	26
United Kingdom	48	34
Italy	30	27
Japan	59	28

Source: United Nations Industrial Development Organization (UNIDO), The Motor Vehicle Industry (ID/78), 1972, p. 8.

TABLE 2.4

Distribution of Sales of the Major
European Automotive Manufacturers, 1973
(percent)

	Domestic Sales	Exports	Overseas Production
Citroen	49	26	25
BLMC	52	27	21
Volkswagen	27	48	25
Fiat	44	27	29
Renault	43	26	31
Peugeot	55	20	25
Daimler-Benz	51	37	12

Note: Data refer to volume, except for BLMC and Daimler-Benz, for which only value data were available.

Sources: Company annual reports.

All the major European firms do almost half or more of their business abroad either through exports or overseas production, with exports accounting for at least 20 percent of total output and overseas production between 21 and 31 percent (apart from Daimler-Benz). The U.S. producers do not export a significant proportion of their U.S. output, but both Ford and Chrysler have about one third of their total production outside the United States and Canada, while General Motors has about one fifth of its production overseas. Compared to the prewar position, this reflects a considerable increase in their foreign involvement for the European producers and a decided shift away from exports and toward overseas assembly in terms of the composition of foreign sales.

A different aspect of the internationalization of the automotive industry is the steps that have been taken recently by the U.S. companies in the integration of their worldwide operations, which have been developed most fully by Ford.[27] Ford has been working toward the increased integration of its European operations since the early 1960s when it bought out the minority shareholders in Ford U.K. with the avowed intention of obtaining greater flexibility of operations.[28]

The setting up of Ford of Europe around 1967 represented a further decisive step. The immediate advantage that the company

gained from this move was the addition of the Escort to the Ford
Werke model range, which improved Ford's weakening position in
the German market. At first, the Escort was assembled at Genk,
Belgium, from British components; later, it was manufactured in
Cologne. The introduction of the Capri showed the advantages of
greater integration of the company's European operations. The
development of the same car for both the British and German markets
meant that it was possible to cut engineering and design time by half.
Further economies could be obtained through the pooling of research
between the two subsidiaries. Ford also gained additional flexibility
in marketing through having two different sources of supply for the
same model, especially in the face of strikes (at least until the
automotive industry unions are able to organize themselves multi-
nationally to meet this threat).

The other U.S. companies have not gone as far as Ford in the
integration of their European operations. Not until late 1970 did
General Motors follow Ford in setting up European headquarters.
It recently opened an automatic transmission plant in Strasbourg,
and it is to be expected that in future there will be greater use of
common design and components between Opel in Germany and
Vauxhall in Britain. Chrysler, after gaining control of Simca and
Rootes in the mid-1960s, was able to increase its exports significantly by integrating its marketing outlets. Integration in production
has not been developed fully, however, partly because of the financial
difficulties faced by the parent company in the United States, which
have resulted in the curtailment of expansion plans. These financial
difficulties also led Chrysler to decide to import the Hillman Avenger
(together with the Mitsubishi Colt) and sell it on the U.S. market as
the Plymouth Cricket rather than to develop a subcompact in the
United States, the tooling costs of which were estimated at around
$200 million.

The decision of Ford and General Motors to produce subcompacts in the United States represents a backward step in the
international integration of their operations. This is especially
true for Ford, which originally had planned to manufacture the
1,600 cc engine in Britain and the 2,000 cc engine in Germany, as
well as importing various other components from Europe. Partly
as a result of the uncertainty of supply because of strikes and partly
because sales reached the minimum output level of 400,000 to
500,000 units required to justify such an investment, Ford decided
to build an engine plant in the United States. It is also certain that
there are political pressures against selling "international" cars
on the U.S. market, which may have encouraged Ford to transfer
operations from Europe.

THE PRESENT STRUCTURE OF THE
WORLD AUTOMOTIVE INDUSTRY

The level of concentration in the major vehicle-producing countries has already been discussed. As was mentioned, all these countries have at least one independent producer, that is, a firm that is not a foreign subsidiary. It is not surprising to find, therefore, that when one looks at the world as one market, concentration is less than in any one country taken in isolation. Nevertheless, it is still true that the industry is dominated by a small nucleus of companies (see Table 2.5). Between them, General Motors and Ford accounted for 38.4 percent of world vehicle production in 1973, while the largest 13 companies in the world made up 87 percent of total output. It is evident that concentration on a national scale has been reflected in concentration in the international market.

The movement toward cross-country mergers has not progressed very far as yet, but this underestimates the extent of links among the world's leading vehicle producers, since the main form that these have taken has been through joint companies or agreements involving no ownership. One of the most significant joint companies linking

TABLE 2.5

Leading Vehicle Producers
(Including Subsidiaries), 1973
(thousands of units)

		Percent
General Motors	8,684	22.9
Ford	5,871	15.5
Chrysler	3,450	9.1
Toyota	2,692	7.1
Volkswagen	2,335	6.1
Fiat	2,278	6.0
Nissan	2,271	6.0
Renault	1,452	3.8
British Leyland	1,161	3.1
Peugeot	795	2.1
Citroen	773	2.0
Toyo-Kogyo	739	1.9
Daimler-Benz	548	1.4
Total	38 million	

Source: Company reports.

major car manufacturers is the Societe Franco-Suedoise de Moteurs in which Renault, Peugeot, and Volvo each has one-third share. The company is intended to produce 1 million engines a year. At first, these will be to the individual specifications of the partners, but eventually it is planned to produce an integrated range. Another important cross-country link through a joint company is that between Citroen and NSU. These two companies have owned Comobil jointly since 1965, which was intended to develop Wankel engine cars, and they set up another company, Comotor, in 1967. In Japan, Toyo-Kogyo and Nissan have collaborated with Ford to build a joint automatic transmission plant. See Figure 2.2 for a diagram illustrating these links among the companies.

Jointly owned companies have also been used to link major car manufacturers within national boundaries. The close cooperation between Renault and Peugeot has been realized in a number of joint companies, the most important of which are Societe des Transmissions Automatiques and Francaise de Mecanique. Similarly, in Germany, Volkswagen and Daimler-Benz for a number of years have had a joint research company going under the grandiose title of the Deutsche Automobil GMBH.

Other agreements, not involving common ownership, can take a number of forms, such as the exchange of parts, production of common parts, or assembly and/or marketing of one firm's vehicles by another. Such agreements tend to be particularly common in the commercial vehicles sector of the industry, possibly because a greater number of small firms have survived than in the case of car production, and it is the first step toward further rationalization of the industry. Thus MAN in West Germany has a production and marketing agreement with Saviem, the commercial vehicles subsidiary of Renault. This involves the exchange of parts between the two firms with MAN producing engines and Saviem supplying truck bodies in return, while MAN also sells Saviem trucks in West Germany through its own dealers. Saviem also has an agreement with the Dutch firm DAF, the Swedish Volvo, and the West German Magirus Deutz in order to develop, produce, and buy their truck components in common.

THE CAUSES OF CONCENTRATION
AND INTERNATIONALIZATION

It was argued in the first section of this chapter that the major factor underlying the increase in concentration in the main producing countries during the interwar years was the effect of economies of scale, leading individual firms to expand output and drive out competi-

FIGURE 2.2

Interpenetration of the Major Automotive Manufacturers, 1975

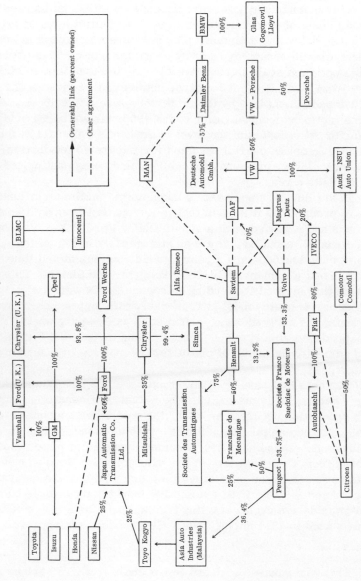

Source: Compiled by the author.

tors in order to achieve lower costs. Can this drive for production economies at plant level explain the developments that have occurred during the postwar period? Such a drive could lead to mergers at the national level followed by a reduction in the number of models produced and an increase in average production volumes. It could also lead to international cooperation in such areas as engine production and to increased exports.

This mechanism, however, depends on either an increasing optimum scale of production over time or an initial level of production that is below the optimum. The evidence on changes in scale requirements in recent years is by no means clear. It is obvious that the optimum scale is considerably greater than immediately before World War II.[29] It appears, however, that most of the increase had taken place by the mid-1950s (see Appendix A), so that the increased concentration of the 1960s cannot be attributed to this factor. Estimates of the level of economies of scale in the industry suggest an overall optimum for integrated production, that is, assembly, pressing, machining, and some casting, of around 400,000 units a year.*

If 400,000 cars per year is taken as the minimum efficient scale of production, it is seen that in Europe in the early 1960s six firms had achieved such a scale: BMC, Ford U.K., Volkswagen, Opel, Renault, and Fiat. If a less stringent definition of the minimum scale of only 200,000 cars a year is used, one might add Vauxhall, Rootes, Ford (Germany), Citroen, Peugeot, and Simca. This suggests that most of the leading European firms were large enough to produce one basic model at reasonably efficient scales of production during the early 1960s. A firm such as Renault, which, in 1961, produced almost 400,000 units of one model, the Dauphine, would gain little in terms of production economies by a larger volume of output.

The data that have been reviewed here are purely technical in their nature, and only indicate the actual cost conditions under which production occurs. As such, the data takes account of tooling costs and fixed capital expenditures, such as those for design and development. These have now assumed a degree of importance far removed from the early days of the industry when Ford was able to put its first car on the market within four months of the company being formed.[30] The U.S. automotive industry now works on a three-year design cycle, starting the sketches for a new model to be introduced in 1971 during 1968. Clay models are approved about

---

*This is discussed in detail in Appendix A where various studies of economies of scale in the industry are compared.

two years before the planned introduction date, after which the cost
of any change in design increases considerably.[31] In Britain, the
development lag seems to be even longer, estimated at between
three and a half and five years.[32] It took Ford four years to develop
the Capri, for example.

Estimates of the design and development costs of a new model
seem to be difficult to ascertain with any degree of accuracy. This
difficulty is illustrated by the different estimates made by two
analysts of Ford's expenditure on the development of the Mustang.
John Kenneth Galbraith[33] puts the engineering and styling costs of
the car at $9 million, with a further $50 million on tooling costs,
while L. J. White[34] suggests a total figure of around $40 million,
roughly equally divided between design and development, and tooling.
In Britain, estimates have put the design, development, and tooling
costs of the Austin Allegro at £17 million and of the Morris Marina
at £15 million.[35] White's estimate puts the cost of design and
development per car at about $100. If these broad orders of magni-
tude are accepted, then taking account of these expenditures would
tend to add to the importance of scale economies, above what would
be expected from technological data, by increasing fixed costs. But
since they only amount to about 5 percent of the total cost for a
successful car, they will not make a great deal of difference.

The key word here is "successful." The costs of failure are
extremely high. In 1970, only four car firms enjoyed profits of
more than $100 million, so that the need to write off development
expenditures of say $30 to $50 million on an unsuccessful car, even
over a period of several years, would be a severe financial strain.
The importance of the increased gestation period between the first
designs and actual production of a model is not so much its impact
on cost curves as its effect on risk. Again, however, the phenomenon of a long gestation period seems to have been characteristic of
the entire postwar period and cannot, per se, be responsible for
the observed developments. In fact, the most recent developments,
such as the use of numerically controlled machine tools and electrical discharge and electrochemical machining in making tools and
dies, and the use of computerized systems to automate the entire
engineering-design function, have led to increased flexibility in the
preproduction period and a reduced lead time.[36] Computer control
of die cutting, for example, has been estimated to cut the average
lag time between approval of the clay model and startup of production
from 21 or 22 months to 17 months.[37]

Since the developments that have taken place in the automotive
industry since 1960 cannot be explained by technological changes in
the area of supply, one must look for an alternative explanation.
The lack of car production during World War II meant that the industry

was faced with very favorable demand conditions in the immediate postwar years both in the United States and Europe. In the United States, this period, which saw used cars selling at prices above the list price for new cars, came to an end in 1953 and would probably have ended sooner had it not been for the effect of the Korean War. In Britain, the return to normal market conditions has been put slightly later, around 1956, [38] having been delayed by the government's policy of putting priority on car exports rather than meeting home demand. A similar situation existed in the other major producing countries in Europe.

As Table 2.6 shows, the rate of growth of new registrations in the major European countries was particularly high between 1950 and 1955, while demand conditions were extremely favorable, and fell in the next five-year period except in the relatively immature Italian market. The first half of the 1960s saw a further fall in growth in all countries except France and the period 1965-71 saw growth decline further in all countries. This slowdown in the rate of growth of the major markets has meant an increase in competition within each national industry.

The increased concentration that has taken place in the U.S. automotive industry since World War II has been analyzed by a number of authors. [39] Here we shall only summarize some of their findings that are relevant. J. A. Menge has suggested that the annual model change has been an important factor in driving the independents out of the U.S. market. These changes impose an additional cost on the smaller firms, which have to replace the dies used for stamping the car body before they are worn out, whereas the larger firms have to change these dies, which have an useful life of up to a million bodies anyway, so that the cost of a style change is correspondingly lower. Since model changes have a considerable effect on sales, the independents found themselves in a vicious circle of being repeatedly forced back along their cost curves away from volumes of production that would justify frequent model changes, by the model changes of the Big Three.

The second important factor is the need to supply a full range of models in order to attract dealers and to prevent customers from changing to another firm when they change price class. This led Studebaker-Packard to attempt to maintain a full line of products after the merger, but the difficulties of doing so at the levels of production that the firm was obtaining led it to abandon the effort after two years.

In Europe, two factors have led to increased competition in the automotive industry. First was the return of a buyer's market in the major producing countries in the late 1950s, leading to the emergence of excess capacity as the unusual postwar conditions were

TABLE 2.6

Average Annual Growth of New Registrations
(Sales) of Vehicles, 1950-71
(percent)

	1950-55	1955-60	1960-65	1965-71
West Germany	17.9	12.4	9.0	5.8
France	17.8	7.1	9.6	5.9
Italy	14.1	17.2	17.0	8.3
United Kingdom	22.4	9.3	5.8	1.8
United States	1.7	-1.6	7.6	1.3

Source: Motor Vehicle Manufacturers Association of the U.S. Inc., 1971 World Motor Vehicle Data, p. 8.

finally eliminated. Second, as was indicated in the previous section, tariff reductions led to a growth of international trade in vehicles, and for the first time the major producers had to face competition from imports in their domestic markets. That this competition was in fact extremely vigorous is illustrated by the discriminatory pricing policies of the companies, which, in their anxiety to penetrate new markets, frequently sold their cars at lower prices abroad than in their domestic markets (see Table 2.7).

From the end of World War II to the late 1950s, an European car firm with a well-protected home market and an excess demand for cars had little need to worry about consumer acceptance of its product. As one observer put it, "Up until the early Sixties, car manufacturers had only one problem: keeping up with demand."[40] The leading firms, such as Renault and Volkswagen, survived and grew, producing only one basic model, and were large enough to reap all the significant economies of scale. Moreover, the favorable market conditions of the 1950s reduced the risk involved in introducing new models. The situation began to change as early as 1954. Until that date, the major car-exporting countries concentrated on different geographic areas, with West Germany, Italy, and France having their main markets in Europe and in its colonies, in the case of France, while the United States supplied the Americas and Britain, the Commonwealth.[41] In 1955, West German companies, particularly Volkswagen, began a vigorous worldwide export drive, and the old pattern of market division started to break down.

The increased competition extended to Europe itself and to the domestic markets of the major producers with the return of a buyer's market and the lowering of tariffs during the late 1950s. Wierzynski has summarized the consequences:

TABLE 2.7

Market Prices of Cars in Foreign Markets
as Percent of Domestic Market Price, 1966

	United Kingdom	France	Germany	Italy	Switzer-land
Mini	n.a.	124	95	95	93
Anglia	n.a.	96	–	100	96
Cortina	n.a.	97	–	126	99
Viva	n.a.	99	86	106	98
Imp	n.a.	108	94	110	97
Citroen DS	153	n.a.	95	120	117
Renault 10	122	n.a.	94	100	108
Volkswagen 1300	141	110	n.a.	116	122
Taunus 12M	162	117	n.a.	112	125
Fiat 500	138	126	101	n.a.	109
Fiat 1500	118	99	82	n.a.	102
Volvo 122S	91	98	77	82	81
Saab Sedan	83	91	69	85	81

Source: J. Paranson, Automotive Industries in Developing
Countries, World Bank Staff Occasional Paper No. 8, 1969, Annex
Table 10.

The new configurations in Europe have led manufacturers
to put a new emphasis on marketing. The accent on
engineering remains, but the shift towards styling, with
annual changes has begun. . . . The life of a given model
is coming down sharply; "facelifts"–small changes in
styling and engineering–don't prolong life expectancy
much any more.[42]

The increase in the range of models offered by the leading
European firms is striking evidence of this. In 1961, Renault
produced only one model, the Dauphine, on a large scale. In 1962,
the Renault 4 and Renault 8 were introduced. Three years later,
the company added two more models, the Renault 10 and the Renault
16, and, in 1968, the Renault 8S and 16TS. 1969 saw the introduction
of the Renault 6-850 and 1970 two more models, the Renault 12 and
the Renault 6-1100. Finally, in 1971, the Renault 12 Estate came
on the market, and since then more new models have been added.
Thus, in the space of a decade, the company moved from complete
reliance on a single model to a whole new range of ten cars.

Renault is only the most spectacular illustration of the general tendency in the European automotive industry. Even a relatively small producer, such as Peugeot, increased its range from two to four basic models between 1960 and 1971. As mentioned above, Volkswagen's efforts to expand its range of models led to the take-over of Auto Union and NSU during the 1960s. Even without including models produced by the Audi-NSU-Auto Union subsidiary, the company had increased its model range from two in 1960 to eight by 1971. The heads of the leading companies are quite explicit regarding their policies of increasing the range of cars that they offer.[43]

On the marketing side there are two reasons why firms require a full line of models. First, there is the observed fact that when customers trade up to a more expensive car, they tend to buy the same make as they owned previously.[44] Thus, if a firm has a gap in its model range it will tend to lose customers who are then difficult to regain. Second, manufacturers prefer exclusive dealerships since this gives them greater control over, and bargaining power vis-a-vis, the dealers. This becomes difficult to impose without a full range since dealers wish to be able to meet the requirements of all customers. As the companies' operations become increasingly international, the need for a wide range of models in order to attract new dealers grows.

As well as the marketing advantages involved in a full line of models, such a policy also reduces risks. As indicated above, the costs of design and development for a new model are considerable and failure extremely expensive. The more competitive environment in which the European car manufacturer has operated for the last decade or more has tended to increase the risk of a new model being unsuccessful. For a one-model company such a failure would probably be fatal, whereas a more diversified firm is able to spread the risk. The future of Chrysler U.K. in the late 1960s hinged very much on the success or failure of the Avenger, and the situation would obviously have been much graver had it been an independent company.

For all the major European companies there is an evident conflict between the need to provide a full range of models and the need for large volumes to take advantage of scale economies. This is partially resolved by giving an appearance of diversity while using common parts in different models in order to attain longer runs. To take the example of Renault again, its range of 11 vehicles (including a van derivative) could be broken down into five different body styles and four different engines. Fiat, which has one of the widest model ranges in Europe, exchanges parts between different models and also has a policy of gradual alterations to keep its models up to date, which cuts both development costs and the gestation lag. Another method used to resolve this conflict is for two companies to get together to produce certain parts, as, for example, the Societe Franco-Suedoise de Moteurs, formed by Renault, Peugeot, and Volvo, which is intended eventually to produce an integrated range of engines.

A full model range and a shorter life for individual models have meant an increased rate of introduction of new models, which again makes life more difficult for the small firm. It is noticeable that mergers often occurred in the 1960s at a time when a new model needed to be introduced. The Chrysler takeover of Rootes came when the British company had recently introduced the Hillman Imp, the tooling for which had cost £9 million, and needed to replace the Minx range, which would have been a severe strain on the firm's financial resources. In fact, the problem can be traced back to an excessive initial dependence on a narrow range of 1,500 cc cars. The merger between BMC and Jaguar also came at a time when the latter needed to introduce a new engine and give a face-lift to most of its models. Similarly, in France, Fiat bought into Citroen when the latter needed to obtain capital in order to finance the introduction of the GS and fill the gap in its range, around 1,500 cc, which happened to be the most popular size class.

Thus it is possible to say that the explanation of concentration in the postwar period does not lie primarily in economies of scale at the plant level as it did before the war. Larger scales of production are not sought in order to reduce production costs but rather to enable a wider range of models to be offered and changes in models to be made more frequently. This drive has been brought about since the late 1950s by the increased competitiveness of the world automotive industry—a result of the slowdown in the rate of growth of demand in the major producing countries and the lowering of protective tariffs.

THE EXPANSION OF THE AUTOMOTIVE
INDUSTRY IN THE UNDERDEVELOPED AREAS

Despite the small share of the underdeveloped countries of Africa, Asia, and Latin America in world vehicle production, which was only 4.9 percent in 1969, and in the number of vehicles registered, which was only 8.8 percent of the world total in the same year, the industry has been growing faster in these areas than in the developed countries. Between 1955 and 1969, the production of the developing countries increased at a rate of 18.9 percent per year, as compared to only 5.7 percent for the developed countries.[45]

TABLE 2.8

Number of Assembly Contracts by
Major Firms, 1968

	Total	Caribbean and Latin America	Asia	Africa
General Motors	24	9	6	2
Ford	32	8	8	4
Chrysler	31	10	9	2
Volkswagen	16	5	3	–
Fiat	28	5	5	5

Source: United Nations Industrial Development Organization
(UNIDO), The Motor Vehicle Industry (ID/78), 1972, p. 8.

The period since 1950 has seen a tremendous expansion of both
assembly and manufacturing operations in the underdeveloped
countries, with nearly 50 countries starting some form of automotive
industry.[46] As Table 2.8 indicates, this has involved a substantial
international extension of the operations of the major international
companies, which have set up assembly plants in countries previously
supplied by exports of assembled vehicles.

The more detailed breakdown of assembly operations by company and country given in the Appendix Table A.1, shows even more
clearly the way in which the operations of the leading companies have
been extended to the underdeveloped countries. Typically, the small
markets of the less developed countries are supplied by a number of
firms, with as many as 10 or more of the 15 firms listed operating
assembly plants either through licensed producers or subsidiaries.

What is the explanation of this rapid expansion of the automotive
industry in developing countries and especially the proliferation of
companies in a number of small markets? Unlike exports, expansion
into these areas through licensing agreements and subsidiaries
cannot be attributed to plant economies. There may, of course, be
economies in the initial stages through supplying parts to a local
assembly plant, although this may be a fairly small and short-lived
gain. There may also be economies for plant design work and some
overheads where plants duplicate production facilities and there is
no gain in terms of plant economies. Model design and development
costs, too, can be spread if the subsidiaries produce the same

models as the parent company.* Where markets are small, however,
the effect on total costs for the firm will be insignificant, especially
if account is taken of the higher costs of local production in the underdeveloped country.

The explanation is to be found in the nature of oligopolistic
competition in the international automotive industry. As has been
shown in the preceding sections, the industry has come to be dominated by a handful of firms at the world level. Competition has not
ceased as a result, but has taken particular forms, such as model
diversification and model changes. The firms in the industry are
all conscious of the interdependence of their actions, but are not in
a position to engage in collusion.

This situation can be clarified in terms of the theory of games.[47]
For simplicity, it is assumed that there are only two players, A and
B (representing two companies). Each player has a choice of two
strategies, either to export finished vehicles to a particular underdeveloped country or to assemble them locally. Because of the
small size of the local market, assembly costs are higher than the
costs of direct exports. If any firm sets up an assembly plant,
however, it will receive tariff protection from competing exports.
The payoffs, which can be assumed to represent rates of return,
can be set out as follows:

		Player A
Player B	Export	Assembly
Export	20, 20	25, 10
Assembly	10, 25	15, 15

As can be seen, the collusive situation is for both firms to continue
exporting. However, each firm has an incentive to set up an assembly plant, because if the other firm does not do so, its profit rate
will be increased. If both firms follow mini-max strategies, however,
they will both assemble locally and both be worse off than in the
cooperative solution. This is the classic case of the "prisoner's
dilemma."

The example is oversimplified in two respects. In the first
place, the situation will not be one of duopoly, but of oligopoly.
This will tend to reduce the likelihood of a cooperative solution being
attained, since it only needs one firm to choose the assembly strategy

---

*General Motors and Ford planned to introduce small cars in
the United States in 1946, but these were canceled and appeared in
1948 as the Australian Holden and the French Ford Vedette.

for all others to be better off if they follow suit. This is just another
way of saying that the more firms there are in an industry, the less
likely they are to be able to arrive at a joint-profit maximizing
solution. The second qualification is that these decisions are not
made once and for all, as in the case of the prisoner's dilemma.
Although a decision to assemble locally might be regarded as
irreversible, at least over a period of several years, the decision
to continue exporting can be changed within a year or two. There
will still be an incentive to set up a local assembly plant if the short-
run profits that can be made before other firms enter are sufficiently
large.

The analysis can be brought nearer to the real world by considering a small underdeveloped country, say Uruguay, which it is
assumed imports fully assembled cars from the United States,
Britain, France, West Germany, and Italy. A company that exports
to Uruguay knows that if one of its competitors should invest in an
assembly plant there, it will obtain tariff protection that would make
finished imports prohibitively expensive. The first company to
invest, moreover, will be able to make large profits until other
firms enter the market, so that there is an incentive to attempt to
preempt the market by entering first. This will be accentuated if
a Japanese company that does not at present export to Uruguay is
interested in setting up a plant in order to break into the market.
Thus, although the optimum situation from the point of view of the
firms at present exporting is to continue to do so because of the
small size of the market, this situation is not stable. If the oligopoly
was sufficiently stable for collusion, either explicit or implicit,
then the result would be different. There would be no local investment until the market was large enough for all (or most) of the firms
to enter.[48]

There is considerable evidence available by now to support
such a model of foreign investment. It has been tested empirically
by F. T. Knickerbocker with data from the Harvard Multinational
Enterprise Project.[49] Using a measure of the extent to which firms
in the same industry followed each other into particular markets,
he concluded that such "oligopolistic reaction" increased with
industry concentration, except at very high levels of concentration
when it fell somewhat as a result of collusion becoming possible.
A second important determinant of the extent of oligopolistic reaction
was the stability of the industry in terms of the number of firms
becoming overseas manufacturers for the first time in the postwar
period.

Knickerbocker's analysis, of necessity, is limited since he
was only able to use data relating to the foreign operations of U.S.

multinational corporations and related these data to data on concentration in the U.S. economy. Looking at the international automotive industry (which, it has been argued, is the relevant unit) rather than the U.S. automotive industry, it appears that the level of concentration and relative lack of stability as a result of the entry of West European and Japanese companies as international producers have given rise to a high level of oligopolistic reaction. This model of defensive investment by international oligopolists in order to protect export markets threatened by local assembly by their competitors is further supported by studies of the decision to invest abroad, based on interviews or questionnaires, which have shown it to be an important motive in many cases.[50] As a result, considerations of market size are not important in the decision of follower firms to expand abroad.[51] In Nigeria, for example, P. Kilby found that there was no necessary relationship between the size of the local market relative to the minimum efficient scale of plant and the decision of foreign firms to set up in certain industries, but that there was a tendency for several firms to follow the first entrant.[52]

It seems, therefore, that oligopolistic interdependence can explain a considerable amount of foreign investment in manufacturing industry. It also seems a plausible explanation of the rapid growth of overseas assembly and manufacturing operations by the major automotive companies in the postwar period. The evidence suggests that many underdeveloped countries could be supplied at a lower cost from the point of view of the companies by exports, but the choice is not usually one between exports and investment, but one between investment and losing the market to competitors. As General Motors Vice-President T. A. Murphy said in evidence to the Senate Subcommittee on International Trade, "There is no question that if General Motors or other U.S. automotive firms were to turn their backs on market participation through overseas facilities, multinational firms based in other countries would be alert and quick to act to fill the need."[53] In practice, the situation is also complicated by the role played by host governments that may actively try to precipitate the decision to invest, either by restricting imports or by playing on the fears of the major companies that a rival will steal a march on them.[54] Host governments also have frequently been persuaded by the large number of companies that have invested in an excessively small market to pass on the costs to the local consumer by providing sufficient tariff protection to enable them to charge correspondingly high prices. Thus, the losses to the companies of failing to achieve a cooperative solution are minimized.

THE OIL CRISIS AND FUTURE DEVELOPMENTS
IN THE INTERNATIONAL AUTOMOTIVE
INDUSTRY

Since 1973, the sharp increase in the price of gasoline has had a major impact on the development of the automotive industry. The most obvious manifestation of this has been the substantial reduction in sales and production of cars in 1974 when the effects of price increases made themselves felt. In that year, production was down on 1973 levels by 22 percent in West Germany, 5 percent in France, 11 percent in Italy, 12 percent in Great Britain, 24 percent in the United States, and 12 percent in Japan. Not surprisingly, demand shifted toward cars with a lower fuel consumption so that, whereas sales of most models fell, those with an engine capacity of less than 1 liter tended to increase. The commercial vehicle market remained much firmer and production increased in France, Italy, and Japan and fell less sharply than car production in the other countries.

It has already been noted that the reduction in the growth of car sales in the main producing countries during the 1960s and early 1970s led to increased competition and concentration in the industry. The recession of 1974 is likely to accentuate this trend, putting pressure on the smaller firms that will find it difficult to maintain their profitability and facing shrinking markets and the attempts of the larger firms to maintain their production levels. Moreover, the smaller firms are less able to carry losses if these are sustained for any length of time. Already the financial difficulties of Citroen in France have led to the government-sponsored takeover by Peugeot and the merger of Berliet with Saviem, together with an injection of F130 million in cash to stave off bankruptcy. In the Netherlands, the national automotive company DAF only survived through being taken over by Volvo, while in the United Kingdom the already serious problems of British Leyland have been accentuated by the crisis.

A number of alternatives face the automotive manufacturers in this situation. Further mergers, both within countries where possible and across national boundaries as in the case of Volvo and DAF, seem likely. Alternatively, the weaker producers may seek closer links with the state, as in the case of British Leyland. A third alternative of diversification into nonautomotive products is difficult because of low profits, which means that firms have only limited funds for new investment. Thus, the most likely outcome of the present crisis for the industry is a reduction in the number of firms and closer links with the state.

One significant aspect of the developments observed in the international automotive industry during 1974 is the continued expansion of car production in a number of peripheral economies despite the recession in the major producing countries. In Brazil, for instance, car production was up by 11 percent and production of all vehicles by 18 percent, while in Mexico the number of cars produced increased by 24 percent over 1973. Other countries in which vehicle output increased were the USSR, Spain, Australia, Czechoslovakia, and Poland. This suggests that another effect of the crisis will be a further internationalization of the automotive industry as production expands outside the traditional centers of the United States, Western Europe, and Japan. Further growth for the major companies is likely to depend increasingly on participation in the automotive industries of Eastern Europe and the underdeveloped countries. Fiat, for instance, saw the sales of its domestic plants drop by 12 percent in 1974, while its production overseas increased by 12 percent.

The need to internationalize further is also likely to accentuate the trend toward concentration among the major companies. Firms such as British Leyland, which has been forced to withdraw from expanding markets in Spain and Australia, are likely to find themselves under increasing pressure at home as their worldwide production falls behind that of more favorably placed companies. Thus, an intensification of competition, both at home and abroad, appears likely in the immediate future until a more tightly knit oligopoly emerges in the industry.

CONCLUSION

This chapter has indicated the way in which an international automotive industry had been formed by the 1960s, in contrast to the primarily national industries of the interwar years. A consequence of this development has been the expansion of the operations of the major companies to a large number of underdeveloped countries, which provide the best prospects for rapid future growth. In order to survive, companies have had to become international, and the need to operate on an international scale has led to further concentration of production. Despite its oligopolistic structure, however, the industry has remained competitive and the struggle between the major producers is occurring in every corner of the world.

NOTES

1. G. Maxcy and A. Silberston, The Motor Industry (London: Allen & Unwin, 1959), p. 11.

THE INTERNATIONAL AUTOMOTIVE INDUSTRY 45

2. R. F. Lanzillotti, "The Automobile Industry," in The Structure of American Industry, 3rd ed., ed. W. Adams (New York: Macmillan, 1961), p. 312.

3. G. Maxcy, "The Motor Industry," in Effects of Mergers, ed. L. Cook (London: Allen & Unwin, 1958), p. 360.

4. S. Hirsch, Location of Industry and International Competitiveness (Oxford: Clarendon Press, 1967), Chap. 2.

5. J. B. Rae, American Automobile Manufacturers (New York: Chilton, 1959), Chap. 1.

6. Lanzillotti, op. cit., Table 2.

7. D. Creamer, "Capital and Output Trends in Manufacturing Industries, 1880-1948," National Bureau of Economic Research, Occasional Paper 41 (New York, 1954). Quoted in Maxcy and Silberston, op. cit., pp. 207-09.

8. D. G. Rhys, The Motor Industry: An Economic Survey (London: Butterworths, 1972), pp. 15-17.

9. Rae, op. cit., Chap. 3.

10. Maxcy, op. cit., Table II.

11. I. Svennilson, Growth and Stagnation in the European Economy (Geneva: Economic Commission for Europe, 1954), p. 15.

12. Maxcy and Silberston, op. cit., pp. 14, 99.

13. Svennilson, op. cit., p. 151.

14. Ibid., pp. 150-51.

15. Ibid., pp. 151-52.

16. Rhys, op. cit., p. 376.

17. L. J. White, The Automobile Industry Since 1945 (Cambridge, Mass.: Harvard University Press, 1971), p. 13.

18. For more details on the elimination of the independents, see C. E. Edwards, Dynamics of the United States Automobile Industry (Colombia, S.C.: University of South Carolina Press, 1965).

19. Letters from Ford U.S. to Ford U.K., quoted in The Economist 197 (November 19, 1960), p. 803.

20. For a detailed theoretical analysis of internationalization, see C. Palloix, "The Internationalization of Capital," mimeographed. Palloix distinguishes the internationalization of the circuit of commodity capital, the circuit of productive capital, and the circuit of money capital.

21. This corresponds to the internationalization of the circuit of commodity capital in Palloix's terminology. Palloix, ibid., pp. 11-12.

22. White, op. cit., Tables A.2 and A.3.

23. W. J. Karssen, "Concentration in the Automobile Industry of the EEC," in U.S., Congress, Subcommittee on Antitrust and Monopoly, Economic Concentration, vol. 7a, 1968, pp. 3915-25.

24. This corresponds to the internationalization of the circuit of money capital in Palloix's terminology. See Palloix, op. cit., pp. 5-9.

25. UNIDO, The Motor Vehicle Industry (ID/78), 1972, p. 8.

26. As early as 1963, the Economist Intelligence Unit commented on this phenomenon. See "Changes in the Ownership of the European Motor Industry," Motor Business 36 (1963).

27. This corresponds to Palloix's concept of the internationalization of the circuit of productive capital. See Palloix, op. cit., pp. 9-11.

28. See letters from Ford U.S. to Ford U.K., op. cit., p. 25.

29. Hoffman estimated an optimum of 100,000 units per year in 1939. See White, op. cit., p. 51. Rhys contrasts the optimum output of presses today of 2 million with a figure of 250,000 before 1939. See Rhys, op. cit., p. 289.

30. See J. K. Galbraith, The New Industrial State (London: Hamilton, 1967), p. 11.

31. For further details, see White, op. cit., Chap. 3.

32. See Rhys, op. cit., p. 300.

33. See Galbraith, op. cit., p. 11.

34. White, op. cit., p. 37.

35. D. G. Rhys, personal communication, 1973.

36. U.S., Department of Labor, Bureau of Labor Statistics, Technological Trends in Major American Industries, Bulletin No. 1474 (Washington, D.C.: Government Printing Office, 1966), pp. 97-102.

37. White, op. cit., p. 33.

38. Rhys, op. cit., pp. 309-10.

39. C. E. Edwards and H. G. Vatter, "The Closure of Entry in the American Automobile Industry," Oxford Economic Papers (1952): 213-34; J. A. Menge, "Style Change Costs as a Market Weapon," Quarterly Economic Journal 76 (1962): 632-47.

40. G. H. Wierzynski, "The Battle for the European Auto Market," Fortune 77 (1968): 119.

41. Rhys, op. cit., p. 383.

42. Wierzynski, op. cit., p. 121.

43. See the statements by Lotz of Volkswagen and Dreyfus of Renault in Wierzynski, ibid., 142.

44. In the United States, between 40 and 70 percent of car purchases are repeats, that is, from the same firm as the previously owned car. See White, op. cit., p. 103.

45. J. Baranson, "International Transfer of Automotive Technology to Developing Countries," United Nations Institute for Training and Research (UNITAR), Research Reports, no. 8 (New York, 1971): 81-83.

46. UNIDO, op. cit., p. 39.

47. For the application of game theory to oligopolistic situations, see M. Shubik, Strategy and Market Structure: Competition, Oligopoly and the Theory of Games (New York: Wiley, 1959).

48. This is similar to White's analysis of the introduction of the compact by the U.S. companies. See White, op. cit., pp. 171-78.

49. F. T. Knickerbocker, Oligopolistic Reaction and Multinational Enterprise (Cambridge, Mass.: Harvard Graduate School of Business Administration, 1973).

50. See F. J. Robinson, The Motivation and Flow of Private Foreign Investment (Stanford, Calif.: Stanford Research Institute, 1961); and Y. Aharoni, The Foreign Investment Decision Process (Cambridge, Mass.: Harvard Graduate School of Business Administration, 1966).

51. Knickerbocker, op. cit., pp. 125-38.

52. P. Kilby, Industrialization in an Open Economy: Nigeria, 1945-1966 (Cambridge: Cambridge University Press, 1969), pp. 53-80.

53. U.S., Senate, Subcommittee on International Trade of the Committee on Finance, 1973.

54. Most of the automotive industry development programs in Latin America involved restrictions on imports of assembled vehicles. A recent example of a host government playing on company fears that a rival will preempt the market is the Lebanonese where the government and local bankers have encouraged British Leyland to set up an assembly plant by suggesting that if it does not do so, the Japanese will. See Counter Information Service, British Leyland: The Beginning of the End? CIS Anti-Report, No. 5, 1973, p. 40.

3

THE SPREAD OF THE AUTOMOTIVE INDUSTRY TO LATIN AMERICA

Chapter 2 discusses the major developments that have taken place in the international automotive industry over the last half century, and more especially since about 1960. Chapter 3 now gives a brief explanation of the way in which these developments have affected the area that is the main focus of interest of this study—Latin America. In this chapter, therefore, the main features of the spread of the automotive industry to Latin America are set out and the chief characteristics of the industries as of the early 1970s are summarized.

THE ASSEMBLY PHASE

The historical origins of the automotive industry in Latin America can be traced back to the first Ford plant set up in Buenos Aires in 1916 (although there had been some previous attempts at local assembly*). Ford was the leading firm in the early development of the industry, opening assembly plants in Chile (1924), Brazil (1925, 1926, and 1927), and Mexico (1926); by 1927, there were 11 Ford companies and branches in Latin America.[1] During the late 1920s and early 1930s, Ford was followed by the other major U.S. companies, General Motors and Chrysler. In some cases, such as the original Ford plant in Argentina, local assembly occurred because of the savings in transport costs that could be made without any tariff protection.[2] By the early 1930s, however,

---

*Between 1906 and 1911, a local entrepreneur, by the name of Anasagasti, had assembled vehicles using Bleriot parts imported from France.

Argentina, Brazil, and Mexico all provided some degree of protection for local assembly. For example, in Argentina in 1931 the tariff on imports of unassembled cars was 30 percent less than that on assembled vehicles and 15 percent less than that on semiassembled vehicles.[3]

As was suggested in Chapter 2, the growth of vehicle exports during the interwar period can be explained by the drive to achieve lower costs in the face of economies of scale on the part of the major companies. Since the most important scale economies were in processes other than final assembly, given a certain volume of demand, local assembly could prove profitable. Estimates for Argentina during the early 1930s suggest that a firm needed sales of about 3,000 to 4,000 cars a year for assembly operations to be worthwhile.[4] Only Ford, General Motors, and Chrysler enjoyed sufficiently large demand; moreover, the European companies that still had room for expansion in their domestic markets were less concerned to find overseas outlets. As a result, the Latin American automotive industry came to be completely dominated by the U.S. companies during the interwar period.

As noted, the traditional division of world markets began to break down around 1954. The implication of this for U.S. hegemony in the Latin American automotive industry is vividly demonstrated by the case of Argentina. In the 1920s and 1930s, the United States accounted for over 90 percent of Argentina's imports of vehicles. The postwar period saw a reduction in U.S. dominance, and, during 1951-54, its share of vehicle imports fell to 61.6 percent. After 1954, the fall became even more pronounced, so that, in 1955-58, the United States accounted for only 22.3 percent of the total. The dollar shortage, gasoline rationing, and, after 1956, lower import duties on small vehicles all tended to favor the European producers. Because the Big Three imported cars from their European (especially German) subsidiaries, these figures exaggerate the reduction in their market share. Nevertheless, they do indicate the way in which Latin America became a battleground in the competitive struggle within the automotive industry.

Another development that had its origins during World War II, when Latin American imports of cars and parts were cut off, was the growth of a substantial industry manufacturing spare parts, in order to keep the existing fleet of vehicles operating. These began as small workshops, operating virtually as cottage industry, but they provided a basis on which a supplier industry could later be developed. In the postwar period, some of these parts began to be used by the assembly plants as original equipment.

The increased competition within the world automotive industry and its extension to Latin America during the 1950s, together with the development of an embryonic parts industry, meant that the circumstances were particularly propitious for governments that wished to develop a local industry during this period. The drive for overseas expansion was such that even relatively small markets (in 1955, the Latin American market absorbed less than 200,000 vehicles, equally divided between cars and commercial vehicles) could not be ignored. Thus, when governments began to use tariffs and local content requirements to cut off imports and started to offer incentives to firms to manufacture vehicles locally, a stream of defensive investments was forthcoming.

In the prewar period, protective measures were not able to do more than shift final assembly to Latin America, the incorporation of local parts being minimal, since the underlying dynamic of overseas expansion was the need of the parent company to achieve economies of scale in production. The new dynamic behind expansion in the postwar period, in which plant economies played a less crucial role, made it possible for the larger countries to enforce extremely high local content requirements and still attract the major multinational companies. (It is interesting to note in this context that both Ford and General Motors had sales approaching 20,000 units a year in Argentina in the late 1920s and continued to assemble vehicles, whereas, in the postwar period, many companies have begun manufacturing operations in Latin America at much lower levels of output.)

Another aspect of the relationship between the competitive struggle in the advanced countries and the development of the automotive industry in Latin America was the export of plants by companies that had been driven out of the industry in the developed countries in order to set up subsidiaries or independent companies. This is illustrated by the case of Industrias Kaiser Argentina, the first company to start manufacturing, as opposed to assembling, motor vehicles on the continent.

Kaiser-Frazer had attempted to enter the U.S. market immediately after World War II, but was one of the first of the independents to be hit as a result of the return of normal market conditions in 1953. Kaiser originally submitted a proposal to set up a factory to the Argentinian government in September 1954 but, with the fall of Perón a year later, some amendments had to be made and the contract was finally signed in January 1956. Kaiser provided the plant that was shipped from the United States in its entirety, and full production was planned at 40,000 vehicles a year with a local content of 60 percent of total vehicle weight. The company setup had a majority local shareholding, part private and part government, while Kaiser had a minority holding. (A similar strategy was followed in setting up Willys-Overland de Brasil.)

In Mexico, a local group of businessmen bought the Borgward plant after that company's failure in Germany in an attempt to set up an independent Mexican automotive company.

GOVERNMENT POLICY AND THE GROWTH OF
THE LATIN AMERICAN AUTOMOTIVE INDUSTRY

A number of factors prompted the governments of the large Latin American countries to develop local manufacture of vehicles and the other countries to require assemblers to incorporate gradually local parts. In most cases the dominating consideration was the need to save foreign exchange, since either vehicle imports were a substantial share of total imports or they were being kept down by quotas or prohibitive tariffs with the result that the supply was extremely restricted. During the 1950s, imports of vehicles and parts accounted for 11 percent of Mexico's total imports,[5] and in Brazil there was a similar proportion during the immediate postwar period (1945-52).[6] In Argentina, on the other hand, vehicle imports were strictly controlled, and, as a result, there was a severe shortage of new vehicles and a deterioration in the age structure of the existing stock. (See Chapter 6.) Over time, these problems were accentuated as the demand for vehicles grew with rising incomes.

Despite the existence of some potential parts suppliers, the incorporation of locally produced parts was extremely limited during the early postwar years. The existing assembly plants were organized in order to assemble imported knocked-down units and failed to act as a catalyst for the development of local suppliers.[7] In Mexico, for example, the few parts that were bought locally, such as tires or batteries, were usually the result of government incentives or requirements. Consequently, there was little saving in foreign exchange as a result of local assembly operations.

A rough estimate of the total amount saved by the Mexican automotive industry in 1961 illustrates this point. The total output of cars assembled in the country in that year, valued at prices in the country of origin, came to $69 million, while direct imports of parts for local assembly were $42.5 million, to which one might add an estimated $5.7 million in indirect imports. The valuation of output was made at prices to the public in the country of origin, however, rather than at wholesale prices, which are the relevant ones for calculating the foreign exchange saving.

A deduction of 20 percent was made to allow for the dealer's margin and local taxes (this would seem to be a very conservative estimate). In order to take account of transport costs to Mexico, this deduction was reduced to 15 percent. (An estimate of 5 percent for the additional costs of delivery to Mexico does not seem excessively low since most vehicles were of U.S. origin.) This reduces the value of local production to $58.6 million and the exchange saving to $10.4 million.

So far, no account has been taken of capital flows resulting from local production. If royalty and license payments are 5 percent of the price to the public of a vehicle, there is a further $3.5 million outflow, leaving a net saving of only $6.9 million to offset against that part of the $10.2 million profit remitted abroad. Assuming that 50 percent of profits were remitted, the total saving for foreign exchange would be only $1.8 million.[8]

A second important motive behind government measures to promote vehicle manufacturing in Latin America was a desire to create new employment opportunities. Assembly plants alone had little employment-generating effect since they depended almost entirely on imports of parts. For example, in Argentina, in 1956, the terminal industry employed 4,449 people,[9] and in Mexico it employed about 4,000 in 1949,[10] increasing to 7,000 by 1960.[11] It was felt, moreover, that automotive manufacture was a particularly appropriate industry to develop from this point of view because of its backward and forward linkage effects that would stimulate the parts industry, the steel industry, petroleum refining, and so on.

A further consideration that recommended the automotive industry for import substitution was its technological progressiveness, which appealed to governments anxious to modernize their industrial structure. The intercountry demonstration effect cannot be left out of the analysis altogether. Given the political rivalry between Argentina and Brazil for influence in Latin America, it was inevitable that if one developed an automotive industry, the other would soon follow suit. Similarly, the development of the automotive industry in these countries both indicated the possibilities open to Mexico and put pressure on the Mexican government to develop its own industry in order to withstand Argentinian and Brazilian efforts within the Latin American Free Trade Area (LAFTA) to open the Mexican market to their car exports.

As a result of these internal pressures and the favorable external environment, the Latin American countries began to require higher levels of local content in their vehicles from the mid-1950s onward. The first country to undertake a systematic development of the automotive industry was Brazil with a decree passed in 1956 that set up the Grupo Ejecutivo de la Industria Automovilística (GEIA) and formulated the norms that were to be applied to the industry.

TABLE 3.1

Local Content Requirements in the Brazilian
Automotive Industry
(percent weight)

1956	35 – 50
1957	40 – 60
1958	65 – 75
1959	75 – 85
1960	90 – 95
1961	95 – 99

Sources: Comisión de Estudios Económicos de la Industria
Automotriz, La Industria Automotriz Argentina; Asociación de
Fálsricas de Automotores, Informe Económico 1969 (Buenos Aires:
ADEFA, 1969), p. 93.

The level of local content aimed at initially was 35 percent
for trucks and 50 percent for cars, rising to 90 and 95 percent by
1960 and 98 and 99 percent, respectively, by 1961, which was, to
all intents and purposes, achieved by 1962 (see Table 3.1). The
basis on which this content was to be calculated was the weight
of the vehicle. Companies setting up in Brazil were offered a
number of incentives, including exemptions from duties for the
permitted imports of parts and from duties and taxes for imported
machinery and equipment, as well as classification as basic industries to qualify for assistance from the National Development Bank.

Argentina soon followed suit with Decree 3693 in 1959, which
set a framework for the organization of the industry over a five-year
period. It gave certain advantages to firms that submitted production
plans for the local manufacture of cars and trucks and met a required
level of incorporation of local parts. Table 3.2 indicates the maximum percentage of the CIF (cost, insurance, and freight) value of
vehicles that could be imported at a preferential rate under the
decree.

In category A, the duty charged on the percentage indicated
in each year was to be 20 percent on the CIF value, while a further
5 percent could be imported at a 100 percent duty and the remainder
up to 60 percent at 300 percent. For the other categories, the
preferential rate was 40 percent and again the remainder up to
60 percent could be imported at 300 percent. A further 10 percent
of the annual amount imported was allowed to cover losses and
replacement of parts with an import duty of 100 percent. In 1960,

TABLE 3.2

Permitted Imports in the Argentinian
Automotive Industry
(percent CIF value)

		1960	1961	1962	1963	1964
A	Commercial vehicles	45	40	35	30	20
B	Cars 190–750 cc	45	40	35	25	10
C	Cars 750–1,500 cc	40	35	30	20	10
D	Cars 1,500–2,500 cc	35	30	25	15	10
E	Cars more than 2,500 cc	30	25	20	15	10
F	Others	20	15	10	5	5

Source: Industrias Kaiser Argentina, La Industria Automotriz Argentina (Buenos Aires: 1963), pp. 34–35.

imports of assembled vehicles were prohibited, although a nominal rate of protection was fixed at between 400 and 500 percent for cars and 35 to 40 percent for trucks.[12]

Foreign firms setting up in the automotive industry also benefited from Law 14,780 of 1958, which had been passed by the Frondizi government to attract more foreign investment to Argentina. This law permitted foreign companies to make their investment in the form of goods and equipment or patents and immaterial goods necessary for the firm's production, as well as in foreign exchange, and guaranteed equal judicial treatment to foreign and local capital. This law led to a substantial inflow of foreign investment to Argentina. Between 1959 and 1961, almost U.S. $400 million was approved by the government, of which 25 percent was in the automotive industry.[13]

The Mexican government, worried by the large variety of makes being assembled in the country (44 in 1960), began to reorganize the automotive industry by prohibiting imports of cars selling at over 55,000 pesos, so that by 1962, the number had been reduced to 22. This was followed by the decree of August 25, 1962 that required 60 percent of the direct costs of vehicles* to be accounted for in Mexico, included in which had to be the engine, by 1964. A further decree in 1963 completely exempted the automotive industry from paying import duties on machinery and equipment for five years

---

*Direct costs is defined as raw materials and parts, lubricants and power used in production, wages of workers employed directly in production, and depreciation.

and on raw materials, parts, and components for four years, followed
by two three-year periods during which exemptions of 50 and 25 percent were granted on imported inputs. Finally, the federal assembly
tax was reduced by 80 percent. The industry remained subject to
government quotas unless a level of local integration in excess of
70 percent was achieved. Thus, by the mid-1960s, there were
three Latin American countries that could be said to be manufacturing
and not assembling vehicles.

This same period, the late 1950s and early 1960s, saw the
development of assembly industries with varying degrees of incorporation of locally produced parts in a number of other countries in the
region. The initial development of an automotive industry in Chile
during the 1950s occurred in Arica in the extreme north of the
country. The area had been declared a free port in the early 1950s,
essentially for political reasons.* However, this did not prove a
very satisfactory mechanism for integrating Arica into the Chilean
economy, the main consequence being the development of a considerable illicit traffic in imported luxury consumer goods.

The government response was to attempt to promote industrial
development in the region, and a number of promotional decrees
were passed that led to several assembly plants being set up in
Arica during the late 1950s and early 1960s. In 1962, Decree 835
attempted to introduce a semblance of order into this system. The
Comisión para el Fomento de la Industria Automotriz was set up
as the government body in charge of the development of the automotive
industry. National content requirements were set on the basis of
FOB (free on board) prices in the country of origin and a certain
percentage for assembly and finishing (see Table 3.3). Equally
significant, vehicles were removed from the list of permitted imports
in January of the same year.

This decree applied only to cars, vans, station wagons, and
pickups, and it was not until Decree 507 of 1966 that similar conditions were laid down for the assembly of chassis for trucks and
buses. This set the local content requirements given in Table 3.4.

Venezuela had a vehicle assembly industry from 1948, but
until 1963, the main source of supply continued to be imports of
completely assembled vehicles. In December 1962, imports were
prohibited almost completely and a local content requirement

------

*It had been taken from Peru in the War of the Pacific in 1884
and many of the inhabitants still looked northward to Lima rather
than toward Santiago. Moreover, it was also a part of the country
where the left attracted considerable support and was thus doubly
sensitive politically.

TABLE 3.3

Local Content Requirements for
Chilean Cars, 1963-70
(percent FOB value)

1963	30.0	1967	55.0
1964	36.6	1968	57.9
1965	41.1	1969	57.9
1966	50.0	1970	57.9

Source: Gamma Ingenieros, Estudio de la Industria Automotriz
Chilena, UNIDO (ID/WG 76/6), 1970, p. 10.

imposed. Initially, this was extremely low, but, by 1969, it had
reached 38.5 percent of the weight of the vehicle for cars. Local
assembly did not begin in Peru until 1965 under a decree issued
two years earlier that required a 30 percent national content to be
achieved within five years of starting production. Colombia relied
mainly on imports for its supply of vehicles for most of the period.
Two firms were set up in the early 1960s under special contracts
with the government, but production only began to achieve significant
levels toward the end of the decade. There are no precise local
content requirements, but in practice it appears to vary between 23
and 30 percent. Of the other Latin American countries, Uruguay
and Costa Rica have some local assembly but at extremely low levels
of output.

The most immediate consequence of these developments was
the mushrooming of firms in virtually every country following the
passing of the various promotional laws. Argentina attracted more
firms than any other country, with 21 automotive manufacturers in
1960. It was closely followed by Chile with 20 (1962); then came
Venezuela (16), Peru (13), and Brazil (11). Only in Mexico, where
two of the firms authorized to produce withdrew, was the number
kept below double figures with eight firms starting production.
(As noted, Colombia did not have any specific automotive industry
legislation.)

It was suggested in Chapter 2 that the nature of competition
in the international automotive industry is such that the decision
of one firm to invest in a particular country will precipitate a
similar decision on the part of a number of other firms, giving
rise to exactly this kind of market fragmentation. It is relevant
here to ask whether government policy could have prevented market
fragmentation. Some writers have suggested that the large number

of firms attracted to the automotive industry in these countries was
the result of excessively generous incentives offered by host governments, 14 and that a better solution would have been achieved if only
a more appropriate level of incentives had been offered.

Such a conclusion implicitly assumes a continuous function
relating the number of firms attracted (or, even more dubiously,
the amount of investment generated, which assumes perfect divisi-
bility of capital) to the level of incentives and, by extension, to the
expected rate of profit. This may be true under conditions of perfect
competition, but under oligopoly the interdependence of firm reactions
makes nonsense of such conclusions, as was seen above. In fact,
the relation between the number of firms entering the industry and
the level of government incentives is highly discontinuous. At a low
level of incentives, no firms are likely to enter, but once a certain
level is reached and one firm finds it profitable to enter, its competitors will tend to follow suit to avoid seeing the market preempted.
This appears to be the characteristic form of oligopolistic behavior
exhibited in the automotive industry.

Of course, it is impossible to know in any given case what
would have happened at a given moment in time had the level of
incentives offered been different from what they were. The uniformity
of the response in the different Latin American countries suggests
that there must be some systematic mechanism at work rather than
merely each country in turn offering excessively generous incentives.
One of the main features of the legislation in each of the countries
concerned was that it was accompanied by measures to ban or
severely limit imports of vehicles, and that this meant that international firms were faced with the choice of either investing locally
or abandoning the market.

TABLE 3.4

Local Content Requirements for Chilean
Commercial Vehicles, 1966-70
(percent FOB value)

4/29/66 to 12/31/66	25.0
1/1/67 to 6/30/67	30.0
7/1/67 to 6/30/68	37.5
7/1/68 to 6/30/69	47.5
7/1/69 to 6/30/70	50.0

Source: Gamma Ingenieros, Estudio de la Industria Automotriz
Chilena, UNIDO (I D/WG 76/6), 1970, p. 10.

The importance of this fact is well illustrated by the statements of F. G. Donner, chairman of General Motors, concerning the decision of his company to invest in Argentina. After World War II, the General Motors Overseas Policy Group concluded that assembly would be economically more sound than manufacturing, given the lack of auxiliary industry and essential raw materials in the country. The reason why this decision was revised was the prohibition of imports. "For General Motors, and a number of other vehicle producers, the question was whether to manufacture in Argentina or abandon the market."[15] Of course, there had been previous periods of severe import restrictions in Argentina. The difference this time was that the creation of a domestic industry threatened to exclude from the market permanently firms that did not invest, since high entry barriers, both natural and artificial, were likely to develop, preventing entry at a later date. This seems to indicate a pattern of interdependent behavior of the kind that was suggested above.

If, then, the oligopolistic international industry leads to a large number of firms wishing to enter the market when an under-developed country begins to develop a local automotive industry, the question then arises of why the host governments did not take direct measures to limit the number of firms entering the industry, for example, through investment licensing. Even such staunch opponents of government intervention as I. Little, T. Scitovsky, and M. Scott admit the need for investment control in such a case and specifically mention the automotive industry as an example.[16] The extent of which governments attempted to screen investment proposals varied from country to country. Argentina and Brazil, for example, were particularly lax, permitting all firms that met the legal requirements to start production. In Mexico, on the other hand, only 10 of the 18 projects put forward to the government were approved, and 2 subsequently withdrew. (Among the firms that submitted proposals but did not start production in Mexico were Peugeot, Volvo, Hillman, Citroen, Toyota, and Mercedes-Benz.)

Despite attempting to screen the proposals submitted, it is noticeable that even the Mexican government failed to reduce the number of companies to the level that the market would have been able to support at a reasonably efficient scale of production. The government ignored detailed work by its own technicians on exactly this point, which showed that the maximum number of models that should be produced in the country was five.[17]

The reason usually given for not limiting the number of entrants is that competition would eliminate the least efficient firms and, at the same time, bring about price reductions.[18] But, as the same semiofficial Mexican study pointed out, the objection to this is that

foreign subsidiaries can produce at a loss in the hope of achieving a
larger market in the future while offsetting these losses against the
tax liabilities of the parent.[19] The real reason for failing to adopt
stricter measures of control is the inability of host governments to
withstand external pressure and the effect that such measures would
have on the "climate for foreign investment."[20]

The effect of the various promotional programs has been a
substantial growth of vehicle production in Latin America. The
output of cars and trucks rose from 60,912 in 1955 to 1,478,150
in 1973, an increase of 24 times in less than two decades.* What
is more, the vehicles produced in 1955 were mainly only assembled
locally, most of the parts being imported, whereas, by 1973, almost
90 percent of local production was manufacturing production, in the
sense of having over 60 percent national content. The increase in
value added in Latin America is, therefore, even more spectacular.
At the same time, there has been a shift in emphasis from commercial vehicles to passenger cars. Whereas in 1955 slightly more than
half of total production was of commercial vehicles, by 1973, passenger cars accounted for approximately two thirds of output (see
Appendix Table B.2).

There was also a sharp rise in the number of vehicles in
circulation in Latin America from 2,727,542 in 1955 to 12,453,934
in 1972, a more than fourfold increase (see Appendix Table B.3).†
Until the late 1950s, the stock of vehicles had grown relatively
slowly at only about 7 percent per year, whereas since then the
rate of growth has been stepped up to about 10 percent. As a result,
the Latin American share of the world's automotive vehicles increased
from 2.7 to 4.4 percent over the period. As might have been expected
from the data on production, passenger cars have shown a more rapid
growth than commercial vehicles.

Local production still has not completely replaced imports of
vehicles to the continent, and, in the late 1960s, these were running
at about 100,000 a year, a relatively small decrease under the circumstances from the 135,000 imported in 1955 (see Appendix Table
B.4). Despite the virtual closure of the two major markets,
Argentina and Brazil, to imports since local production began,
other countries, mainly Mexico and the Central American republics,

---

*These figures refer to seven countries in Latin America—
Argentina, Brazil, Colombia, Chile, Mexico, Peru, and Venezuela—
which account for virtually all the area's vehicle production.

†The figures refer to Bolivia, Ecuador, Panama, Paraguay,
Uruguay, and the member countries of the Central American Common
Market, as well as the seven countries mentioned in the previous
footnote.

have continued to absorb a significant number of foreign cars and commercial vehicles.

AN OVERVIEW OF THE CURRENT
LATIN AMERICAN AUTOMOTIVE INDUSTRY

It is convenient to separate the countries of Latin America into three groups according to the technological level and degree of local integration of their automotive industries, since, as will be seen in later chapters, such technological differences have important economic repercussions in terms of economies of scale, capital intensity, and so on. The local content requirements imposed in the major Latin American countries have already been discussed and are summarized for convenience in Table 3.5.

The first group that can be identified are those countries that have almost complete local integration, producing the engine, other parts and subassemblies, and body stamping. Both Argentina, with a local content requirement of 96 percent for cars and 90 percent for commercial vehicles (calculated on a standard value-weight relation for each group of parts), and Brazil, where, until 1972, the requirement was 98 percent for trucks and 99 percent for cars (measured as a percentage of total vehicle weight), fall into this category. In Brazil, the local content was reduced in 1972 in order to permit greater flexibility in the interchange of parts between foreign subsidiaries. Both the engine and the stamped body parts are generally produced by the terminal manufacturers, that is, the assembly companies.

Mexico, although it by now has a market almost as large as that of Argentina, comes into the intermediate group. As in Argentina and Brazil, the engine, other parts, and subassemblies are produced locally, but body stampings are mainly imported. The local content requirement is 60 percent of the direct cost of the vehicle, which has enabled the subsidiaries of U.S. companies in Mexico to follow the annual model changes of the parent rather than having to keep the same model in production for several years, as in Argentina and Brazil.

The third, somewhat heterogeneous, group includes Colombia, Chile, Peru, and Venezuela. These have in common the import of both body stampings and engines, but some local production of various other parts. Local content varies from 23 to 30 percent in the case of Colombia and to 70 percent in Chile. It should be noted, though, that the Chilean figure includes a 5 percent allowance for final assembly, and special legislation regards parts imported from other LAFTA countries as local content. In effect, therefore,

TABLE 3.5

Degree of Local Integration in the
Latin American Automotive Industry, 1973

Group	Country	Local Content	Measurement Basis
1	Argentina	Cars 96 percent; commercial vehicles 90 to 93 percent	Value
	Brazil	Cars 85 percent; commercial vehicles 78 to 82 percent[a]	Value
2	Mexico	Average 65 percent	Direct cost
3	Colombia	23 to 30 percent	Value
	Chile	70 percent[b]	Value
	Peru	25 to 35 percent	Value
	Venezuela	45 percent	Value

[a]Imports only permitted if compensated for by exports.

[b]Parts imported from other LAFTA countries considered as local content when compensated for by exports. Actual local content varies from 27 to 72 percent.

Source: Ministerio de Fomento, Dirección de Industrias, Algunos Aspectos Sobre la Integración Latinoamericana de la Industria Automotriz (Bogota, 1973).

the terminal firms in these countries are assemblers, importing the body stampings and engines from the parent company or its affiliate in another country and buying other parts from local suppliers (although the Unidad Popular government planned to take the step to manufacturing production in Chile).

This grouping by level of national integration also reflects the ranking of countries by size of automotive industry, whether measured in terms of the number of vehicles produced, the value of production, or the numbers employed in the terminal industry (see Table 3.6). Argentina and Brazil together accounted for almost 70 percent of the vehicles produced in Latin America in 1973. These two countries are also the most important in terms of value of output and employment generation. Mexico accounted for about 19 percent of the vehicles produced in the region and is only slightly behind Argentina in terms of value of output (although this does not take account of the higher import content of Mexican vehicles). The remaining four countries accounted for less than 12 percent of total output and have correspondingly low levels of employment.

TABLE 3.6

Production and Employment in the
Latin American Automotive Industry, 1973

Country	Units Produced	Value of Production	Number Employed (millions of $ U.S.)
Brazil	729,136	1,946.6[a]	88,625
Argentina	293,742	1,369.6	50,626
Mexico	283,250	1,137.6	35,551
Venezuela	96,951	170.5[a]	7,463
Peru	31,741	155.1	3,154
Colombia	26,315	49.0[b]	1,599[b]
Chile	17,015	n.a.	4,550

n.a.: not available.
[a]1972.
[b]1969.

Sources: Industry trade association publications.

A similar ranking emerges if one considers the relative
importance of the industry within each country. In Argentina and
Brazil, the automotive industry represents an important part of
the total economy and especially the industrial sector, accounting
for about 4 percent of GNP and 12 percent of industrial production
in both countries during the early 1970s.[21] In this respect, too,
Mexico occupies an intermediate position with the industry, accounting for almost 7 percent of the total value of production in the manufacturing sector in 1973.[22] Of the other countries, it has been
estimated that the value of production of the automotive industry
in Chile in 1969 was 2.8 percent of manufacturing output[23] and
in Venezuela in 1968 it came to 4.4 percent of total manufacturing
output.[24]
    A further feature of the Latin American automotive industry
that deserves comment at this point is the extent to which it has
been penetrated by the major international companies. Table 3.7
ranks 13 companies according to their size in the world market
and gives the output of their vehicles in each of the major Latin
American countries. Reading along the rows, it is possible to see
the spread of each company's Latin American operations. Thus,
for example, Chrysler has affiliates in all seven countries listed

TABLE 3.7

Total Vehicle Production by Firm in Latin America, 1973

Firm	Argentina	Brazil	Chile	Colombia	Mexico	Peru	Venezuela	Total	Percent of Worldwide Production
General Motors	29,681	140,567	–	–	37,170	–	17,911	225,329	2.6
Ford	62,374	147,986	–	–	44,512	9,897	29,337	284,209	4.8
Chrysler	27,671	36,826	24	11,406	47,864	6,096	21,817	155,505	4.5
Toyota	–	645	–	–	–	8,867	3,840	10,581	0.4
Volkswagen	–	365,472	–	–	87,361	–	5,244	466,944	20.0
Fiat	66,648	–	5,232	1,690	–	–	2,099	75,669	3.3
Nissan	–	–	440	–	24,635	6,025	1,814	32,914	1.4
Renault	41,892a	–	1,650	11,453	15,912	–	6,695b	77,602	5.3
BLMC	–	–	2,039	–	–	–	780	2,819	0.2
Peugeot	29,102	–	1,562	–	–	–	–	30,664	3.9
Citroen	17,489	–	6,068	–	–	–	–	23,557	3.0
Daimler-Benz	7,689	32,564	–	–	–	–	2,702	42,955	7.8
American Motors	4,236	–	–	–	16,993	–	3,227	24,456	
Total	293,742	729,136	17,015	26,315	283,250	31,741	96,951	1,478,150	
Percent	19.9	49.3	1.2	1.8	19.2	2.1	6.6	100.0	

aIncludes 8,016 Torinos; Industrias Kaiser Argentina and Renault also produce Rambler and Jeep under license.
bIncludes unspecified number of AM vehicles.

Source: Industry trade association publications.

and Renault produces in five countries. Until recently, Ford and
General Motors operated in six countries, but the closure of their
plants in Chile and Peru as a result of government rationalization
policies has left them with plants in only four countries, the same
number as Fiat and Volkswagen.

If the rankings of the companies in Latin America are compared
with their rankings worldwide, one sees that Volkswagen is relatively
more favorably placed in Latin America, while Ford also comes
ahead of General Motors. Other points to be noticed are the relatively
poor performance of the Japanese companies, since only local production is included and they have relied more on exports from Japan,
and of British Leyland, which has chosen to concentrate its efforts
in the Commonwealth. The spread of operations seems to suggest
that there is no agreed division of the Latin American market between
the major companies as has been observed in some other industries.

It is also worth noting that, apart from Volkswagen and possibly
Daimler-Benz, their Latin American operations are strictly marginal
from the point of view of the major automotive manufacturers. Latin
American production usually amounts to less than 5 percent of the
worldwide output of these companies. The importance of the continent
has been increasing, however, and, as was suggested in Chapter 2,
the oil crisis may accentuate this tendency. Volkswagen, which has
20 percent of its production in Latin America, mainly from its large
Brazilian subsidiary and Mexico, may foreshadow the development
of the other companies. At present, however, no other firm has a
Latin American subsidiary of a substantial size relative to the parent
company.

Table 3.8 indicates the insistence of both General Motors and
Ford on having 100 percent ownership of their subsidiaries. (The
apparent exception of Ford in Brazil is due to having bought Willys-
Overland do Brasil.) Chrysler has shown a greater willingness to
opt for less than complete ownership and even minority participation,
while some of the other companies, notably Renault, have used
licensing. What is not seen in the table are the changes that have
been taking place over time with a tendency for foreign ownership
to rise as capital participation replaces licensing and majority
ownership replaces minority holdings.

The preceding tables give some idea of the extent to which
the fragmentation of the Latin American markets between a large
number of companies has continued, despite host government hopes
to the contrary. The full extent of this fragmentation is not captured
because of the exclusion of a number of firms. If each company in
each country is considered separately, there were a total of 73
terminal firms in the Latin American automotive industry in 1972.
Of these, 22 had an annual output in that year of less than 1,000

TABLE 3.8

Percentage Equity in Affiliate

Firm	Argentina	Brazil	Chile	Colombia	Mexico	Peru	Venezuela
General Motors	100	100	–	–	100	–	100
Ford	100	51	–	–	100	–	100
Chrysler	100	92	License	80	91	100	100
Volkswagen	–	80	–	26	100	License	License
Fiat	89	–	99	–	–	–	40
Toyota	–	100	–	–	–	100	License
Renault	40*	–	50*	49	License	–	License
BLMC	–	–	53	–	–	–	–
Nissan	–	–	60	–	100	75	License
Peugeot	93	–	50*	–	–	–	–
Daimler–Benz	100	100	–	–	–	–	License
Citroen	91	–	100	–	–	–	–
American Motors	8*	–	–	–	46	License	100

*Same company.

Sources: Banque Francaise et Italienne pour l'Amérique du Sud, "L'industrie Automobile en Amérique Latine," Etudes Economiques, no. 3 (1972); J. Behrman, The Role of International Companies in Latin American Integration; Autos and Petrochemicals (Lexington, Mass.: D. C. Heath, 1972), Appendix A; company reports.

vehicles, while a further 21 had an output of between 1,000 and 10,000.[25] At the other end of the scale, only three firms had production figures of more than 100,000 vehicles, with another three between 50,000 and 100,000.

CONCLUSION

This chapter has described the origins and development of the automotive industry in Latin America, indicating the relationship between the growth of the industry on the continent and the tendencies in the international industry of which it forms a part. It has shown the way in which the oligopolistic structure of that industry, together with the policies adopted by host governments to promote the development of a local industry, gave rise to a large number of relatively small-scale producers being set up and the persistence of this structure to the present. It has also indicated the existence of three different levels of automotive industry development in the area: total integration, integration excluding major body stampings, and local assembly with the incorporation of some parts. The remainder of this study concentrates on three case studies, Argentina, Mexico, and Chile, one from each of the three groups identified. This will permit a more detailed consideration of the key features of the development of the Latin American automotive industry during the 1960s.

NOTES

1. M. Wilkins and F. Hill, American Business Abroad (Detroit: Wayne State University Press, 1964), pp. 145-49.

2. Ibid., p. 91. This may also have been the case with the Ford plant in Mexico. Wilkins and Hill state that Ford's head in Mexico was able to negotiate important concessions of railway freight rates, customs duties, and taxes for the company, but the original investment decision may have preceded this (p. 147).

3. G. Wythe, Industry in Latin America, 2nd ed. (New York: Columbia University Press, 1949), p. 119. If one estimates that the value added in the assembly of completely knocked down vehicles represents 10 percent of total costs, and that the value added in assembling semiknocked down vehicles is 5 percent, then this tariff would represent an effective rate of protection in the region of 300 percent.

4. D. M. Phelps, The Migration of Industry to South America (New York: McGraw-Hill, 1936).

5. Jorge Orvananos Lascurain, "Aspectos de la Demanda y Oferta Automotriz" (professional thesis, Instituto Tecnológico Autónomo de México, 1967), Chap. 2b (ii).

6. Economist Intelligence Unit, "The Brazilian Motor Industry," Motor Business, no. 18 (1959): 28-36.

7. This is the conclusion of a study of the procurement practices of U.S. firms operating in the Mexican automotive industry. See G. S. Edelberg, "The Procurement Practices of the Mexican Affiliates of Selected United States Automobile Firms" (D.B.A. thesis, Harvard University, 1963).

8. The value of output at prices in the country of origin was calculated using AMIA (Asociación Mexicana de la Industria Automotriz) data for the average prices of five different size groups of cars in their country of origin and weighting them by an estimate of their market share in 1961. A similar estimate of the foreign exchange saved in 1960 put the sum even lower at U.S. $1.3 million. See C. Sánchez-Marco, Introduction to the Mexican Automobile Industry (Paris: OECD Development Centre, 1968), pp. 7-8.

9. Consejo Nacional de Desarrollo (CONADE), La Industria Automotriz (Analisis Preliminar) (Buenos Aires, 1965), Table 23.

10. Carlos Octavio Gómez y Linares, "Papel de la Política Fiscal en el Desenvolvimiento de la Industria Automotriz" (professional thesis, Universidad Nacional Autónoma de México, 1970), Chap. 2b.

11. Asociación Mexicana de la Industria Automotriz (AMIA), "La Industria Automotriz de México en Cifras" (Mexico City: 1972), p. 69.

12. S. J. Parellada, La Industria Automotriz en la Argentina, UNIDO (ID/WG 76/9), 1970, p. 174.

13. "The Motor-Vehicle Industry in Latin America," Bank of London and South America Quarterly Review 2 (1962): 124.

14. See, for example, O. Altimir, H. Santamaria, and J. Sourrouillo, "Los Instrumentos de Promoción Industrial en La Postguerra," Desarrollo Económico 6 (1966): 99-105.

15. F. G. Donner, The World-wide Industrial Enterprise: Its Challenge and Promise (New York: McGraw-Hill, 1967), pp. 64-67.

16. I. M. D. Little, T. Scitovsky, and M. Scott, Industry and Trade in Some Developing Countries: A Comparative Study (Oxford University Press for OECD, 1970), p. 342.

17. Nacional Financiera, Elementos para una Política de Desarrollo de la Fabricación de Vehículos Automotrices en México (Mexico City, 1960).

18. See G. M. Bueno, "La Industria Siderúrgica y la Industria Automotriz," El Perfil de México en 1980, vol. 2 (Mexico City: Siglo XXI, 1971), p. 95.

19. Nacional Financiera, op. cit., p. 56.

20. King suggests that to have refused to allow General Motors and Ford to continue operating in Mexico would have seriously harmed the country's image with foreign investors. See T. King, Mexico, Industrialization and Trade Policies Since 1940 (Oxford: Oxford University Press for OECD, 1970), pp. 61-62. It is, of course, difficult to get any hard facts on the pressures brought to bear on host governments, but some general suggestions are indicative. In 1961, the Argentinian government revised the automotive industry promotional legislation through Decree 6567. The most significant changes involved were an increase in the permitted imported content of cars over 2,500 cc and a measure to make it easier to introduce new models. It appears that part of the motivation behind these changes was to give an added incentive to U.S. companies to start producing passenger cars in Argentina. In Mexico, it is believed that the Japanese government applied pressure in favor of Nissan's investment proposal being accepted. There is a striking similarity between the behavior described here and that that has been observed in South Africa. Here, too, no attempt was made to limit the number of firms, and the explanation given was that the "exclusion of firms from some countries while those from other countries were granted exclusive manufacturing rights might have had political implications," and that the exclusion of any of the existing foreign subsidiaries would have been interpreted as enmity toward foreign investors. See S. J. Kleu, "Import Substitution in the South African Automobile Industry" (D.B.A. thesis, Harvard University, 1967), pp. 223-53.

21. Figures given by Asociacão Nacional dos Fabricantes de Vehiculos Automotores (ANFAVEA) for Brazil; for Argentina, see Banque Francaise et Italienne pour l'Amérique du Sud, "L'industrie Automobile en Amérique Latine," Etudes Economiques, no. 3 (1972): 9.

22. AMIA, op. cit.

23. Gamma Ingenieros, Estudio de la Industria Automotriz Chilena, UNIDO (ID/WG 76/6), 1970, p. 2.

24. Hector Hurtado, La Industria Automotriz en Venezuela, UNIDO (ID/WG 76/7), 1970, p. 6.

25. R. Jenkins, "International Oligopoly and Dependent Industrialization in the Latin American Motor Industry," unpublished (Cambridge, 1974).

4

A MODEL OF THE DEVELOPMENT OF THE SECTOR OF PRODUCTION IN A PERIPHERAL ECONOMY

In Chapter 3 the fragmentation of the Latin American automotive industry among a large number of firms and the predominant position enjoyed by the major international companies were described. The main body of this work is an analysis of the way in which this structure has been generated in three countries, Argentina, Chile, and Mexico, and some of the further consequences to which it has given rise. This chapter presents a model of structural change within an industry for an underdeveloped economy. In the chapters that follow, empirical evidence is presented to support the theoretical generalizations made and to illustrate the specific operation of the model in each of the three cases.

A GENERAL OVERVIEW: THE GROWTH OF THE SECTOR OF PRODUCTION

The analysis of the development of an individual industry over time, or, as A. Cotta calls it, "the growth of the sector of production,"[1] has been a relatively neglected area of economic theory. This, no doubt, reflects, to some extent, the neglect of dynamic analysis on the part of microeconomic theory, which has remained tied by the limitations imposed by the static, or at best comparatively static, approach.[2] Industrial organization theory has been noticeably reluctant to go beyond description and classification of different market structures, to make generalizations about changes over time within an industry.[3] Conventional economic theory, therefore, does not have much to offer in the way of models to analyze the problem under consideration.

One exception, however, is the product cycle theory. This theory has been used by certain authors in the context of international trade and capital flows, but it also has a wider applicability.4 According to this theory, products, like men, have a life cycle passing from infancy through maturity to old age. When a product is first introduced, it is characterized by high unit costs and a relatively limited market. Production processes tend to be labor intensive, techniques change rapidly, and production runs are relatively short since constant modifications are being made to the product. For these reasons scientific and engineering expertise are essential if the product is to be successful, and the factor limiting entry into the industry is know-how rather than capital.

The industry at a certain point passes into a growth phase with sales beginning to expand rapidly and mass production techniques being introduced with a consequent increase in the capital-labor ratio. The number of firms in the industry rises as new firms are attracted by the growing market and entry is made easier by the expiry of patents and the acquisition of manufacturing skills. Casualties and mergers also tend to increase since many of the entrants are ill-equipped to supply the market. Management, defined to cover administrative skills and marketing, now becomes the crucial labor input.

Ultimately, the exhaustion of new markets and the appearance of substitutes lead to a slowing down of the rate of growth of sales and possibly a reduction in demand. Production techniques in this period become even more capital intensive because of the large quantity of specialized machinery and the optimal size of plant increases making economies of scale an important factor in determining the competitive strength of individual manufacturers. The number of firms tends to decline, and since there are few new innovations, unskilled and semiskilled labor are the most important human inputs.

This model cannot be applied directly to the development of an industry in a dependent underdeveloped economy, but it is possible to suggest an alternative scheme concentrating on the same basic variables. Typically, the initial source of supply of a particular product comes from imports rather than from a large number of small manufacturers. In this case, local operations will only involve sales and servicing so that the capital investment required is low. This initial phase will also tend to be associated with a diversity of sources of supply. In contrast to the initial phase of the product cycle in a developed country, the key human input will be knowledge of the local market rather than engineering skill. Moreover, the dependence on imports means that supply may well fluctuate in response to changes in the particular country's balance of payments position.

For many products it is possible to move from importing the finished good to local assembly of imported parts. Such a development may occur fairly early in a country's evolution when transport costs and tariff barriers make it profitable. This can be done with a minimum increase in capital investment at fairly low levels of output. It tends to create additional employment compared to the case where the assembled product is imported, and hence holds some appeal for host country governments, although it can easily give rise to cases of negative value added at international prices.*

Not all products are such that they can be assembled from imported parts; for these, only two stages may be identified, imports or local production. With assembled products, however, local assembly of imported parts represents an intermediate stage between importing the finished product and manufacturing it locally using locally produced parts. This last stage requires a much greater investment in fixed assets than either of the previous two stages since the transformation of materials generally requires more machinery and equipment. It also involves a much larger scale of production than is necessary for assembly, which tends to lead to greater concentration. It creates major new sources of employment while at the same time freeing the supply of the product from its previous dependence on the balance of payments position; and a sudden upsurge in sales can be a result of this.

In the manufacturing phase of an industry's development, access to foreign technology becomes a crucial factor. As long as products are imported or only assembled locally, the operations that take place in the underdeveloped country do not involve very complex processes since the technology is already embodied in the imports. What is more, since local value added is low, the competitive disadvantage of using inferior techniques is small. The transition to manufacturing production not only increases local value added and hence the importance of efficiency in production but also requires the use of complex techniques that are not usually possible to develop locally.

The need for foreign technology gives a new role to international corporations in the development process. The companies that previously supplied the market with imports are able to take advantage of the fact that their trademarks are already well known

---

*Negative value added occurs when the output of an industry valued at international prices is less than the value of the inputs used at international prices. This situation is most likely to arise in assembly processes where local value added at domestic prices is relatively small when these activities are heavily protected.[5]

and of their ability to mobilize local and foreign sources of credit, as well as almost always receiving various forms of government incentives. As Furtado points out, there is an initial stage of high profits when the product becomes freely available, and then, "Once supply returns to normal, the market tends to be controlled by one or more financially powerful groups, nearly always linked to the international consortia that had traditionally controlled imports."[6] It is this phenomenon that recent writers on Latin American development have labeled the "new dependence."[7]

COMPETITION WITHIN AN INDUSTRY:
THE STEINDL MODEL

The previous discussion illustrates broad lines along which an industry might be expected to develop in a peripheral economy. Further analysis of the problems posed in Chapter 3 requires the development of a model of intraindustry competition that will explain the unequal growth rates of different firms. These questions have been tackled by Josef Steindl in his two major books.[8] The remainder of this section will be devoted to an exposition of Steindl's model of competition within an industry.

Steindl bases his arguments on the existence of significant cost differentials between firms within the same industry, claiming that the existence of considerable cost differentials is of crucial importance to the theoretical analysis of price formation.[9] These cost differences are related to the size of firms, and their primary cause is to be found in the existence of economies of scale.[10] This assumption gives rise to the concept of the marginal producer, which is the highest cost producer in an industry, analogous to the least fertile land under cultivation in Ricardo's theory of land rent. In Steindl's formulation, the scarcity of big units of capital plays the role of the scarcity of better land. In an industry where competitive pressure is acute, the marginal firm earns only normal profits, whereas in an industry where entry is difficult such firms may earn a surplus. Thus, it is necessary to distinguish between "competitive" industries, where there is freedom of entry and exit and excess capacity is eliminated in the long run by price-cutting, and "monopolistic" industries, where this mechanism is not operative.

In addition to the assumptions concerning cost differentials and the marginal producer, the other assumptions made are that firms invest only in their own industry (an assumption that is later relaxed), that firms invest because they have saved in the past, and, finally, that the rate of growth of the market is exogenously given for the industry as a whole.

Let us consider first the case of an industry where the marginal producer earns only normal profits. Larger firms, tending to have higher profit margins as well as a higher rate of profit (unless the increase in the capital-output ratio with scale more than offsets the higher profit margin), will accumulate funds at a faster rate than small firms. Three alternative situations can be distinguished. First, the internal accumulation and hence the expansion of the large firms may be no faster than the rate of growth of the market, so that large firms are not increasing their market share and new entries are maintaining the share of small firms (since it is assumed that marginal firms do not accumulate). Second, large firms expand faster than the industry as a whole and then they increase their market share, but small firms may still be able to grow in absolute terms. Finally, the rate of growth of the favorably placed firms may be so fast relative to the growth of demand, or their initial market share may be so large, that they are only able to expand by driving out marginal producers.

The three alternative situations can be expressed algebraically as follows:

$$x'_f < x'; \qquad x'_d > x' \tag{a}$$

$$x' > x'_d > 0; \quad x'/S_f > x'_f > x' \tag{b}$$

$$x'_d < 0; \qquad x'/S_f > x'_f \tag{c}$$

where x' is the rate of growth of the market, x'_f the rate of growth of favorably placed firms, x'_d the rate of growth of marginal producers, and S_f the market share of favorably placed firms.

In order to expand their market share, the favorably placed firms must undertake a "sales effort," which can take the form of heavier advertising expenditures or price or quality competition. Such a sales effort will result in a reduction in the net profit margin of these producers and hence the funds available for internal accumulation. If one then assumes that new capacity involves lower costs than existing capacity as a result of technical progress, one can identify two factors in the dynamics of the industry's development. These are cost reductions by progressive firms, which tend to increase the profit margin by expanding the cost differential between them and the marginal producer, and the excessive internal accumulation by the former, which leads to the elimination of high cost firms and tends to reduce the profit margin.

Figure 4.1 helps to illustrate the interaction of these two factors. The output of the various firms is arranged in the declining order of their costs, from left to right along the horizontal axis.

FIGURE 4.1

The Steindl Model of Intraindustry Competition

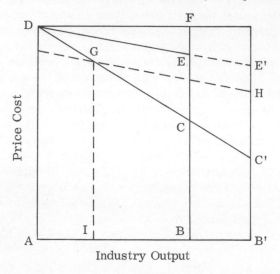

Source: Compiled by the author.

The cost curve of the industry is given by CD. If EF represents
the sales effort, then the price curve is given by DE. If progressive
firms expand output from B to B', costs fall to C' and the profit
margin increases to C'E'. This is the first of the two effects considered above. If this leads to a higher level of internal accumulation
than can be supported by the expansion of the industry as a whole,
there is a competitive struggle and the price line is driven down to
GH, thus eliminating the high cost producers AI and driving down
the profit margin of the most progressive firms to C'H.

In a monopolistic industry, marginal firms earn abnormal
profits since they tend to require capital equipment on a scale that
makes it impossible to refer to them as small firms. Moreover,
since they are not small, marginal firms are likely to have larger
financial resources and hence are able to offer more resistance to
any attempt to drive them out of the industry. This increases the
costs to the progressive firm in attempting to increase its market
share and thus reduces the incentive to do so. In many cases,
therefore, the sales effort required for expansion would be so large
as to offset the advantage obtained by innovation and accumulation.
As Steindl puts it, "Oligopoly is grit thrown in the mechanism of
competition previously described."[11]

INTRAINDUSTRY COMPETITION IN A
PERIPHERAL ECONOMY

As was indicated above, the key factor underlying cost differentials for Steindl was economies of scale in conjunction with size
differences between firms. Although he does not emphasize the fact,
his data indicating a positive correlation between size and gross
profit margins refer to plants, and it is an assumption on his part
that interplant cost differences are reflected in differences between
firms.[12] In the case of a dependent industry in a peripheral economy,
however, the essential factor distinguishing favorably placed firms
is not their size of plant but their foreign ownership. This may be
thought of as the size of the total operation into which the individual
company is integrated, since foreign subsidiaries are part of a
worldwide unit, while locally owned firms are, at the most, part
of a national conglomerate. This is clearly not the same concept
as the technical economies of scale that Steindl sees as the primary
cause of cost differentials.

There are a number of reasons why one might expect foreign
subsidiaries that are part of a worldwide organization to enjoy lower
costs than national firms in the same industry. These derive in the
main from the scale of the total operation and the increased flexibility
that access to an international parent company and its affiliates gives.
(Chapter 7 discusses two examples of this flexibility at work in the
cases of Chile and Mexico.) Two of the most general advantages
enjoyed by subsidiaries are access to the parent company's technology
(understood in a wide sense to include trademarks, marketing skills,
administrative skills, and so on) and to its financial support.[13]

Generally, only the multinational corporations are in a position
to undertake large-scale industrial research, and local firms in the
periphery are obliged to rely on licenses in order to obtain the technology that would be expensive to develop locally.* In order to bring
out the significance of this fact, it is necessary to consider briefly
the nature of the international market for technology.

It has now come to be recognized that the market for technology
does not approximate the perfect competition model. This is partly

---

*This obviously does not apply to all industries but only to
those high technology industries normally considered dynamic.
It should also be borne in mind that one is considering the cost to
the individual firm of developing its own technology. Divergences
between private and social cost might mean that it would still be in
the national interest to develop the technology locally.

a consequence of the inherent ambiguity in any market for information, since the perfect competition model assumes perfect knowledge.[14] It is also a consequence of the empirical fact that international transfers of technology usually occur in sectors dominated by international oligopolists.[15] C. Vaitsos has argued that the marginal cost of transferring technology from the point of view of the firm making the transfer is zero, since it already possesses the technology that has been developed for other markets, or close to zero where there are some local adaptation costs. On the other hand, the marginal cost to the recipient of developing an alternative is either very large or even infinite.[16] Between these two limits the price is set by relative bargaining strength.

Jorge Katz[17] has developed a model of bilateral monopoly to determine the price at which technology will be sold by a monopolistic supplier to a recipient that enjoys a monopoly position in the supply of a final good in the domestic market. The point is that part of the monopoly profit that the final good producer is able to make by its position in the domestic market is appropriated by the technology supplier. The supplier cannot, however, appropriate the whole of the benefit of his customer's monopoly position since an increase in the royalty charged as a percentage of sales will lead to a reduction in output and an increase in the price of the final good. The only way in which the technology supplier can secure the entire monopoly profit available is through direct investment.

J. Katz assumes a single monopolist in both the technology and the final goods market. In practice, oligopoly is a more likely situation, and this will affect the price according to whether competition is stronger in the technology market or in the product market (on the supply side). Even so, it remains true that the foreign investor appropriates the whole of the monopoly profit available from facing a downward sloping demand curve, while the licensed producer yields part of this profit to the licensor. Since royalty and licensing charges of 5 percent on sales are common, this factor can lead to significant cost differentials between foreign subsidiaries, which do not have to pay for technology supplied by the parent company, and nationally owned firms, which do.[18]

Technology is usually thought of as know-how related specifically to production. In this context, however, one is interested in a much broader spectrum of advantages that a foreign firm enjoys over local competitors. Thus, trademarks, technical assistance in administration, the use of advanced marketing techniques, and so on must be included. The local firm has to obtain these in exactly the same way as it must obtain technical assistance in production and design, rights to use blueprints, and so on.[19] Without them, the local firm suffers a productivity disadvantage. With them, it has to cede part of its profit to the foreign supplier.

The second important source of advantage to foreign subsidiaries is differential access to capital. This can take two forms: either access to debt and equity capital on preferential terms reflected in lower interest charges and higher share prices or greater access to credit reflected in a higher gearing ratio. As far as the first form is concerned, the scale of the multinational corporation gives it a double advantage. It is able to raise capital in countries where interest rates tend to be lower, whereas national firms are usually forced to raise capital locally since they are virtually unknown outside the home country.[20] Moreover, even when foreign firms raise capital in the country where their subsidiary operates, as they often do,[21] they are able to do so on more favorable terms than their national competitors because of the security the parent company represents.[22]

Suppose that a nationally owned company must pay an interest rate of 16 percent on capital it raises locally, while a foreign subsidiary can obtain capital at an 8 percent rate of interest either locally or abroad. Assume further that both companies have a debt-equity ratio of 1 and a capital-output ratio also of 1. Then the additional cost of capital to the local firm represents a cost disadvantage of 4 percent on sales. With a capital-output ratio of 2, then the cost disadvantage would be increased to 8.

In this example it was assumed that the gearing ratios for foreign subsidiaries and local firms were the same. In practice, the backing of the parent company means that a subsidiary is not subject to the same restrictions on its gearing ratio as a locally owned enterprise. Thus, where local finance is available at low real rates of interest, the foreign subsidiary may use a high gearing ratio in order to increase its rate of return on the parent's own capital.[23] This can be illustrated by maintaining the assumption that local companies must pay a rate of interest of 16 percent and that foreign subsidiaries pay only 8 percent and introducing an assumed rate of return on total assets of 20 percent for all firms and a debt-equity ratio of 2:1 for foreign subsidiaries and 1:1 for local firms. It can then be shown that local firms will have a rate of return of 24 percent on their own invested capital as compared with 44 percent for foreign firms. Thus, the combined effect of differences in the cost of finance and its availability can be considerable.

The differential costs of capital and technology would appear to be the most significant sources of cost differentials between firms in dependent economies. What then of the other major inputs into the productive process, labor and materials? It is possible that the overall size of multinational corporations gives their subsidiaries greater bargaining power vis-a-vis both their suppliers and their

labor force. In theory, this could lead to lower prices for their
materials and lower labor costs as a result of lower wage rates.

Lower prices could arise where suppliers are also multinational in the scope of their operations so that the customer is able
to use its purchases in the home market as a lever in order to obtain
better terms from the supplier in other markets where they both
operate. Lower labor costs could arise from the creation of a docile
labor force through threats to move production elsewhere* and a
greater ability to withstand union pressure for wage increases since
the company's operations in any one country is only a small part
of its total activities, whereas unions are still fragmented by national
boundaries.

There does not appear to be any empirical evidence to support
the hypothesis that subsidiaries have used their potential bargaining
power in this way. As far as labor is concerned, the evidence
suggests that foreign firms tend to pay their workers higher wages,
thus creating a privileged elite within the local working class.[24]

Although it has been argued that differences exist in the cost
of technology and finance to locally owned firms and foreign subsidiaries, it must be emphasized that these are not necessarily
reflected in differences in the payments actually made by the two
kinds of firms. While the payments made by national firms reflect
the cost to them of the inputs that they use, the same cannot be held
to be true for wholly owned subsidiaries, since charges appearing
as royalties in company accounts are a way of transferring resources
from the affiliate to the parent, which has no connection with the cost
of the technology provided. Similarly, where the parent provides
loan capital to a subsidiary, the financial charges that the latter
has to pay may bear no relation to the opportunity cost of capital to
the multinational corporation as a whole. This, needless to say,
makes it difficult to test the underlying relationships empirically.

The above analysis concentrates on one particular type of
inc .stry, namely, that in which foreign and local firms both produce
basically similar products using similar foreign techniques. This
seems to be a fair characterization of the so-called "dynamic"
industries ("so-called," as "dynamic" refers not to their actual
performance, which may be quite undynamic, but to the expectation,
based on the experience of the developed countries, that they would
be dynamic). Another broad type of industry is that in which foreign
subsidiaries compete with local artisan-type production, where both
the technology and the product are different for the two groups of

---

*Compare Henry Ford II's threat to the workers at Dagenham
to concentrate Ford's expansion on the continent.

firms. In a dynamic industry, it is possible to concentrate on differences in the costs of inputs, whereas in the second case comparison
of the two groups of firms would be much more complicated, requiring
consideration of both technology and the demand side.

In summary, it is possible to say that economies of scale (as
they can be referred to in the broad sense of scale in its global context) accruing to favorably placed firms in a peripheral economy
tend to be pecuniary economies, whereas in a developed economy
they are real economies. The modification of the Steindl model in
order to apply it to a dependent economy requires changes in the
behavioral as well as the structural hypotheses.

BEHAVIORAL ASSUMPTIONS OF THE MODEL

The key behavioral assumptions made by Steindl are that firms
invest what they have saved in the past and that they tend to do so in
their own industry because it is easier to expand in a branch of production with which one is already familiar than to go into new industries. In view of recent developments in the advanced capitalist
economies (especially the formation of conglomerates), the latter
assumption has come to be extremely doubtful in the context in which
it was formulated, as Steindl himself has admitted.[25]

The only model of foreign investment that shares Steindl's
behavioral hypothesis is the gambler's earning theory associated
with Barlow and Wender, Penrose, and others, according to which
profits made abroad are reinvested locally. This may be a reasonable assumption during the early stage of a national company's
transition into a multinational corporation,[26] but ceases to be a
rational model for corporate behavior once international operations
have become widespread.[27] Moreover, the empirical evidence does
not support the assumption of subsidiary independence but is consistent with a model of global maximization.[28] Thus, instead of
the firm's investment decisions being made on the basis of past
profits, they are made on the basis of future profit expectations
compared to those in the other countries in which it operates and
the total available resources of the parent company.*

If the gambler's earning hypothesis is rejected as a model of
behavior for the foreign subsidiary, then it is necessary to introduce
an alternative behavioral postulate that will relate the rate of expansion of these firms to internal conditions in the country that is being

---

*This model applies to the expansion of existing capacity rather
than the initial investment decision.

studied, making <u>ceteris</u> <u>paribus</u> assumptions concerning conditions
elsewhere for the time being.

It is then possible to identify a number of important variables.
First, there is the current and past rate of profit of the firm, which
is an indicator of expected future profits. Second, the rate of growth
of the market determines the ease with which firms are able to
expand. Third, there is the cost to the firm of driving out its competitors in order to increase its market share, which is determined
by the profit rate of marginal firms and the cost advantage of favorably
placed firms, as well as the financial strength of marginal firms.
Finally, one must introduce a risk factor that leads foreign corporations to limit the amount of their own capital transferred to the
subsidiary, particularly during the early stages of the investment.[29]

The main points can be shown diagramatically as in Figure 4.2.
In the initial situation, the total output of the industry is AC, AB of
which is produced by local firms and BC by foreign firms. As in
Figure 4.1, firms are ranked according to costs, with the difference
that there is now a sharp discontinuity in the cost curve corresponding
to the cost differential between local and foreign firms. If the market
is expanding by, say CM, then foreign firms are able to expand their
output by an equal amount without reducing the sales of locally owned
firms.

Given a stagnating market, however, if foreign firms wish to
expand output to BM, then the output of local firms must be reduced
by AP. In order to do this, prices must be lowered from HK to RV.
(This may also be thought of as a sales effort of KV per unit rather
than a price-cut.) In deciding whether or not to undertake such an
expansion, the profit-maximizing firm must compare the area
JTUN, which represents the profit lost as a result of the price-cut
(or sales effort), with UELV, the gain from the expansion. This
can be seen to depend on the profit margin of the marginal firm
that gives the amount by which prices have to be cut or sales effort
increased to effect a given increase in output, the initial profit of
foreign firms, and the lowering of costs as a result of the expansion.*

Despite their complexity, the above relationships represent
an oversimplification as far as the behavior of a foreign subsidiary
is concerned, ignoring as it does the effects of the parent company's
liquidity and its alternative opportunities for investment elsewhere.
It is, however, an improvement over the gambler's earning theory.
In the case of locally owned companies, Steindl's assumption that

---

*Figure 4.2 suffers from being a tool of comparative statics.
It is also impossible to show the financial strength of different firms
in two dimensions.

FIGURE 4.2

Intraindustry Competition in a
Peripheral Economy

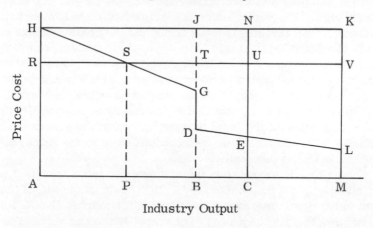

Source: Compiled by the author.

firms expand by reinvesting the profits that they have earned in the
past would seem satisfactory. The possibilities of outside finance
are limited by the low degree of development of the capital market
in most underdeveloped economies so that firms expand by plowing
back profits.[30]

THE COMPLETE MODEL

It is now possible to set in motion a dynamic two-sector model
of structural change within an industry in a peripheral economy.
The nature of interfirm cost differentials has been identified and
behavioral assumptions have been made about the investment decisions
of the two groups of firms. All that remains is to link these to the
changes over time in demand and supply conditions, which were
discussed at the beginning of this chapter, and which are exogeneous
from the point of view of the model of competition. It was pointed
out that the startup of local production in underdeveloped economies
was likely to be followed immediately by a rapid growth of sales
where there had previously been import restrictions. It was also
indicated that local manufacturing tended to be associated with
increasing capital intensity and scale requirements. Firms require
more working capital to finance local suppliers and more fixed
capital for their own operations. Similarly, the rate of royalty pay-

ment on sales increases with local content since royalties are frequently not charged on imported components.

In the initial period of rapid growth of the industry, prices tend to be high, possibly up to the tariff barrier, and profits are correspondingly high. The capital intensity of production is low so that local firms do not find themselves at a great cost disadvantage compared to foreign subsidiaries. Moreover, their greater knowledge of the local environment gives them certain advantages over subsidiaries so that they are able to earn a more than adequate rate of return.[31] The rate of growth of the market is sufficiently great for both groups of firms to expand at the desired rate, especially since a lack of knowledge of the local market may make foreign companies reluctant to risk much of their own capital, even to the extent of preferring licensing agreements.

Over time, however, two factors enter to influence the dynamic of the situation. On the demand side, if the rate of growth of the market slows down, increased competition for market shares tends to drive down the rate of profit. Let us put it another way. The rate of growth of the two sectors taken together must, in the long run, equal the exogenously given rate of growth of demand. Since the rate of growth of supply is a function of the rate of profit in the two sectors and the changing level of capital intensity, then these variables must be adjusted to bring about the equality of supply and demand. But the rate of change in capital intensity, it is assumed, is also an exogenous variable, so that the entire burden of adjustment falls on the profit rates. Thus a slowdown in the rate of growth of demand tends to lead to a fall in the rate of profit.*

On the supply side, two factors appear to be important. First, there is a tendency for the cost disadvantage of local firms to increase over time. This is in part owing to the increasing level of capital intensity, either through an increase in fixed investment or in working capital, which affects nationally owned firms to a greater extent than local firms because of the higher cost of capital to them (discussed above) and, in part, because of increased royalty payments. This increase in cost disparity is, as was suggested above, an incentive for foreign firms to expand at the expense of locally owned firms. The second factor is the change in the perception of risk on the part of the foreign companies as they become more familiar with the local

---

*"Tends," since in certain periods exogenous changes in the capital-output ratio may be sufficient to offset demand changes. Also, if the changes in capital intensity are not to be exogenous, changes in the rate of growth of demand may be offset by changes in capital intensity.

environment, which makes them prepared to make a greater capital contribution, manifesting itself in a more rapid growth of subsidiaries and a replacement of licensees by joint ventures and joint ventures by wholly owned subsidiaries.

Let us suppose for the moment that the rate of growth of demand is unchanged, perhaps because it is controlled by the government through a quota system, prices also being controlled. Then the changes described in the previous paragraph will lead unambiguously to an increase in the rate of growth of foreign firms, since demand growth and profit rates remain unchanged. This will lead to increased competition and tend to drive down profits. Thus, a new equilibrium will be established with a lower rate of growth for domestic firms and a higher rate of growth for foreign subsidiaries. If now it is assumed that the rate of growth of demand slows down, then this serves only to accentuate the process described above.

So far the analysis has assumed implicitly constant returns to scale and full (or at least constant) utilization of capacity for all firms. Although economies of scale have not been assigned the role of primum mobile in our model as they were in that of Steindl, they do undoubtedly exist and reinforce the tendencies described above. Thus, economies of scale, by reducing the costs of expansion, increase the incentive to expand market shares. There is a cumulative process whereby an initial cost advantage leads to a faster rate of growth and thus larger scale, which further increases the original cost advantage.

Underutilization of capacity plays a similar role to economies of scale (indeed, it may be thought of as its short-run equivalent). This is likely to be particularly important in industries where there are significant plant indivisibilities so that capacity tends to be expanded ahead of demand. Fajnzylber makes the point that in dynamic industries, foreign subsidiaries tend to build excess capacity in order to obtain an optimum scale of plant and then use various mechanisms in order to increase utilization.[32] In view of their limited financial resources, local firms may well be unable to both invest in an optimum scale plant and undertake the necessary expenditures in terms of advertising or consumer credit to achieve reasonable levels of utilization. Thus, they are forced to adopt suboptimal positions.[33]

CONCLUSION

This chapter has presented a model of competition and growth within a sector of production that can be used to explain the development of the Latin American automotive industry during the 1960s.

Three main features have been identified in the operation of the model. The first is the change involved in the move from importing or assembly operations to local manufacturing, particularly the increased capital requirements and importance of foreign technology that this implies. Also on the supply side, there is the existence of significant cost differentials between foreign subsidiaries and national firms as a result of the advantage that the former enjoy in terms of access to finance and technology. Finally, on the demand side, there is the rate of growth of the total market that determines the expansion possibilities for firms and the degree of pressure toward the elimination of some existing firms. In Chapters 5 and 6, some evidence is presented to illustrate these points in the context of the automotive industry in Argentina, Chile, and Mexico.

NOTES

1. A. Cotta, "The Growth of the Sector of Production," in Problems of Economic Dynamics and Planning: Essays in Honour of Michel Kalecki (Oxford: Pergamon, 1966), pp. 79-105.

2. The "new theories of the firm" represent a partial exception to this generalization, but, although they attempt to provide a dynamic analysis of the individual firm, they do not go beyond the single firm, that is, they do not deal with industry dynamics. For a discussion of these theories, see R. Marris, "An Introduction to Theories of Corporate Growth," in The Corporate Economy: Growth, Competition and Innovative Potential, ed. R. Marris and A. Wood (New York: Macmillan, 1971), pp. 1-36.

3. Bain, for instance, in his basic text, Industrial Organization, states that no single pattern of concentration typifies all industries. Rather, he believes that a fairly common situation is one where initially there are a fairly large number of small firms, concentration then increasing in maturity, reaching a peak that is subsequently maintained or falls off slightly, but in either case tends to stabilize at a relatively high level. This, significantly, is the only aspect of industrial structure about which Bain even attempts such a generalization. See J. Bain, Industrial Organization, 2nd ed. (New York: Wiley, 1968), pp. 159-62.

4. The following summary of the product cycle theory is based on S. Hirsch, Location of Industry and International Competitiveness (Oxford: Clarendon Press, 1967), pp. 16-42. See also R. Vernon, "International Investment and International Trade in the Product Cycle," Quarterly Journal of Economics 80 (1966): 190-207.

5. See I. M. D. Little, T. Scitovsky, and M. Scott, Industry and Trade in Some Developing Countries: A Comparative Study (Oxford: Oxford University Press for OECD, 1970), pp. 423-27.

6. C. Furtado, Economic Development of Latin America: A Survey from Colonial Times to the Cuban Revolution (Cambridge: The University Press, 1970).

7. F. Cardoso and E. Faletto, Dependencia y Desarrollo en America Latina: Ensayo de Interpretación Sicológica (Mexico: Siglo XXI, 1971); V. Bambirra, "Integracion Monopolica Mundial e Industrialización: sus contradicciones," Sociedad y Desarrollo 1 (1972); O. Caputo and R. Pizarro, Imperialismo, Dependencia y Relaciones Económicas Internacionales (Santiago: Centro de Estudios Socio-Economicos, 1970); T. dos Santos, El Nuevo Carácter de la Dependencia (Santiago: Centro de Estudios Socio-Economicos, 1968).

8. See his two major works, Small and Big Business: Economic Problems of the Size of Firms (Oxford: Blackwell, 1945) and Maturity and Stagnation in American Capitalism (Oxford: Blackwell, 1952). A model which is similar to that of Steindl in many respects has been developed by P. Sylos-Labini. Unlike Steindl, who emphasizes accumulation, Sylos-Labini's main concern is with the determination of the equilibrium price under oligopoly. Consequently, although the issue of intraindustry competition and the elimination of small firms is discussed by Sylos-Labini, it is not as fully developed as in Steindl's writings. For clarity of exposition, the discussion has been couched entirely in terms of Steindl's model. It is also worth mentioning here that Sylos-Labini's analysis is carried out in terms of a homogeneous oligopoly, but he indicates that it can be extended to differentiated oligopoly. See P. Sylos-Labini, Oligopoly and Technical Progress (Cambridge, Mass.: Harvard University Press, 1962), pp. 53-56.

9. Steindl, Maturity, op. cit., p. 18.

10. Steindl, Small and Big, op. cit., pp. 13-21; Maturity, op. cit., pp. 18-40.

11. Steindl, Maturity, op. cit., p. 55.

12. Ibid., p. 37. In fairness to Steindl, it should be pointed out that, in Small and Big, op. cit., pp. 14-15, he mentions the importance of economies of scale in industrial research and other factors that are related to firm rather than plant scale.

13. An empirical study comparing the factors perceived as obstacles to their expansion by local and foreign (United States and Canadian) firms in El Salvador indicated the availability of capital and the availability of technical and administrative skills as the two areas where the advantage of foreign firms was most marked. See W. J. Bilkley, Industrial Stimulation (Lexington, Mass.: Heath Lexington Books, 1970), pp. 171-74.

14. K. Arrow, "Economic Welfare and the Allocation of Resources for Invention," in The Rate and Direction of Inventive Activity: Economic and Social Factors, National Bureau for Economic Research (Princeton, N.J.: Princeton University Press, 1962), pp. 609-25.

15. This is well established for technology transfers through direct foreign investment. See J. N. Behrman, Some Patterns in the Rise of Multinational Enterprise, Research Paper 18 (University of North Carolina, 1969). The same appears to be true for all contractual transfers of technology. See United Nations, Conference on Trade and Development (UNCTAD), Major Issues Arising from the Transfer of Technology to Developing Countries (TD/B/AC. 11/10), 1972, pp. 7-10.

16. C. V. Vaitsos, Transfer of Resources and Preservation of Monopoly Rent, Center for International Affairs, EDR No. 168 (Harvard University, 1970), pp. 17-23.

17. J. Katz,"Importación de Tecnología, Aprendizaje Local e Industrialización Dependiente," Centro de Investigaciones Económicas, Documentos de Trabajo No. 59 (Instituto Torcuato di Tella, 1972), pp. II 7-18.

18. For Argentina, see Katz, ibid., pp. VIII 11-15. For Mexico, see M. S. Wionczek, G. M. Bueno, and J. E. Navarrete, "La Transferencia Internacional de Tecnología al Nivel de Empresa: El caso de México," mimeographed (Mexico: Fondo de Cultura Económica, 1974), pp. 91-94. It should be noted that a royalty of 5 percent on sales implies a higher rate on the value added by the firm, and may be greater than the profit margin that remains after the royalty has been paid.

19. F. Fajnzylber, Estrategia Industrial y Empresas Internacionales: Posición Relativa de América Latina y Brasil, ECLA, UN E/CN 121 12/ (1970), pp. 125-26.

20. S. Rose, "The Rewarding Strategies of Multinationalism," Fortune 78 (1968): 100-05, 180-82.

21. See M. Z. Brooke and H. L. Remmers, The Strategy of Multinational Enterprise: Organization and Finance (London: Longman, 1970), Chap. 2, p. 6. U.S. manufacturing subsidiaries in Latin America raised 40 percent of their capital from local external sources (more than in any other area) in the period 1957-65. See Fajnzylber, op. cit., Chap. 2.

22. See D. Chudnovsky, Empresas Multinacionales y Ganancias Monopólicas (Buenos Aires: Siglo XXI, 1975).

23. Ibid.

24. It is well known that workers of foreign companies in the export sector in underdeveloped economies are often paid higher wages than prevail in the economy as a whole; for example, the case

of the Chilean copper miners. It also appears that even within one industry, foreign companies pay higher wages. See R. C. Maddox, Wage Differences Between U.S. and Guatemalan Industrial Firms in Guatemala, Studies in Latin American Business no. 10 (University of Texas, 1971).

25. See Josef Steindl, "On Maturity in Capitalist Economies," in Problems of Economic Dynamics and Planning: Essays in Honour of Michel Kalecki (Oxford: Pergamon, 1966), pp. 423-32.

26. See Rose, op. cit.

27. For a criticism of the gambler's earning theory, see S. Hymer, "The International Operations of National Firms" (Ph.D. thesis, Massachusetts Institute of Technology, 1960), pp. 169-79.

28. Stevens has carried out an econometric test of this hypothesis. See Guy V. G. Stevens, "Fixed Investment Expenditures of Foreign Manufacturing Affiliates of U.S. Firms," Yale Economic Essays 9 (1969): 136-98.

29. See Y. Aharoni, The Foreign Investment Decision Process (Cambridge, Mass.: Harvard Graduate School of Business Administration, 1966), especially Chap. 6.

30. G. di Tella, "The Behaviour of the Firm with a Financial Restriction," Journal of Industrial Economics 27 (1969): 119-31.

31. Bilkley concluded that the areas where local firms apparently enjoyed an advantage over foreign firms were those related to the superior contacts and better knowledge of local conditions of the former. See Bilkley, op. cit., p. 171.

32. F. Fajnzylber, Sistema Industrial y Exportación de Manufacturas, ECLA (E/CN. 12.), 1970, pp. 280-98.

33. See di Tella, op. cit.

5

AUTOMOTIVE INDUSTRY TECHNOLOGY, SUPPLY CONDITIONS, AND COST DIFFERENTIALS

It was argued in Chapter 4 that the development of the Latin American automotive industry could be explained by a model of intraindustry competition. This chapter concentrates on two of the main features of the model that relate to the supply side of the industry's development, that is, the changeover from assembly to manufacturing and the existence of cost differentials between foreign subsidiaries and local firms.

As was discussed previously, there is a tendency for the capital intensity and technological complexity of production to increase as an industry moves from assembly operations to full manufacturing. This generalization is made more specific by reference to the technology of the automotive industry. It will be shown that the introduction of automotive manufacture requires a considerable increase in investment on the part of firms that wish to continue production. This is a reflection of the rising capital requirements that result from the greater capital intensity and higher minimum scale requirements of the other processes involved in production as compared to assembly.

In the latter part of this chapter, the existence of significant cost differentials between foreign subsidiaries and locally owned firms is discussed. Since these differences are related to the preferential access to capital and technology enjoyed by subsidiaries of multinational corporations, it is to be expected that the differential will widen with the introduction of manufacturing production, as well as the rising capital requirements and technological level that this involves.

TECHNOLOGY

It is possible to identify a number of stages of automotive industry development.[1] In the first stage, local activities related to the automotive industry are confined to distribution, servicing, and possibly the production of some replacement parts, such as batteries and tires, while the vehicles themselves are imported "on wheels," that is, fully assembled. During this phase, the supply of vehicles comes from a variety of different sources and there may be significant competition.

Transport costs or tariffs may soon lead to assembly plants being set up. It is only a small step to move on to the final assembly of semiknocked down (SKD) vehicles, which can be carried out in rudimentary buildings with a minimum amount of machinery and equipment. Capital requirements tend to increase when the vehicles are painted locally and, at a more advanced stage, with completely knocked down (CKD) assembly, which includes local welding and body-building shops. The necessary capital investment is, nevertheless, still within reach of local entrepreneurs, and often the assemblers are the previous importers. The protection received from imports and the limited number of firms setting up plants imply a reduction in competition, and this, taken together with the fact that the greater part of the final product is imported from a parent company or licensor, gives considerable scope for over-pricing.[2]

As was seen in Chapter 3, the impact of purely assembly operations on the local economy tends to be limited. There is little if any saving in foreign exchange, and the effect in terms of backward and forward linkages and employment creation is small. It has been estimated that the labor and materials required to pack a Renault 10 cost as much as it would to assemble the car.[3] Even with a minimal incorporation of local parts of, say, 5 or 10 percent, there may not be any significant foreign exchange saving, especially when it is remembered that the system of deletion allowances practiced by the exporting firms reduces the gains from omitting items from a CKD pack.* Table 5.1 indicates the situation with a 5 percent local content.

---

*This is the system by which the omission of a part from a CKD kit leads to a reduction in the price of the pack of less than the value of the omitted part. This leads to the logical possibility that a firm imports an empty CKD pack and pays, say, 50 percent of what it would pay for a complete pack.

TABLE 5.1

Savings in Foreign Exchange from
Local Assembly
(dollars)

	Imports	SKD	CKD
Ex-factory price	1,000	980	950
Minor deletions		-50	-50
	1,000	930	900
Packing and FOB charges	{ 40	110	{ 100
Freight and insurance		80	
Total	1,040	1,120	1,000

Source: A. S. El Darwish, "The Establishment of an Automotive Industry in Developing Countries," in UNIDO, Establishment and Development of Automotive Industries in Developing Countries (ID/36 vol. 2, 1970), pp. 59-72, Table 2.

The first locally manufactured parts to be incorporated are those, such as batteries or tires, that already have been developed in order to meet the demand for replacements. The sum total of these parts, however, would only account for between 5 and 10 percent of a vehicle's price. There is a limitation on the use of local parts at this stage since basic parts, such as bearings, cannot be bought locally unless main parts, for example, engines, are imported in unassembled form, which would increase their volume and consequently transport costs. There are some other parts that can be supplied locally with little additional investment. Examples of such parts are shock absorbers, small stampings, and electrical parts that in many cases can be produced by existing manufacturers. The incorporation of these items, taken together with an allowance for assembly costs, permits the achievement of a local content of about 35 percent in this stage of automotive industry development. This is illustrated by the following cost breakdown (in percent) of a low-cost, medium-sized car found in a Chilean study:[4]

Wheels and tires	4.4
Windows	1.6
Brake operating system	1.2
Upholstery	7.0
Raw material for paint	2.9

Radiator	1.9
Small mechanical parts	3.4
Body accessories	4.6
Total	27.0

Add to this an estimated 5 to 10 percent for assembly costs, and the total is in the region of 35 percent.

During this period, the industry finds itself with increased requirements of working capital in order to finance the newly developed local suppliers. Dependence on local parts may prove a new source of supply bottlenecks and lead to excess capacity in the terminal sector. On the other hand, new sources of employment are created.

Further local integration involves the engine and transmission, which raises content to some 60 percent. Finally, local stamping of the major body parts brings the industry properly into the final stage of development with an almost entirely domestically produced vehicle.* It is only in the later stages of local integration that the terminal manufacturer becomes involved in machining, pressing, and possibly foundry activities. In the previous stage, the terminal producer is still basically an assembly plant, although in some cases it may integrate backward into part production. The essential difference between this and the import and CKD assembly stages is that the terminal plant now buys some parts locally instead of importing them.

Since an increase in national content involves the introduction of new production processes at the local level, it has repercussions on economies of scale, investment requirements, and costs in the automotive industry. The different processes undertaken in an integrated car factory, that is, assembly, machining, stamping, forging, and casting, are subject to different cost schedules and, hence, scale requirements. It is generally agreed that economies of scale are most significant, and the additional costs of low volume

---

*It should be noted that these figures are only estimates of the shares of the various groups of parts in the cost of the final product and will not correspond exactly to the percentages in particular countries or individual firms. They do not necessarily conform with the local content requirements set down in government legislation since these are measured in a variety of ways. There are also differences between individual models; for example, the use of an overhead camshaft engine in the Fiat 128 increased the share of the engine in total cost relative to the body, which is made from four major pressings.

operations, therefore, greatest, in the stamping process, which requires expensive dies and presses. Machining is also subject to large-scale economies, but to a somewhat lesser extent than stamping. The other processes also have decreasing costs, especially foundry work (see Appendix A).

As a result, the disadvantages of small-scale production tend to increase with local content. Up to a level of local content of about 20 to 25 percent, different scales of production make relatively little difference to costs over a range of 8,000 to 50,000 units a year (see Figure 5.1). Above this level, the disadvantages of small scale becomes more important. Finally, when local content exceeds 65 percent, they are overwhelming, reflecting again the importance of scale economies in body stamping. This is the pattern that one would have predicted from the nature of the basic production processes.

Not only do the different processes involved in vehicle production enjoy differing economies of scale, they also require different initial investments. At an output of 10,000 cars a year, it has been estimated that the investment for an assembly plant would be around $6.4 million. Partial integration, involving some machining and foundry operations, would increase investment requirements to $19.1 million. A fully integrated factory, however, would involve a total investment in the region of $49 million, of which $15 million would be in the machining department and $21.1 million in stamping.[5] During the initial stages of local integration, when the changeover is made from CKD assembly to use some local parts, the terminal firm does not need to make much additional capital outlay (at least as far as investment in fixed assets is concerned). Further integration to include the engine and bodywork, on the other hand, means the creation of machining and stamping departments and hence a considerable increase in investment.

CHANGES IN SUPPLY CONDITIONS IN
ARGENTINA, CHILE, AND MEXICO

From the general features of automotive industry technology discussed above, it is to be expected that the developments of the 1960s in Argentina, Chile, and Mexico would have increased the capital requirements of the automotive industry considerably. This is likely to be most marked in Argentina, which has the highest level of local integration, and least striking in Chile. An indication of the extent to which this has occurred can be obtained from several different sets of data. First, it is possible to observe the growth of investment in the industry during the period in which local content

FIGURE 5.1

Cost Increase as a Function of Local Content

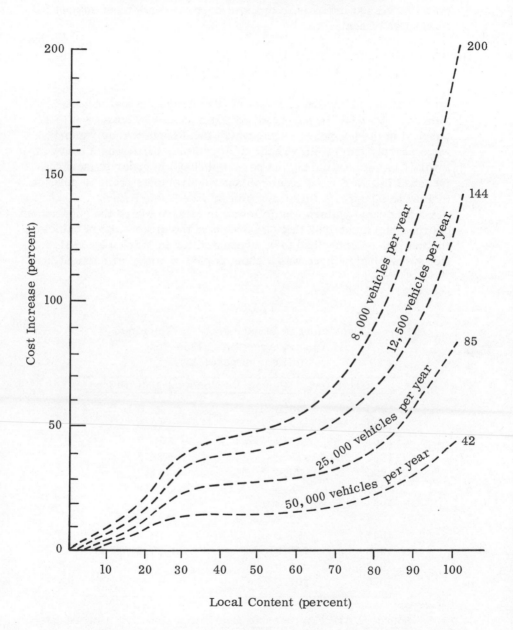

Source: Asociación de Fabricas de Automotores, Informe Económico 1969 (Buenos Aires: ADEFA, 1969), p. 24.

was being increased. Second, the increase in the amount of capital
employed per unit produced can be calculated. Finally, the relationship between variable and fixed costs can be estimated as an indication
of the increased importance of those cost elements most subject to
economies of scale.

The Time Profile of Investment

The broad pattern of investment in Argentina and Mexico is
similar. As would be expected, investment in the industry is
bunched in the few years during which local content requirements
were sharply increased. Thus, in Argentina, there was a heavy
level of investment during the period 1960-63 in order to meet the
increase in government local content requirements from 40 percent
in 1961 to 90 percent three years later (see Table 5.2).

The same pattern was followed in Mexico where the government
decreed in August 1962 that 60 percent of the direct cost of vehicles,
including the engine, had to be accounted for in Mexico by 1964.
Not surprisingly, there was a short period of heavy investment in

TABLE 5.2

Investment in Fixed Assets by Terminal
Plants, Argentina, 1959-70
(millions of pesos ley)

	Current Prices	Constant 1960 Prices
1959	20.0	22.3
1960	42.0	42.0
1961	56.0	50.7
1962	110.0	76.3
1963	90.0	51.3
1964	48.7	23.9
1965	55.8	19.6
1966	87.8	24.9
1967	94.9	20.9
1968	118.2	23.9
1969	245.9	47.8
1970	407.2	n.a.

Sources: ADEFA, Informe Estadístico, no. 588 (August 28,
1974), Table 12, and own elaboration using BCRA implicit price
deflator for total investment in fixed assets.

TABLE 5.3

Annual Increase in Fixed Assets,
Mexico, 1961-69
(millions of pesos)

	Current Prices	1960 Prices
1961	21	21
1962	15	14
1963	105	93
1964	594	511
1965	286	229
1966	154	117
1967	147	109
1968	133	98
1969	81	58

Sources: Asociación Mexicana de la Industria Automotriz,
"La Industria Automotriz de México en Cifras" (Mexico City: 1972),
p. 69, and own elaboration using Bank of Mexico implicit price
deflator for investment in fixed assets.

1964 and 1965 while firms endeavored to build the necessary capacity
to meet these requirements. As Table 5.3 indicates, almost 60
percent of the total investment in fixed assets by the Mexican automotive manufacturers during the 1960s occurred in the two years
1964 and 1965.[6]

The Chilean automotive industry remained essentially an
assembly industry throughout most of the 1960s. Consequently,
the value added in the terminal industry was low and virtually all
the parts and components that make up the vehicle were bought,
either from the parent company and its affiliates or from local
suppliers. It has been estimated that the terminal sector accounted
for only 16.8 percent of the total costs of Chilean cars in 1969, the
remainder being distributed in the following manner: 29 percent
local materials, 11.8 percent imported from other LAFTA countries,
and 42.4 percent imported from outside LAFTA. Despite government local content requirements, therefore, the Chilean terminal
producers have not found it necessary to make major investments
in fixed capital.

As Table 5.4 indicates, it was only from 1970 that investment
appeared to increase sharply, reflecting important new investments
in productive capacity, particularly the expansion of the Citroen
plant in Arica and the new factory at Los Andes built by Automotores
Franco-Chilena, a joint venture between Renault and Peugeot.

TABLE 5.4

Annual Increase in Fixed Assets,
Chile, 1964-70
(millions of escudos)

	Current Prices	1965 Prices
1964	6,732	8,684
1965	11,188	11,188
1966	3,264	2,481
1967	16,890	10,303
1968	17,289	8,126
1969	37,190	12,645
1970	76,499	19,125
1971	101,886	20,377
1972	228,145	n.a.

Note: The firms were Citroen, Chilemotores (Ford), EMSSA
(BMC), Federic (NSU), Fiat, Imcoda (Skoda), Importsur (Volvo),
Nissan, Indauto (Renault), Indumotora (General Motors), Nun y
German (Chrysler), San Cristobal (Peugeot), and Teona (CM).
Between them, they accounted for 95.1 percent of total production
in 1963 and 100 percent in 1972. The original data came from the
balance sheets of the companies and were adjusted to achieve a
common closing date.
Source: Oficina de Planificacion Nacional (ODEPLAN),
Cuentas Nacionales de Chile, 1960-71 (Santiago: ODEPLAN, n.d.),
Tables 6 and 15, and author's compilation.

The Capital Intensity of Production

The increased investment brought with it an increase in the
capital intensity of production and therefore in the total amount of
capital required to produce a given output. This was partly a result
of a higher proportion of in-plant manufacture and partly a result of
the more capital-intensive nature of the processes introduced. Any
attempt to measure capital-output ratios at an industry level is faced
with a number of problems. While the measurement of output can
be reasonably unambiguous, the measurement of capital is fraught
with difficulties. A number of alternatives have been used by
different authors. These can be divided broadly into three categories:
those using the value of the stock of capital, those using depreciation,
and those using a physical index, such as installed horsepower or
electricity consumed.[7]

Each approach is subject to particular problems and none represents an entirely satisfactory measure. The valuation of capital will be subject to competitive distortions, which make it possible for the same physical capital to be valued differently at different times or different places. This is a particularly salient point in discussing an industry where foreign investment and foreign technology are important elements, so that the value placed on a particular item of physical capital is either a monopoly price charged by a technology supplier or a transfer price charged by a parent company to its subsidiary. Depreciation calculations can be based either on an assumed standard rate of depreciation, given a value of the capital stock, in which case the same objections apply as did in the case of the first measure, or on the actual depreciation of individual firms, in which case it becomes an arbitrary measure depending on the particular accounting practices of the firms studied. Finally, installed horsepower or electricity consumption, although much easier to measure unambiguously, may not be a good proxy for capital. Because it does not indicate the mechanical efficiency of machinery, similar horsepower or electricity consumption figures may be associated with completely different physical capital. Moreover, with electricity consumption figures, there is the additional complication that they do not take into account capacity utilization; thus, physical capital and this proxy may diverge even further.[8]

Strictly speaking, what is relevant from the point of view of the argument being developed here is that the capital outlays that firms were required to make increased as a result of the rising content requirements imposed by governments. Thus, the relevant measure of capital intensity is one based on the value of the stock of capital, whether or not this represents an increase in capital intensity in physical terms. The problem of dealing with the investment of foreign companies in their local subsidiaries (mentioned above) makes this a less than completely satisfactory measure. As a check, therefore, a second measure of capital intensity based on electrical energy consumed has also been used.

Table 5.5 shows four indicators of the capital intensity of the Argentinian automotive industry, the first three based on the output and the fourth on value added. These indices all agree in showing a considerable increase in capital intensity over the period, the increase being more marked in the case of the capital stock measurements than in the case of electricity consumption. The increase observed in the ratio of capital to value added indicates the increased capital intensity of the production processes, so that the increase observed in the other measures cannot be attributed solely to a higher level of vertical integration.

TABLE 5.5

Capital Intensity in the Argentinian
Automotive Industry, 1959-64

	Capital per Unit	Capital/ Output	Kilowatt-hour Output	Capital/ Value Added
1959	794	0.20	458.6	0.49
1960	537	0.12	636.6	0.74
1961	812	0.18	578.6	0.77
1962	1,312	0.28	633.9	1.47
1963	2,478	0.53 (0.32)	980.0	1.91
1964	1,863	0.45	820.7	1.66

Source: Consejo Nacional de Desarrollo (CONADE), "La
Industria Automotriz: Análisis Preliminar" (Buenos Aires: CONADE,
1966), and own elaboration.

One further point deserves comment, namely, the sharp rise
in all indices in 1963 and the subsequent fall in 1964. This reflected
a substantial decline in vehicle production in 1963 of about 20 percent
compared with 1962 that led to considerable excess capacity in that
year. An alternative calculation, based on full capacity utilization,
gave a capital-output ratio of 0.32 as opposed to the actual ratio of
0.53, indicating a steady increase in capital intensity through to
1964. Thus, it seems reasonable to conclude from these figures
and the previous discussion of automotive industry technology that
the period of increasing local content in the Argentinian automotive
industry during the early 1960s was accompanied by an increase in
the amount of capital required to produce a given number of vehicles.

In Mexico, as in Argentina, there is evidence to support the
contention that capital intensity rises sharply as the automotive
industry makes the transition from assembly to manufacturing.
In the Mexican case, as has already been seen, this occurred during
the years immediately following the 1962 decree. Table 5.6 shows
that the capital-output ratio, whether measured in terms of the
value of output or the number of units produced, and the ratio of
capital to value added more than doubled between 1963 and 1965.
Unfortunately, it has not been possible to obtain a continuous series
for electricity consumption, but the available figures are consistent
with the estimates in the other three columns. During the second
half of the decade, when local content remained unchanged, capital
intensity declined somewhat as output expanded without any major
new investments.

Unlike the two preceding cases, there was no evidence of a tendency for capital intensity to rise in Chile; indeed, there appears rather to have been a fall during the mid-1960s and a subsequent recovery toward the end of the decade (see Table 5.7). Data on electricity consumption for the industry as a whole are not available, but the figures for one of the leading firms, Citroen, confirm the general pattern, with electricity consumed per car produced falling until 1968 and then starting to increase.

As was indicated previously, the Chilean industry remained an assembly industry during the 1960s despite an increasing incorporation of locally produced parts. As a result, the greater part of the assets of the terminal firms was in the form of working capital, either stocks or short-term credits.[9] Working capital grew much faster than fixed assets. In the four years to 1969, fixed assets increased by only 30.8 percent in real terms as compared to 234 percent for working capital.[10]

It is tempting to attempt a comparison of capital intensity in the three countries considered. In doing so, however, the problems of measurement discussed earlier are further compounded owing to different accounting practices, different prices of both capital goods and vehicles, and the difficulties of finding suitable exchange rates for local currencies. Any comparative analysis of the three cases,

TABLE 5.6

Capital Intensity in the Mexican
Automotive Industry, 1960-69

	Capital per Unit	Capital/ Output	Kilowatt-hour Output	Capital/ Value Added
1960	440	0.17	n.a.	0.38
1961	416	0.17	n.a.	0.39
1962	421	0.16	n.a.	0.40
1963	435	0.16	241	0.35
1964	888	0.28	268	0.63
1965	1,101	0.33	n.a.	0.86
1966	1,043	0.30	421	0.95
1967	1,032	0.30	n.a.	1.08
1968	964	0.27	417	0.82
1969	899	0.25	n.a.	0.77

Source: Asociación Mexicana de la Industria Automotriz, "La Industria Automotriz de México en Cifras," (Mexico City: 1972), pp. 69-71. Secretaría de Industria y Comercio, and own elaboration.

TABLE 5.7

Capital Intensity for 13 Chilean Automotive
Manufacturers, 1964-72

	Capital per Unit ($)	Capital/ Output
1964	766	0.12
1965	897	0.14
1966	964	0.15
1967	820	0.11
1968	491	0.09
1969	496	0.10
1970	607	0.12
1971	n.a.	0.16
1972	n.a.	0.07

Source: Corporación de Fomento, company accounts, and
own elaboration.

therefore, must be extremely tentative. Bearing this in mind, it
might be suggested that the changeover from assembly operations
increases the value of fixed assets required per car produced to
over $1,000 and raises the capital-output ratio above 0.25. This
took place in Argentina in 1962, in Mexico in 1964, and has yet to
occur in Chile.

In comparing Argentina and Mexico, one could expect the
higher level of local content in the former to give rise to a higher
level of capital intensity, a view confirmed by all the indicators
used. In Chile, capital intensity is significantly lower than in the
other two countries, although in the mid-1960s it was higher than
expected. But this could be explained by different accounting practices or higher relative prices for fixed assets, which would inflate
the figures for capital intensity. As noted earlier, calculations
such as these are extremely tricky, and their interest lies in the
fact that they are consistent with the conclusions drawn in the
earlier part of this section.

The Structure of Costs

The previous section suggested that the amount of capital
required to produce a given output increased as a result of the
transition to manufacturing production. In the earlier discussion,

it was seen that such a step would also increase the importance of
economies of scale since new processes of production are introduced.
Thus, not only does the capital intensity of production increase but
so, too, does the disadvantage of low volumes of output, creating
a double tendency toward an increase in the total capital needed by
a firm.

One of the main factors leading to economies of scale in production are large initial costs (see Appendix A). It is to be expected
that an increase in local content requirements in the automotive
industry will result in a rise in the share of fixed costs in total
costs.[11]

The available data for Argentina (see Table 5.8) are not
sufficiently detailed to make an exact estimate of the share of fixed
costs. This would require a more detailed breakdown of labor,
administration, finance, and sales costs. It would also require
the subtraction of profits from the last row of the table. Nevertheless, the figures do give some indication of the changes that took
place between 1960 and 1967.

From the table, there appear to have been three major changes.
First, nationally produced materials were substituted for those
previously imported, leading to an increase in the share of the
former, while the total share of material inputs in costs remained
more or less constant. This was obviously a direct result of the
government's local content measures. Second, the share of administrative, finance, and sales costs fell by more than half. This can
be attributed to the doubling of output over the period, thus spreading

TABLE 5.8

Cost Structure of the Argentinian
Automotive Industry
(percent)

	1960	1967
Local materials	35.1	52.3
Imported materials	28.0	11.2
Labor	11.3	12.5
Other inputs (energy, and so on)	1.1	1.8
Administration, finance, sales	16.4	7.8
Profits, depreciation, interest	8.1	14.4

Source: Asociación de Fabricas de Automotores (ADEFA),
Informe Económico 1969 (Buenos Aires: ADEFA, 1969), pp. 7-10.

the cost of administrative overheads, which had to be incurred from the outset, over a greater volume. Finally, payments to capital, that is, profits, depreciation, and interest, almost doubled their share of costs. Thus, although the data are not as detailed as they could be, they do suggest that fixed costs have increased.

A clearer picture can be obtained from the Mexican data. These, again, show an increase in the share of national materials at the expense of imported materials between 1960 and 1969. It has also been possible to estimate the share of fixed costs, which increased more than fourfold over the period. Table 5.9 gives a much better idea of the differences between an assembly and a manufacturing industry, since the Mexican automotive industry in 1960 was still quite clearly in the assembly phase, whereas in Argentina by that year the industry was already in transition.

The case of Citroen in Chile provides confirmation of the hypothesis that fixed costs tend to increase with local content. Between 1968 and 1974, the local integration of the models considered rose from 38.6 to 64.8 percent, on the Chilean government's definition. This manifested itself in terms of actual costs to the firm in a substantial fall in the share of foreign parts and an increase in the share of locally purchased parts. At the same time, there was a substantial increase in fixed costs, which almost trebled their share of the total* (see Table 5.10).

TABLE 5.9

Cost Structure of the Mexican
Automotive Industry
(percent)

	1960	1969
Local materials	12.7	42.0
Imported materials	66.1	30.4
Labor	9.9	14.9
Other variables	8.8	1.6
Fixed	2.5	11.1

Sources: Banco de México, La Estructura Industrial de México en 1960 (Mexico City: 1967), pp. 215-18; Asociación Mexicana de la Industria Automotriz, unpublished data; and own elaboration.

---

*Although figures have been adjusted to make them comparable in the case of the two years for each country, they are not comparable between countries.

TABLE 5.10

Cost Structure of a Chilean Car
(percent)

	1968	1974
Foreign parts	50.4	33.6
Local parts	26.0	31.1
Other variables	14.0	8.4
Fixed	9.7	26.9

Source: Based on data provided by Oficina de Planificación Nacional. The vehicles in question are the Citroen A2L in 1968 and the Citroen AX in 1974.

COST DIFFERENTIALS

In this section some initial evidence is presented to support the hypothesis that significant cost differentials of the kind discussed in Chapter 4 do in fact exist as between local and foreign firms in the Latin American automotive industry. Ideally, one should like a complete breakdown of costs for each company in order to analyze interfirm differences in costs.[12] Such a study, especially had it been attempted for all three countries under consideration, would have involved a complete study in itself, and since the intended scope of this work is much wider, would not have been justified. Moreover, it is extremely doubtful whether a single researcher could have obtained all the information necessary for such a project, considering the suspicion with which some companies view such investigation of their activities. This presents particular problems in both Argentina and Mexico where foreign subsidiaries, whose shares are not quoted on the local stock exchange, are not obliged to publish their balance sheets. Therefore, in the section that follows, the investigation has been restricted to a comparison of those cost elements that the a priori analysis above has suggested as significant sources of cost differentials.

A further difficulty arises from the nature of the problem being analyzed. As noted in Chapter 4, it is by no means easy to isolate the gains to a multinational corporation of the operations of a subsidiary in a particular country. Since transactions between parent and subsidiary are not usually of an arm's-length nature, the declared profitability of a subsidiary is not necessarily an accurate indicator of the contribution it makes to the international company's global profits. Payments such as royalties, which appear as costs from the point of view of the subsidiary, are profits from the point of view of the multinational corporation. Moreover, practices such as transfer pricing make it difficult to estimate costs of production for the subsidiary, particularly where the products being sold are specific to the firm and do not have a market price. Similarly, interaffiliate loans may be made at rates of interest above the opportunity cost of capital to the parent company. Problems such as these mean that a comparative analysis of costs can at best only be suggestive of the underlying situation, which may be distorted by transfer accounting.

Bearing all this in mind, it is not to be expected that an examination of the declared rates of return of locally owned and foreign firms will necessarily indicate that the latter are more profitable. Six foreign subsidiaries and three firms with majority local ownership for which data were available were compared for 1964 and 1965. The firms were Citroen, Ford, General Motors, Chrysler, Fiat, and Mercedes-Benz (foreign owned) and Industrias Kaiser Argentina (IKA), Industria Automotriz Santa Fe (IASF), and Siam di Tella (locally owned); and the average rate of return on capital plus reserves was calculated for both groups.* As can be seen from Table 5.11, the foreign firms made higher profits in 1964 and showed substantial profits in 1965 when the local firms had a loss.

Since the declared profitability of foreign subsidiaries is such a poor indication of their contribution to the parent company, this

TABLE 5.11

Profitability* of Selected Argentinian Firms,
1964–66
(percent)

	1964	1965
Local firms (declared)	12.9	-3.8
Foreign firms (declared)	16.0	25.8
Foreign firms (effective)	22.4	32.3

*Rate of return on capital plus reserves.
Sources: Company balance sheets and own elaboration.

---

*Mercedes-Benz, IKA, and IASF had a financial year ending on June 30, so the averages of two financial years were taken to get figures for calendar years.

TABLE 5.12

Profitability of Selected Chilean Firms, 1970
(percent)

	Declared Profits	Effective Profitability Assuming Overpricing of	
		25	10
Local firms	4.9		
Joint ventures	-11.2	9.8	-0.7
Foreign firms	-2.9	48.4	23.1

Sources: Company balance sheets and own elaboration.

gives no idea of the cost advantage enjoyed by subsidiaries, except that effective profitability is almost certain to be greater than declared profitability. Overpricing of imported intermediate inputs is not likely to have been a very significant factor in the Argentinian automotive industry because of the relatively high local content requirements, which had reached 90 percent by 1964, limiting the scope for such practices. Moreover, since under the Argentinian legislation, content was measured in value terms rather than by weight, as in Brazil, increasing the price of imported parts would reduce the quantity that could be imported. This, together with the high costs of producing locally those parts that could no longer be imported, acted as a disincentive to overpricing. The lack of any data on overpricing is not likely, therefore, to be an important omission.

Royalty payments, while representing costs to locally owned firms, are part of the effective profits of foreign subsidiaries. In the third row of Table 5.11, therefore, the rate of return for the six foreign subsidiaries has been recalculated to include royalties as well as declared profits.* As a result of including royalty payments, the rate of return of foreign companies increased considerably, making it significantly higher than that of the locally owned companies in both of the years considered. Even these figures may underestimate the effective profitability of foreign subsidiaries, since it has not been possible to allow for other channels of profit repatriation.

---

*Royalty payments were estimated on the basis of the payments actually made by some companies and on extrapolation for other companies from the percentage royalty on sales paid in later years.

As in Argentina, a number of Chilean automobile manufacturers were selected and grouped according to ownership. The larger number of firms made it possible to distinguish three groups: 100 percent locally owned firms, joint ventures, and 100 percent foreign firms. The firms selected were Nun y German and Imcoda (local), British Leyland, Indauto, and Automotres San Cristobal (joint ventures), and Citroen, Fiat, General Motors, and Nissan (foreign).* The declared rate of return on capital plus reserves was found to be positive only for the locally owned firms, while the joint ventures and foreign subsidiaries had losses. There certainly appears to be no reason on this evidence for supposing that foreign firms are more profitable than their local competitors, a conclusion that was supported by a general study of the largest manufacturing firms in Chile that found that the profitability of foreign subsidiaries was similar to that of local firms.[13]

As was indicated above, calculations of the profitability of foreign investment from the point of view of the parent company should also include royalty payments made by the subsidiary. It appears that such payments have not been widely used by car assemblers, however, possibly because the Comisión Revisora de Contratos de Regalias, set up in 1967, has put a maximum royalty of 5 percent on the "despiece" value of national integration for the assembly of vehicles.

Unlike Argentina, where the high level of local integration meant that there was relatively little scope for overpricing of intermediate inputs, Chilean car assemblers are heavily dependent on parts imports from parent companies or associated producers so that this possibility cannot be ignored. This requires consideration of the pricing policies of multinational automobile companies regarding the CKD packs they export. As was mentioned above, the normal practice is for a price to be set for the entire CKD pack and then a deletion allowance is granted for those parts omitted from the pack, which tends to be less than the share of that part in the pack's total value. One possibility is that the deletion allowance for a part is based on its marginal cost, whereas the entire pack is priced at average cost. Another possibility is that the deletion allowance equals the cost of production of the part but does not include the profit margin.[14] All this points to the difficulty of determining what exactly is the world market price for the CKD pack of a particular firm and so to determine the extent of overpricing.

---

*British Leyland's financial year closed on June 30 so the averages for 1969-70 and 1970-71 were used.

In the particular case of Chile, one does have some basis on which to work. The Chilean legislation, under which the automotive industry operates, specifies local content requirements in terms of the "despiece" value of the vehicle. This is a breakdown of the FOB price of the vehicle in the country of origin allocating a certain percentage of the total cost to each part and component. If a foreign company wished to overvalue some part it intended to import, there would have to be a corresponding undervaluation of some other part. If the other part were also to be imported, then the company would have gained nothing by overpricing the first part. If, on the other hand, it were to have been produced locally, the total number of locally produced parts would have to be increased in order to attain the required content level. Consequently, the scope for overpricing seems rather limited.*

However the foreign subsidiary does not import CKD packs at FOB prices, but at CIF prices. Therefore, the prices actually paid do not necessarily correspond with those indicated in the "despiece" value of the car. In practice CIF prices in Chile appear to be about 50 percent above FOB prices.[15] Most reasonable estimates of these charges for vehicle exports do not put them above 20 to 25 percent.[16] Peugeot, for example, in the tender it submitted to the Chilean government for the franchise to build a medium-sized car, indicated the breakdown in Table 5.13 for CKD pack imports from France. Taking the FOB price as 100 and the CIF price as 150, it would appear, therefore, that between 17 percent (25/150) and 20 percent (30/150) of the CIF value of parts imported represents overpricing; or, to put it another way, parts are overpriced by between 20 percent (25/125) and 25 percent (30/120).

TABLE 5.13

Cost of Imported CKD Pack in Chile

	U.S. $	Percent
CKD	466.90	100
Packing	32.60	7.0
Freight	48.54	10.4
Insurance	3.74	0.8

Source: Corporación de Fomento, unpublished data.

---

*The whole question is complicated, however, by the need to allocate overheads.

In the second and third columns of Table 5.12, the effective return to the foreign company has been calculated, first assuming what appears to be a reasonable estimate of overpricing of 25 percent, and then with a much lower rate of only 10 percent, as a sensitivity text in view of the lack of any direct evidence on the level of overpricing. In the first case, the rate of return for foreign subsidiaries is increased to almost 50 percent, while overpricing of only 10 percent would give a return of over 20 percent. For joint ventures, the rate of return on the foreign company's own capital (which was slightly more than half of the total share capital) was calculated. This turned a large loss in terms of declared profits into an effective profitability of almost 10 percent with an assumed overpricing of 25 percent and a small loss with overpricing of only 10 percent. This second finding suggests that there are considerable gains to the foreign company from complete ownership, while the general conclusion must again be that wholly owned subsidiaries have a significant cost advantage over their local competitors.

The Mexican data, which cover the eight firms in operation throughout the period under consideration, provide confirmation of the higher profitability enjoyed by foreign subsidiaries. A comparison of declared profits indicates a higher rate of return for this group of firms from 1969 on. If royalties are also included in the calculation, as was argued above, foreign firms had higher returns from 1968.

As in the case of Chile, the fact that Mexican vehicles have a substantial import content makes it necessary to consider the possibility of declared profits underestimating effective profitability because of transfer pricing. Data on two Mexican firms (Automex and Ford) indicated that, in 1964, the output of the two companies, valued at international prices, was less than the tradable value of the imported and local parts that they incorporated.[17] Since the prices of local parts already had been adjusted to take account of the higher cost of such parts compared to world prices, the only reasonable explanation appears to be that the prices of the imported parts are also higher than the international market price. (An alternative explanation is that some parts got lost in transit, but this does not seem very plausible.) This is consistent with what is known about the system of deletion allowances used by the automotive manufacturers.

The assumption that transfer pricing may be an important source of income is given further support by the finding that some technology contracts in the automotive industry specify a 10 percent markup on the price of components sold to the Mexican firm over the price of original equipment. The rate of return of foreign subsidiaries, therefore, was recalculated using an assumed level

of overpricing of 10 percent of the value of imported parts. As
indicated in Table 5.14, this resulted in a substantial increase in
the rate of profit, which contributed to a further divergence between
the profitability of the two groups of firms.

It is equally difficult to unravel the elements that account for
the differences in the profitability of foreign subsidiaries and local
firms as it is to illustrate the existence of those differences. In
Chapter 4 it was suggested that better access to capital, both in
terms of being able to borrow more and of being able to obtain
finance on better terms, was one of the key advantages enjoyed by
foreign subsidiaries. For several reasons, it is not easy to show
this empirically. First, better access to capital is a factor affecting
only the supply of funds to the two groups of companies, whereas
actual gearing ratios are affected not only by the supply of funds
but also by the demand for external finance of each firm. Thus,
foreign firms, which generate more funds internally because of
their higher profitability, have, as a result, a lower demand for
external funds. It cannot be predicted a priori, therefore, how
gearing ratios would differ. In the early years of a firm's existence,
before it has been able to accumulate much capital internally, or
during periods of major expansion relative to the existing size of
the firm, the difference should be easier to see.

Second, it is not easy to say much regarding access to funds
from a comparison of interest payments. A large part of a foreign
subsidiary's debt may be held with the parent company, so that
interest charges are a form of interaffiliate transfer pricing,
determined by the need to move funds within the international firm.
Thus, high interest rates paid by such firms may represent a method
of repatriating capital rather than the high cost of capital, per se.
The lack of any systematic relationship between interest payments
(deflated by liabilities) and ownership, which was found in the three
cases studied, does not necessarily contradict the hypothesis that
the opportunity cost of outside finance differs for the two groups
of firms, and, as will be seen in Chapter 7, shortage of capital
played an important part in the failure of a number of companies.

Bearing in mind these difficulties, an attempt was made to
compare the gearing ratios of foreign and local firms. For Argentina,
the date chosen for such a comparison was June 30, 1962, this being
the earliest date for which information was available for sufficient
companies. It was found that the average gearing ratio for three
local firms (Industria Automotriz Santa Fe, Industrias Kaiser
Argentina, and Siam di Tella Automotores)* was 1.52. For the

---

*For Siam, the average for 1961 and 1962 was used since the
financial year ended on 31 December.

TABLE 5.14

Profitability of Selected Mexican Firms, 1966–73
(percent)

	1966	1967	1968	1969	1970	1971	1972	1973
Local firms	11.5	6.6	6.7	8.0	-3.8	-17.9	-11.1	-3.6
Foreign firms	4.9	-5.0	5.2	9.6	10.3	6.7	6.1	8.5
Foreign firms (profits & royalties)*	7.1	-2.9	7.6	11.4	12.2	9.0	8.7	11.7
Foreign firms (profits & royalties + 10% average overpricing)	17.8	7.1	18.5	19.0	19.9	17.8	18.2	n.a.

*Royalty payments in 1966–67 and 1969–70 were calculated on the basis of the ratio of royalties to sales found in 1968.

Sources: Asociación Mexicana de la Industria Automotriz, unpublished data and own elaboration.

industry as a whole, the gearing ratio was 2.32,[18] implying that
foreign subsidiaries have gearing ratios considerably higher than
those found for the local firms. The evidence, therefore, does
indicate a considerable difference in gearing ratios between foreign
and local firms.

For Chile, the latest year for which data were available, 1970,
was chosen for comparison, because this, as indicated earlier,
permits three groups of firms to be compared and because, despite
some of the firms having existed for a number of years, considerable
investments were being made. The results here are even more
striking than those for Argentina, and confirm the findings of a study
of foreign investment in Chilean industry, that foreign firms tend
to commit less of their own capital and rely more heavily on outside
finance than their Chilean counterparts.[19] The same nine firms
were selected as before in considering profitability. It was found
that the unweighted average of the gearing ratio was a remarkable
7.49 for the four foreign subsidiaries considered. If one looks at
the other two groups of firms, the joint ventures have a gearing
ratio of 4.54, while the local wholly owned companies have the
lowest gearing ratio of all at only 1.20. Another feature of the
financial structure of vehicle producers in Chile that bears on the
access to capital of different firms is the virtual absence of long-
term liabilities, particularly in the case of locally owned firms.
In fact, the only firm to use long-term debt on a significant scale
has been Citroen, although the other foreign-owned firms also used
some.

In Mexico there is an interesting new element in the situation.
In 1965, the gearing ratio of the foreign subsidiaries operating in
the Mexican automotive industry was 1.24, somewhat less than the
average for the industry as a whole, which stood at 1.44 in that
year.[20] This appears to contradict the initial hypothesis, especially
since the year in question represented an early stage in the development of the industry when, according to the earlier argument, it
might have been supposed that significant differences would exist
between local and foreign firms.

A more detailed examination reveals that, in fact, it is
possible to distinguish two types of firms among those that have
majority Mexican ownership, namely, those with state participation
and those that have private Mexican capital. The former have a
gearing ratio that is much higher than for the industry as a whole,
2.41, while the latter have a lower than average gearing, only 0.82.

The high gearing of the former group of companies can be
explained by the advantages that state ownership give to the two
companies, Dina and VAM, in terms of access to credit, either
because government credit was channeled to these firms or because

private sources of credit considered government backing as good a
guarantee of their loans as the backing of a foreign parent. The
private Mexican firms are in the same position as their Argentinian
and Chilean counterparts with lower gearing.*

Another indication of access to capital is the share of interaffiliate loans in a company's total liabilities. The wholly owned
subsidiaries in Mexico tend to have a much higher percentage of
their liabilities in the form of loans from the parent company, for
example, Ford, 95.3 percent; General Motors, 51.3 percent;
Volkswagen, 42.6 percent; whereas Automex, which only had a
minority foreign shareholding, only got 15.3 percent of its total
loans from its foreign affiliate.[21] As was mentioned earlier, this
does not show up necessarily in the form of lower interest charges
as it may be used as a form of interaffiliate transfer pricing.
Unfortunately, the data are not available to determine the extent
to which the liabilities of subsidiaries take the form of interaffiliate
loans in Argentina and Chile.

Nevertheless, as has been seen, there is suggestive evidence
to support the hypothesis that foreign subsidiaries do enjoy better
access to outside sources of finance than do their local competitors
in all three countries considered. This is most evident from the
higher gearing ratios characteristic of foreign subsidiaries, as
well as from other indicators, such as the proportion of long-term
liabilities and the percentage of liabilities that are loans from the
parent company. Unfortunately, this is not reflected in differences
in interest payments between different types of firms.

Apart from access to capital, the other major factor contributing to differential costs, it was suggested in a previous chapter,
was access to the parent company's technology. The latter appeared
either directly as royalty payments or indirectly incorporated in
the costs of imported parts. Again, it is difficult to measure with
any precision the advantage this represents from the point of view
of the subsidiary. For the purpose of comparison, the royalty
payments made by local firms can be regarded as an additional cost
and any such payments by foreign subsidiaries can be ignored since
they form part of the effective profitability of the parent.

---

*It is, of course, possible that the higher gearing ratios of
foreign subsidiaries compared to local firms is a result of factors
other than preferential access to capital. It may be the case that
local firms are prepared to raise capital by issuing shares on the
local stock market, whereas a foreign company, which wishes to
maintain complete ownership of its subsidiary, prefers to borrow
locally.

One point that needs to be made in this context is that royalty payments are often made on a scale that increases with local content. What appears, therefore, as a low rate of royalty payments in relation to the sales of the local company often represents a much higher proportion of the value added and a substantial part of the total profit before paying royalties. As local content, and hence value added, increase, the royalty charge increases as a percentage of the firm's total sales.

It is often difficult to obtain data on the amount of royalties paid, especially payments from subsidiaries to parent companies. In this case, as indicated above, the problem can be partly avoided since it is only payments by locally owned companies that are relevant, and these are often more willing to disclose the sums involved. In the Argentinian case it was possible to obtain an estimate of royalty payments as a percentage of sales for the three local companies for which estimates of profitability and gearing were given earlier. The largest of these, Industrias Kaiser Argentina, made royalty payments, which amounted to about 2 percent of the total value of sales in 1968, to American Motors, Kaiser-Willys, and Renault. Of the other two companies, Industria Automotriz Santa Fe paid a rather high rate of 5 percent of sales to DKW, while Siam di Tella paid an estimated 3 percent for its BMC license.

In Chile it is necessary to take an additional factor into account, namely, the high cost of imported parts as a result of transfer pricing. Overpricing of intermediate inputs can be thought of as a form of payment for technology, like royalties, since it arises from the dependence of a local firm on a foreign technology supplier. As was seen earlier, this represented a considerable amount and should be considered as a cost from the point of view of the local firm. To this sum must be added the further costs in terms of any royalty charges that have to be paid by the local firm. Nun y German, for example, paid royalties of about 1.5 percent on sales in 1970, but this accounted for more than 30 percent of the company's profits before paying royalties.

In Mexico the rate of royalty charges was roughly similar to those found in Argentina. One estimate puts them at between 3.5 and 5 percent on sales, although higher rates may be charged in the case of more sophisticated components.[22] Any overpricing of imported components would have to be added to the royalty payments in order to arrive at the total cost disadvantage of locally owned firms.

CONCLUSION

This chapter has sought to establish two main points. First, it was seen that policies that raised the local content of vehicles

produced in underdeveloped countries led to an increase in the capital
intensity of production and in the economies of scale to which the
automotive industry is subject. Together, these two factors have
led to considerable increases in the total amount of capital required
by an automotive manufacturer. Even in Chile, which remained at
a lower level of local content, there was a growing need for working
capital to finance suppliers. Second, some evidence was presented
to support the hypothesis that foreign subsidiaries enjoyed a cost
advantage over local firms as a result of the better access they have
to capital and technology.

NOTES

1. A similar classification of stages in the development of
the automotive industry in underdeveloped countries can be found
in I. Griffiths, The Motor Industry in Developing Countries: Patterns
of Growth and Location, Makerere Institute of Social Research,
EDRP no. 143 (1968), pp. 5-16.
2. Overpricing refers here to the practice of charging subsidiaries or licensees prices that are above the competitive world
price for inputs supplied by the parent company or licensor. The
work that brought this to the attention of development economists
is C. V. Vaitsos, Transfer of Resources and Preservation of
Monopoly Rent, Center for International Affairs, EDH No. 168
(Harvard University, 1970).
3. F. L. Picard, The Rationale of the Gradual Development
of the Automotive Industry in Developing Countries. From Assembly
of Imported Parts to Complete Local Production, UNIDO (ID/WG.
13/3), 1968, p. 23.
4. Quoted in UNIDO, The Motor Vehicle Industry (ID/78),
1972, p. 48.
5. Economic Commission for Latin America (ECLA),
Prespectivas y Modalidades de Integración Regional de la Automotriz
en América Latina, ECLA/DI/DRAFT/92, División de Desarrollo
Industrial (1973), Table 2.5.
6. Although not strictly relevant to the point under consideration, that is, the increased capital requirements of the terminal
industry, it is of interest to note that investment in the automotive
parts industry also followed the same pattern. In Argentina, almost
40 percent of the total investment in the parts industry between 1960
and 1967 (both years inclusive) was in the two years 1961 and 1962,
while in Mexico, the total assets of the parts industry more than
doubled between 1962 and 1964, from 2,000 million pesos to 4,500
million pesos. See Comisión de Estudios Económicos de la Industria

Automotriz, La Industria Automotriz Argentina: Informe Económico 1969 (Buenos Aires: ADEFA, 1969), Table 11; and Manuel Franco Rosas, "Problemas y Perspectivas de la Industria Automotriz en México" (Thesis, Universidad Nacional Autónoma de México, 1971), Chap. 1.

7. See, for example, Mario M. Cortes, "Technological Absorption and Unemployment: A Comparative Analysis" (Ph.D. thesis, Washington University, 1973), quoted in D. Felix, "Technological Dualism and Late-Late Industrializers: On Theory, History and Policy" (Paper delivered at the Economic History Association Annual Meeting, Atlanta, September 1973), p. 4, who uses mainly installed horsepower; J. Katz, Importación de Tecnología, Aprendizaje Local e Industrialización Dependiente, Centro de Investigaciones Económicas, Documentos de Trabajo No. 59 (Instituto Torcuato di Tella, 1972), pp. VI 3-6, who uses the value of the capital stock; and C. Cooper, Employment, Incomes and Equality: A Strategy for Increasing Productive Employment in Kenya (Geneva: 1972), pp. 446-52, who uses depreciation.

8. For a further discussion of these points, see R. Sutcliffe, Industry and Underdevelopment (Reading, Mass.: Addison-Wesley, 1971), pp. 140-46.

9. Instituto de Costos, Estudio Sobre la Industria Automotriz (Santiago, 1969), Anexo 28.

10. Ibid., Chap. 2b.

11. It has been observed in the motor industry in advanced countries that the more vertically integrated a firm, the higher the ratio of fixed to total costs. See G. Maxcy and A. Silberston, The Motor Industry (London: Allen C. Unwin, 1959), pp. 62-63.

12. An example of the kind of analysis that we have in mind is the study of the Argentinian tractor industry by José María Dagnino Pastore and others, the third volume of which is devoted entirely to a comparison of the cost structure of the different firms. José María Dagnino Pastore et al., La Industria del Tractor en la Argentina, Centro de Investigaciones Económicas, Trabajos Internos, No. 21 (Instituto Torcuato di Tella, 1966).

13. See L. Pacheco, "La Inversión Extranjera en la Industria Chilena" (professional diss., University of Chile, 1970), Chap. 7.

14. See S. J. Kleu, "Import Substitution in the South African Automobile Industry" (Thesis, Harvard University, 1967), pp. 67-73, for this and other examples.

15. See Felix Gil Mitjans, "Un Modelo de Programación de la Industria Automotriz Chilena" (Thesis, Universidad de Chile, 1969), Table C; and Instituto Chileno del Acero, Problemas y Perspectivas de la Industria Automotriz Chilena (Santiago, 1969), Anexo II.

16. See J. Behrman, The Role of International Companies in Latin American Integration; Autos and Petrochemicals (Lexington, Mass.: D. C. Heath, 1972), on the relatively low costs of transporting parts.

17. C. Sanchez-Marco, Industry Study, Cost-Benefit Analysis of Car Manufacturing in Mexico (1) (Paris: OECD, Development Center, 1968), Tables VI and IX.

18. C. M. Jiménez, "Contribución al Estudio Crítica sobre la Política de Radicación de Capitales en la República Argentina: La Industria Automotriz" (Ph.D. thesis, University of Buenos Aires, 1964), Chap. 2b (i). Average figures for 1961 and 1962 were again used.

19. Pacheco, op. cit., Chap. 4.

20. Emilio Kawage Vera, "La Industria Automotriz y la Política Gubernamental" (professional thesis, Universidad Autónoma de México, 1968).

21. Rafael Vizcaino Velasco, La Industria Automotriz Mexicana: Análisis Evaluación y Perspectivas (professional thesis, Escuela Superior de Economía, 1969), Chap. 4.

22. M. S. Wionczek, G. Bueno, and J. E. Navarrette, "La Transferencia International de Tecnología al Nivel de Empresa: El Caso de México," mimeographed (Mexico: Fondo de Cultura Económica, 1974), pp. 92-93.

6

THE DEMAND FOR CARS AND DEPENDENT INDUSTRIALIZATION

It was noted in Chapter 4 that the rate of growth of market demand was an important element in explaining the extent to which competition led to an increase in concentration within an industry. If expansion is rapid, then it will enable all firms to grow and perhaps even encourage new firms to enter the industry. When a market is stagnating or only growing slowly, however, foreign firms can only grow by driving out other companies, and there will be a tendency for increased concentration and denationalization.

In this chapter, the characteristic features of the demand for cars in underdeveloped countries are discussed, and the typical pattern of growth of demand over time traced. The analysis concentrates on the market for passenger cars to the exclusion of that for commercial vehicles. This seems justified since the dynamic role in automotive industry development almost always has been played by the former (with the exception of the socialist bloc and the earliest phase of development in some countries). Moreover, the passenger car sector is, analytically, the more interesting of the two since it is here that the distinction between developed and underdeveloped countries is most marked.

THEORETICAL CONSIDERATIONS

The most significant characteristic of the car from the point of view of demand is that it is a consumer durable. In economic terms, this means that the product is not entirely consumed during the period in which it is bought. In other words, at any given moment in time there is a stock of cars in existence on the roads that is different from the new purchases of cars over, say, the

preceding 12-month period. Consequently, most of the models that
have been used to analyze and predict car demand in the developed
countries are based on the stock-adjustment principle.[1] New car
purchases are a function of the difference between the existing number of cars in circulation at the end of the previous period and a
desired, optimum stock of cars and the rate of depreciation.

Although it is possible to apply the same kind of model to
underdeveloped countries, it is necessary first to consider a number
of important characteristics that differentiate the demand for cars
in such countries. The models that explain the demand for cars in
terms of a few variables, such as income, price, and the existing
stock, represent a simplification of a much more complex phenomenon. A satisfactory formulation would need to take account of a
number of other variables, such as the cost of car ownership (and
not just the price of new cars), the cost and availability of alternative forms of transport, the development of the road network, the
extent of consumer credit, advertising, expectations, the time
pattern of the development of ownership of consumer durables,
and the distribution of income.[2] It appears from the goodness of
fit of the equations used in developed countries that the omission
of these variables is not serious, either because they have remained
constant or because they are well approximated by the included
variables. In other cases some of these variables, such as credit
terms, have been explicitly included.[3] It cannot be assumed a priori,
however, that the same will apply in underdeveloped countries.

The usual model applied in the developed countries makes the
desired car stock (S*) a function of income and price, and demand
for new cars a proportion of the difference between desired and
actual stocks.

$$X_t = a(S^*_t - S_{t-1}) - dS_{t-1} \tag{1}$$

$$S^*_t = m + bY_t + cP_t \tag{2}$$

where X is the demand for new cars, Y is income, and P is price.

The desired car stock is also a function of the development of
the road network and the availability and cost of other forms of
transport. Whereas in developed countries these may be relatively
unchanging, in underdeveloped countries it is not possible to make
the same assumption. Therefore, it may be necessary to introduce
a time trend to catch these variables. The advantage of using a
time trend in this context, rather than a more direct proxy, is that
one can thus also catch the typical pattern of growth of demand for
a new commodity, which is partly a function of the availability of
complementary commodities (such as roads on which to drive cars)

but also a function of the diffusion of knowledge and changes in consumer tastes.[4] Thus, we may rewrite Equation 2 in the form

$$S^*_t = m + bY_t + cP_t + gt \qquad\qquad\qquad (3)$$

Another feature that usually has been ignored in car demand
studies in developed countries but that may be important in underdeveloped countries is the distribution of income. If one thinks of
the desired stock of cars, S^*, as the maximum level of car ownership
(the term used by Roos and von Szleiski), then it can be seen more
clearly that this will be determined by the number of households
with an income above a certain minimum required for car ownership;
that is, it will be a function of both income level and distribution and
not just per capita income as was previously assumed. This does
not present much of a problem when income is fairly equally distributed and does not change significantly over time. If, however,
there are sharp discontinuities in income distribution, or if it
changes during the period under study, then per capita income will
not be such a good explanatory variable. As income increases,
the number of households pushed over the threshold of car ownership
will vary. Thus, a highly unequal income distribution may give rise
to rapid initial growth of demand, but a subsequent slowing down
because increases in per capital income do not bring many additional
households over the threshold. Similarly, regressive changes in
favor of upper and middle income groups will increase the number
of potential consumers, while income increases for the lowest
income groups will not. Where cars are mass consumption goods,
explicit inclusion of income distribution is likely to be a less
important consideration than where car ownership is just beginning
to penetrate the upper and middle income groups.

One of the few studies of car demand in an underdeveloped
country to consider income distribution explicitly is one of Brazil
by the Confederacão Nacional da Industria.[5] The following equation
was used to forecast the growth of car sales:

$$1 + q = (1 + r)^{\alpha} / (1 + p)^{\alpha - 1}$$

where q is the potential rate of growth of the car stock, p is population growth, r is the rate of growth of GNP, and α is Pareto's
income distribution coefficient (the parameter of the income distribution curve calculated as the elasticity of the number of income
receiving units to the lower income limit). A higher value of α
implies a more equal distribution of income, so that, given the
above equation, greater income equality tends to lead to a faster
potential rate of growth of the car stock.[6] In view of the criticisms

that have been leveled at Pareto's law, however, this does not appear to be a very satisfactory method for dealing with the effects of income distribution on the demand for cars.

The demand for a consumer durable can be divided into two components, that part that goes to increase the stock of the product and that that goes to replace existing units. In the specific case of cars, part of sales goes to increase the number of vehicles on the road, while the remainder goes to replace scrapped vehicles. The relative importance of these two components of demand differs greatly between developed and underdeveloped countries. For example, in the United States, in the mid-1960s, scrappage represented 70 percent of new registrations; that is, of total sales, 70 percent went to replace scrapped units, while only 30 percent contributed to an increase in the number of vehicles in circulation. In Britain, in 1965, scrappage was 42 percent of new registrations. The equivalent ratio for Argentina in 1965 was about 10 percent and that for Mexico 7.2 percent in the same year.

Another respect in which the demand for cars in underdeveloped countries may differ from that in developed countries is in the proportion accounted for by business demand for passenger cars. This is particularly important in the earliest stages of the development of car ownership. Data for South Korea[7] in 1965 indicated that 66.5 percent of all cars registered in the country were either business or government vehicles as compared to only 19 percent in Britain.[8] Unfortunately, there are no corresponding figures available on the share of business registrations in the total stock in the Latin American countries that interest us, but, bearing in mind the considerably higher level of car density in those countries, it would probably be much lower than in South Korea.

By far the most important factor to be taken into account when considering car demand in an underdeveloped country as opposed to a developed country is the question of constrained supply. This can be ignored in developed countries where the greater flexibility of the economy means that, when they do arise, supply constraints are of short duration. In an underdeveloped country, on the other hand, they can persist over long periods because of a low capacity to import or bottlenecks in certain key sectors, for example, electricity, or, in the case of the automotive industry, the parts industry.

Supply constraints assume a special significance in the case of consumer durables, since, unlike the case of nondurable consumer goods, they give rise to a backlog demand for the goods concerned. In terms of the model discussed above, there is a growing divergence between the desired and the actual stock of vehicles in circulation. In cases of particularly severe shortages prolonged over a considerable period of time, the stock of vehicles may fall as scrapped units are not replaced, while per capita income and the desired stock of vehicles increase. The classic example of this process is Argentina where the number of cars per 1,000 inhabitants fell from 24 in 1928 to 19 in 1958, despite the growth of income during the period.

Backlog demand is not necessarily identical with repressed demand, although the two concepts have been confused. Backlog can arise with or without repressed demand, as the latter is conventionally understood. The best way of bringing out the distinction between the two concepts is through some simple examples.

The first possible situation is one where the supply of cars is controlled either by import quotas or by production quotas and prices are also controlled by government policy. In this case, if the demand at the fixed price exceeds the given supply, or to put it another way, if the market clearing price is in excess of the controlled price, then there will be repressed demand that will manifest itself in waiting lists for cars, advance payments, and other forms of nonprice rationing. This will also clearly lead to backlog demand, since there will develop a divergence between the actual stock and the desired stock of cars.

A second situation is again one with a supply constraint in the sense that the government attempts to keep down the level of car sales. But, in this case, it uses the price mechanism to do so, either directly by using import duties rather than quotas or indirectly with import or production quotas, by allowing prices to rise to the level that equates demand with the available supply. This is not a situation of repressed demand in the conventional sense, but it is one of backlog demand in the sense of a gap between actual and desired car stocks.

The last situation that can be identified is one where neither supply is restricted nor prices controlled. This is the usual situation of developed countries and here there is neither repressed nor backlog demand.

Figure 6.1, a diagramatic representation, can help to clarify the different situations even further. Let us suppose that in period 0, given the existing stock of cars and the level of income in the country concerned, the demand for new cars is given by the line DD_0. Supply is limited by the government to the level S_0. The first example, discussed above, is that where the price of cars is also controlled at the level $\bar{P}$, below the market clearing price P_0, and the indicated repressed demand is given by MN. In the second case, prices are allowed to rise to the level P_0 so that repressed demand is eliminated. In the third case, supply is increased to S_1 so that repressed demand is also eliminated.

FIGURE 6.1

"Repressed" and "Backlog" Demand

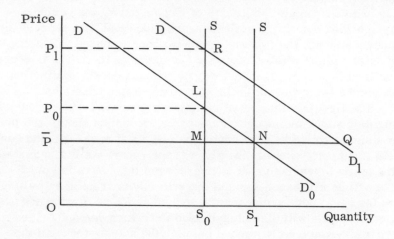

Source: Compiled by the author.

So far, however, the analysis has been confined to one period, so that it has not been possible to discuss whether or not there is also backlog demand in these cases. As was mentioned above, DD_0 was drawn for a given level of income and stock of cars. Over time, however, these factors will change, increases in income pushing the curve outward and increases in the stock of cars pushing the curve inward. If there is a backlog of demand, the stock will not grow sufficiently fast to match the growth of income and the curve will be pushed outward to DD_1. If supply remains constrained at S_0, repressed demand at the official price $\bar{P}$ increases from MN to MQ and the market clearing price rises from P_0 to P_1. This shift in DD as a result of backlog demand will occur independently of whether or not it is accompanied by repressed demand and will continue as long as a backlog exists.

The same point can be made with a numerical example. Suppose for simplicity that the demand equation takes a log-log form:

$$\log X_t = a \log Y_t - b \log P_t - c \log S_{t-1}$$

a, b, and c are thus the elasticities of demand with respect to the variables to which they are attached. Let us assume for the sake of the example that a = 3, b = 1, and c = 2. Assume further that Y_t is growing at a rate of 5 percent per year. In the long run both new purchases and stock must grow at the same rate. If this is assumed initially to be 5 percent, then P_t can remain constant.

Rates of Growth of Variables

Year	Y_t	X_t	S_t	P_t
0	5%	5%	5%	0
1	5%	4%	4.8%	1.0%
2	5%	4%	–	1.4%
.	.	.	.	.
.	.	.	.	.
.	.	.	.	.
.	.	.	.	.
n	5%	4%	4%	3%

If the rate of growth of supply is reduced to 4 percent, then the market clearing price rises initially by 1 percent and the rate of growth of the stock of cars falls below 5 percent. Eventually, the rate of growth of the stock of cars falls to the new equilibrium rate of 4 percent. The rate of growth of market clearing prices will then level off at 3 percent per year. It makes no difference if actual prices are allowed to rise by this amount or not; there will be a backlog of demand in either case.

Whether or not repressed demand exists together with the backlog demand, the effect is the same when the supply constraint is removed. Either way demand is very buoyant for a period while this backlog is being met. In the case where there is no repressed demand, because prices have been allowed to rise to the market clearing level, this can be thought of simply as a price effect, since the startup of local production, for example, is likely to be accompanied by a fall in price compared to the previous import price plus duty.[9] In practice, some combination of the two cases is likely to be found. In the first case there is no visible price effect but queuing and so on are eliminated and the gap between the desired and actual stock closed.

Having defined backlog demand in this way, it is not simple to identify when it may have existed and even more difficult to attempt to quantify it. The problem arises from the fact that the phenomenon is not necessarily accompanied by queuing and that it is not easy to know how high prices have to be to choke off demand so that there is no repressed demand observable.

One approach to the problem is that of international comparisons. It is assumed initially that the most important single factor determining the level of car ownership within a country is its per capita income. The regression line relating car density to income was calculated using the data available for 26 capitalist economies. The use of cross-section analysis in such a situation presents a number of problems. A regression calculated in this way may simply be the result of linking points on each country's individual growth path relating car density to income.

For a curve derived from cross-section data to be meaningful, it is necessary to postulate a universal relationship between the two variables. This is a strong assumption but may not be implausible in economic terms. What it does imply is that as incomes rise, consumption follows the same pattern in all countries. This is the equivalent of saying that, as a result of the international demonstration effect, the desired level of car density is the same in countries at the same level of income. In fact, it would appear that the international demonstration effect is very strong in the case of passenger cars.

If it were the case that no universal relation existed between income and the number of vehicles in circulation, but that the relationship observed using international cross-section data was simply the result of linking points on individual country curves, then this observed relationship would show no constancy over time. If, on the other hand, there was such a universal relationship, then the curve would not change significantly over a number of years.

The hypothesis that a universal relation exists was tested by calculating the regression equations relating the log of the number of cars per 1,000 inhabitants to the log of per capita gross domestic product for 26 countries on which data were available both for 1958 and 1969. The equations thus derived were as follows:

$$1958 \quad \log S = 1.63 \log Y - 3.10 \quad\quad r^2 = 0.83$$
$$\quad\quad\quad (0.16) \quad\quad\quad (0.44)$$

$$1969 \quad \log S = 1.74 \log Y - 3.38 \quad\quad r^2 = 0.90$$
$$\quad\quad\quad (0.11) \quad\quad\quad (0.33)$$

These were tested to see if the coefficient of log Y, that is, the income elasticity of the number of vehicles in circulation, had changed significantly over the period, and it was concluded that it had not.

It has already been mentioned, in discussing the demand for new cars, that per capita income is by no means the only factor determining this demand, and the same is true of the stock of cars. The most important variable, apart from income, is likely to be the cost of car ownership, composed of the purchase price of the car and its running cost over its entire lifetime. It has not been possible to find any data on international comparisons of the cost of running a car, so that the purchase price of a new car has been taken to represent the cost of car ownership. Using data for 16 countries in the mid-1960s, it was found that introducing the price variable, the data for which were admittedly not very good, did not add anything to the explanatory power of the regression using only per capita income.

It seems possible, therefore, to use the equations presented earlier to give a rough indication of the expected level of car ownership in a country, given its per capita income. If the actual car density falls well below the predicted level, this would be a priori evidence of backlog demand.

Taken together, these factors tend to make the pattern of demand found in the car market of the underdeveloped countries rather different from that found in developed countries. As has just been seen, there is likely to be a significant upward time trend in the demand for cars in underdeveloped countries, as the road network develops and the use of cars becomes more widespread. This would not be the case in the developed countries since they have already passed through the comparable phase in the development of the car market. Thus, the number of cars in circulation and even the number of new registrations may continue to grow in recession years when per capita income falls. This tendency for growth independently of income and price movements is likely to be accentuated during the early years of the development of the industry in many countries because of the existence of considerable backlog demand along the lines just described.

It is not clear what the consequences of the various individual characteristics of the market for vehicles in underdeveloped countries will be for the income and price elasticities of demand. A. Nowicki has suggested that income and price elasticities will tend to be higher in underdeveloped countries than in developed countries.[10] He bases his argument on the differential weights of expansion and replacement demand in the two groups of countries. If one assumes that the income elasticity of demand for increases in the stock of vehicles is the same in developed and underdeveloped countries, and that the rate of scrappage is less sensitive to income changes than new demand, then the higher weight of the latter in underdeveloped countries will make total demand more sensitive to income changes.

It is not clear that either of these assumptions holds, however. In the first place, the tendency for demand to grow regardless of changes in income, the greater importance of demand for cars for business as opposed to private use, and the more unequal income distribution may mean that the income elasticity of demand for new car purchases is not the same in developed and underdeveloped countries. Moreover, despite the relative importance of replacement purchases in the advanced countries, demand still fluctuates considerably from year to year, reflecting perhaps the role of expectations and the ability to postpone the acquisition of a new car, which may make a replacement market more volatile.

In developed countries, the high proportion of demand that goes to replace scrapped units tends to dampen the price elasticity of demand, since used cars tend to be traded in when making new purchases. It is not necessarily true, however, that the lower ratio of replacement to expansion demand in underdeveloped economies will lead to a higher price elasticity. The fallacy here lies in equating sales to new owners with sales that increase the number of cars in circulation. In practice, new cars tend to be bought by previous owners and those who are buying for the first time tend to buy used cars. Even if it were true that a higher proportion of new car buyers were entering the market for the first time in underdeveloped countries, one could still not conclude that this would lead to a higher price elasticity without taking into account a number of other factors. The importance of business demand or the importance of supply constraints might make demand relatively inelastic with respect to small changes in price.

INCOME DISTRIBUTION AND THE
DEMAND FOR CARS

In the previous section it was indicated that the distribution of income was an important variable in explaining the growth of car ownership in underdeveloped countries. Since it is unfortunately rather difficult to include it in an econometric model of car demand, the general pattern of ownership or expenditure by income group will be discussed before going on to consider the growth of demand and changes in demand conditions in each country individually. Unlike the developed countries where car ownership is by now widespread, in the underdeveloped countries a mass market has not developed and ownership reaches down only as far as medium-sized business owners and professional workers. As Nowicki puts it, "a country which shows signs of having mass consumption in motor cars is becoming a developed country."[11]

In Argentina, the most developed of the countries under consideration, more than half the households covered by a family expenditure survey in 1963 spent virtually nothing on car purchases, accounting for only 5 percent of total expenditure on cars, while

TABLE 6.1

Expenditure on Cars by Income Group in
Argentina, 1963
(thousands of pesos)

Family Income	Percent Families	Percent of Car Expenditure	Cars as Percent of Total Expenditure
Less than 200	53	5.3	0.5
200 to 350	29	23.1	2.5
350 to 750	15	38.4	5.1
More than 750	3	33.2	10.9
Total	100	100.0	3.3

Sources: Camara Industrial de Fabricantes de Autopiezas de
la Republica Argentina, Estudio Técnico-Económico de la Industria
Nacional de Transporte (Buenos Aires, 1970), pp. 232-35. Comisión
de Estudios Económicos de la Industria Automotriz, La Industria
Automotriz Argentina, Informe Economico, 1969 (Buenos Aires,
1969), pp. 197-98.

more than 70 percent of such expenditure is made by the top 18 percent of households. Thus, even in this country, with its large middle
class, the car is still by no means a mass consumer good. Families
with an income below 70,000 pesos do not spend on cars, while those
between 70,000 and 200,000 pesos spend only 0.5 percent of their
total expenditure on cars. It is only in the highest income group,
which accounts for 3 percent of all families, that the proportion
rises above 10 percent (see Table 6.1).

The Mexican case (Table 6.2) shows a high concentration of
automobile ownership among the highest income groups. The lowest
76 percent of families by income account for only 14 percent of all
the cars owned in the country, while the highest 9 percent, with
40 percent of total income, own 59 percent of all cars. It can be
seen from these figures that cars, as would be expected of a luxury
consumer durable, are more highly concentrated than total income.
Even these figures underestimate the extent to which car ownership
is concentrated, since they refer only to the number of units owned,
whereas the lower income families will tend to have secondhand
cars and cheaper models and the high income groups will have newer
and larger cars. Data on car ownership that took account of the
value of the vehicles owned or data on new purchases would show
even higher concentration.

TABLE 6.2

Ownership of Cars by Income Group
in Mexico, 1963

Family Income (pesos monthly)	Percent Families	Percent Total Income	Percent Cars Owned
Less than 1,500	76.01	35.4	14.2
1,501 to 3,000	15.00	24.7	26.8
3,001 to 4,500	4.55	13.0	15.6
4,501 to 10,000	3.56	17.6	32.5
More than 10,000	0.88	9.3	10.9

Source: Banco de México, S. A., Encuesta sobre lugresos y Gastos Familiares en México, 1963 (Mexico City, 1966).

Unfortunately it was not possible to obtain statistics of car sales or ownership by income group for Chile. As an approximation, data on the consumption of transport equipment in general had to be used, which tend to underestimate the true extent to which car ownership is concentrated, since they include other items, such as bicycles, which tend to be consumed by lower income groups. Even so, the figures in Table 6.3 show that car purchases only assume a significant proportion of total expenditure for the top 5 percent of households and that these account for more than 75 percent of total

TABLE 6.3

Expenditure on Transport Equipment by
Income Group in Chile, 1969

Family Income (sueldos vitales)	Percent Families	Percent of Car Expenditure	Transport Equipment and Percent of Total Expenditure
0 to 2	31.2	0.5	0.1
2 to 4	35.0	1.1	0.1
4 to 6	14.6	8.1	1.2
6 to 8	14.3	14.8	1.6
More than 8	4.9	75.5	13.2

Source: S. Pitar and E. Moyano, Redistribución del Consumo y Transición al Socialismo, Cuadernos de la Realidad Nacional no. 11 (1972), pp. 25-44.

purchases of transport equipment. The lowest two thirds of all
households consume only 1.6 percent of the total, which in all likelihood includes no cars whatsoever.

These three studies, despite the differences in the concepts
they employ (car ownership, sales), all show that car ownership
in Latin America is concentrated in the hands of a small minority
of the population, while the vast majority is virtually excluded from
participating in this market. The second point that emerges is the
discontinuity in car consumption, which increases sharply as a
percentage of total consumption in the upper income groups. In the
two studies that refer to car purchases (that is, those on Argentina
and Chile), more than 10 percent of total expenditure by the highest
income group is on cars, while the proportion is significantly less
among lower income groups. (This would seem to indicate a lack
of trickle down from the high income groups as far as car consumption
is concerned.)

THE DEMAND FOR CARS IN SOME
LATIN AMERICAN COUNTRIES

This section attempts to utilize some of the theoretical concepts
discussed in previous sections in order to analyze the pattern of
growth of car output in a number of Latin American economies and
the factors contributing to it. Where possible, econometric analysis
is used, but emphasis is given to statistical material of a more
descriptive nature.

As has already been seen, a number of factors may underlie
the growth of output. As with all commodities, there is both an
income elasticity and a price elasticity effect. There is also an
added factor derived from what has been called backlog demand,
that is, the adjustment of the car stock to its normal level, below
which it has been kept by a supply constraint. In the early stages
of the industry's development, this is likely to be the most important
factor at work in a number of countries. Finally, there is the
import-substituting effect of replacing cars previously imported,
the importance of which depends on how far imports were permitted
before the initiation of local production.

Of the three countries to be considered, Argentina and Chile
are obviously cases where imports of cars have been subject to
severe restraint so that there is an a priori reason for supposing
that the supply constraint and backlog demand have been important
factors. This is not so readily apparent in Mexico, which has
enjoyed a more favorable balance of payments position since World
War II and has been able to maintain imports and local assembly at

relatively high levels. Nevertheless, even Mexico had a considerably lower number of cars in circulation in 1960 than might have been expected on the basis of international comparisons.

Argentina

As was indicated above, Argentina appears as a classic case of a country where control of imports of cars over a long period of time led to a considerable divergence between the actual and desired number of vehicles in circulation. As Table 6.4 indicates, the crisis of 1929 brought a sharp fall in the country's car imports. Up to 1956, the main method used to restrict imports of cars was a quota system, which was subsequently replaced by high tariff duties. Car prices rose considerably in real terms from 1929 onward, especially after World War II. Thus, small cars in the early 1960s cost between 1.6 and 2.5 times more than in 1929 and medium and large cars varied from 2.8 to 4.3 times the 1929 price.[12] Presumably the differential was even higher during the 1950s before the start of local production. These comparisons, it should be remembered, take no account of quality and design improvements over the period.

If the stock of cars in Argentina in 1960 is compared with the level predicted on the basis of international comparison, it appears that it fell short by more than 40 percent. Another consequence and indication of the shortage of new vehicles from the 1930s onward was the lengthening of the life of the existing vehicles. Whereas in 1933 more than half the cars in Argentina were less than 5 years

TABLE 6.4

Imports of Cars into Argentina, 1920-54

1920-24	105,854
1925-29	267,766
1930-34	70,443
1935-39	125,334
1940-44	36,150
1945-49	48,985
1950-54	25,759

Source: Asociación de Fabricas de Automotores (ADEFA), Industria Automotriz Argentina (Buenos Aires, 1970).

old and all cars were less than 10 years old, by 1954 the situation
had so deteriorated that 65.7 percent of all cars were more than
15 years old and only 7.3 percent were less than 5 years old.[13]
This lengthening of the life of cars meant that the real stock of
vehicles in circulation, taking account of depreciation, was less
than the apparent stock calculated simply in numerical terms.

Until 1960, imports had been the major source of cars in
Argentina. Nevertheless, the absolute level was low and fluctuating.
The only years during the 1950s in which they surpassed 15,000 were
in 1951 and 1958. Import substitution, in the literal sense of the
phrase, therefore, did not provide much scope for the growth of
local production. The initial backlog demand and the age structure
of the existing stock, on the other hand, did. The number of cars
per 1,000 inhabitants rose from 23 in 1960 to around 75 by 1971.
By 1967, the proportion of cars less than ten years old had risen
to 70 percent compared to less than 25 percent in 1954 and less
than 40 percent in 1960.[14]

It is impossible to say exactly when the initial backlog demand
was eliminated. Some industry sources put the elimination of excess
demand as early as the end of 1962,[15] but it is difficult to disentangle
the effect of the recession in general economic conditions from the
secular evolution of the automotive industry. By 1969, however,
the car density in Argentina was higher than its expected level by
almost 20 percent.

These developments had a number of market manifestations.
New car prices fell by almost 25 percent in real terms between 1960
and the mid-1960s. At the same time, used cars, whose value
depreciated by only 5 percent per year up to 1960, began to depre-
ciate at a faster rate.[16] As Table 6.5 indicates, there was a
considerable increase in depreciation rates up to 1963 that continued
during the mid-1960s.

The same forces of increased supply and competition that
tended to drive down the prices of new cars and the trade-in values
of secondhand cars also led to increased utilization of sales finance.
Initially, the manufacturers found little need to extend credit to
their customers in order to sell their cars. But between 1959 and
the first half of 1963, the percentage of total units sold for which
credit was granted rose from 32 to 84 percent, while the average
period for which credit was extended lengthened from 10 to 24 months
and the monthly interest rate fell from 2.0 to 1.6 percent.[17] In the
mid-1960s, the normal deposit was estimated at between 40 and
50 percent of the car's price.[18] This was a period during which
the manufacturers or their dealers began to set up finance companies
in order to provide credit to their customers. One of the earliest

TABLE 6.5

Relative Prices of New and Used Cars
in Argentina, 1963–66

Year	New	Age (years)			
		1	2	3	4
1963	100	84	80	76	72
1964	100	82	78	74	70
1965	100	78	73	70	66
1966	100	73	68	63	59

Source: Asociación de Concesionarios de Automotores de la
República Argentina, El Concesionario de Automotores en la Argentina 2 (Mar de Plata, 1967).

established companies, Permanente, which operated on behalf of
IKA, grew rapidly during the first half of the decade, especially
between 1963 and 1964.

In order to try and gain further understanding of the factors
contributing to the growth of car production in Argentina during
this period, a statistical demand function was estimated for the
years 1960 to 1971. A stock adjustment model of the form discussed
above incorporating a time trend was used.

$$X_t = aY_t + bP_t + cS_{t-1} + dt \qquad (1)$$

In order to avoid the problems posed by multicolinearity
between income, price, and stock, first differences of the variables
were taken and the equation became

$$DX_t = aDY_t + bDP_t + cDS_{t-1} + d \qquad (2)$$

The equation was estimated using both absolute and per capita values
of sales, income, and stock, the best fit being obtained with the
latter, which gave the equation

$$D(X/N)_t = 31.35 D(Y/N)_t - 0.02 DP_t - 0.36 D(S/N)_{t-1} + 1.56$$
$$(7.06) \qquad\qquad (0.04) \quad\;\; (0.14) \qquad\qquad (0.63)$$

$$R^2 = 0.79$$

A number of interesting observations can be drawn from this
equation. In the first place, per capita income, car density, and

the constant term are all significant. If one assumes a rate of
depreciation of the stock of cars of 2 or 3 percent per year, then
the adjustment coefficient can be estimated at slightly less than
0.4, remembering that the coefficient c is composed of the rate of
depreciation minus the adjustment coefficient. The estimated income
elasticity at the mean values of the variables comes to approximately
3.1. The calculated price elasticity of demand is extremely low,
only 0.3 and not significantly different from zero, although it does
have the correct sign. The constant term in the equation is significant, indicating an upward trend in demand not explained by income
and price changes. In fact, this appears to be the most important
factor explaining the growth of output during the period, followed by
the growth of per capita income.

It is of interest to compare these findings with the results
obtained in a number of studies of car demand in the United States.
Ten studies quoted by L. White[19] found income elasticities ranging
from 1.0 to 4.0, with 3.0 as a center point, and price elasticities
between -0.5 and -1.5. The lower income elasticities were obtained
using variables such as Roos and von Szelski's "supernumary income,"
rather than total income, as the independent variable. Where
personal disposable income was used, the elasticity estimates were
all greater than 3. The Suits study, which is the one most akin
in its methodology to the equation used here, suggested an income
elasticity of 4.59.[20] As Suits points out, the use of first difference
analysis tends to bias the income elasticity upward and the price
elasticity downward. Thus, it appears clear that the income elasticity of demand is lower in Argentina than in the United States, and
that the price elasticity is also probably lower.

As the initial backlog of demand was eliminated in Argentina,
it was to be expected that further growth in output would come to
depend more closely on growth of income. In fact, the correlation
coefficient between per capita income and car sales per head
increased from 0.62 in the period 1960-65 to 0.85 for the entire
period 1960-71. This suggests that from the mid-1960s onward the
expansion of the market came to depend on the growth of the economy
as a whole. This, in turn, led to a slowing down of the rate of
growth of both car production and the number of cars in circulation.
Whereas car production grew at an average of 27.2 percent per year
between 1960 and 1965, it fell to 6.4 percent for 1965-73.

Another indication of the reduced dynamism of the industry
is obtained if one compares annual changes in car output to changes
in gross domestic product (GDP).* As can be seen from Table 6.6,

---

*A similar pattern is found in the case of commercial vehicles.
The rate of growth of commercial vehicle output slowed down from

TABLE 6.6

Growth of Car Output and Gross Domestic
Product in Argentina, 1960-73

	Cars (percent)	GDP (percent)	Cars/GDP
1961	95.0	7.1	13.4
1962	15.8	-1.7	+
1963	-16.9	-2.4	7.0
1964	52.1	10.4	5.0
1965	16.7	9.1	1.8
1966	0.1	0.7	0.1
1967	-2.6	2.5	–
1968	-1.8	4.6	–
1969	19.6	8.4	2.3
1970	9.1	4.4	2.1
1971	15.6	3.7	4.2
1972	4.0	3.8	1.1
1973	9.2	4.8	1.9

Key: + Increase in numerator accompanying decrease in
denominator. - Decrease in numerator accompanying increase in
denominator.

Sources: Banco Central de la República Argentina (BCRA)
data as quoted in Fundación de Investigaciones Economicas Latinoamericanas, Indicadores de Coyuntura (Buenos Aires), various
issues; ADEFA, 1974 Industria Automotriz Argentina (Buenos Aires:
ADEFA, 1975); and own elaboration.

not only does the coefficient relating the growth of car output and
GDP fall significantly in the second half of the decade but one gets
a new phenomenon of car output falling in years when GDP increased
(1967, 1968), whereas in the first half of the decade, car output
increased while GDP fell (1962). The same tendency for the rate
of growth to fall during the second half of the decade was also evident
in the case of the number of cars in circulation. The reduction from
14.1 percent per year in 1960-65 to 10.4 percent per year in 1965-73

4.5 percent per year in 1960-65 to 2.5 percent per year in 1965-73.
There was also a tendency for the ratio of changes in commercial
vehicle output to changes in gross fixed investment to decline during
the 1960s. See Appendix Table A.12.

was not, however, on such a dramatic scale as that observed for output.*

Chile

The Chilean situation cannot be described in the same terms as the Argentinian one, of a severely restricted supply of cars being eased as a result of the setting up of local production facilities leading to the elimination of the backlog of demand that had built up during the period when imports were the major or only source of supply. Until 1960, the supply of new cars in Chile depended entirely on imports that fluctuated around 2,500 units a year between 1955 and 1960. As a result, the number of cars in circulation grew by an average rate of only 3.6 percent per year and the number of cars per 1,000 inhabitants remained more or less constant at around 7.5. Those cars that were imported were subject to a tax of 200 percent on their FOB value from 1956 onward. Thus, in 1960, the stock of cars in Chile was extremely low relative to the country's per capita income, less than 40 percent of the level that would have been expected on the basis of international comparison.

The startup of local production in 1960 by no means removed the supply constraint, as it did in Argentina, although it did increase the apparent consumption of cars threefold. Supply remained constrained for a number of reasons. First, since the local content requirement was only 30 percent in 1963, the industry was still highly dependent on imports during the early years of its development. Second, as the foreign exchange constraint was removed through increasing national integration to 57.94 percent in the late 1960s, a new restriction came into play with the limited capacity of suppliers to provide parts.[21] Firms replying to the Rol Industrial annual questionnaire in the period 1967-70 gave deficiencies in the quantity or quality of inputs as an important factor causing underutilization of capacity.[22] A third problem derived from the special agreement with Argentina by which Argentinian-produced parts qualified as local content if compensated for by exports of Chilean parts. This has introduced another bottleneck, and some firms mentioned the difficulties of increasing these exchanges as a further cause of excess capacity.[23]

Despite an average annual increase of slightly less than 10 percent in the number of cars in circulation in Chile during the 1960s,

---

*For commercial vehicles the period of most rapid growth of number in circulation was 1959-64. The rate of growth fell from 7.9 percent per year in 1960-65 to 6.1 percent per year in 1965-73.

the evidence seems to suggest that, for the greater part of the period, supply fell short of demand. Official and semiofficial bodies have suggested that the demand for cars had not been met up to 1968 or 1969.[24] This is borne out by the fact that for the greater part of the period, consumers had to wait a long time and make advance payments for cars, especially those models in greatest demand, such as the Mini or Renault 4. Moreover, some of the manufacturers were able to finance part of their operations by requiring advance payments from dealers. Not surprisingly, no firm mentioned a deficiency of demand as a cause of excess capacity.[25] The existence of official price control from 1966 onward meant that supply had to be rationed through queuing rather than through the price mechanism.

Nevertheless, there were some signs that from about 1967 onward, market conditions were easing as supply and demand came increasingly into balance. One indication is that the average period for which credit was granted increased from 6 months in 1966, 9 months in 1967, 12.7 months in 1968, and to 14 months in 1969. Another is the growth of credit outstanding at the beginning of each year from 44 million escudos in 1967 to 246 million escudos in 1969, at 1969 prices.[26] This is confirmed by evidence on the initial deposit and length of the period for which credit is extended both to dealers and to the public for various models.[27]

These trends were reversed with the election of the Unidad Popular in 1970. The large increase in effective demand and the inflationary climate led to an upsurge in the demand for cars. By 1971, all sales were being made for cash, and there was such a long waiting list for cars that the government was forced to intervene, setting up Estanco Automotriz to deal with the distribution of cars. This situation persisted until the military coup of September 1973, but the deflationary policies pursued by the junta led to a sharp reduction in demand, the reemergence of sales credit, and considerable sales difficulties for the motor companies.

The main factors underlying the growth of car production in Chile were the substitution of imports by locally produced vehicles in the early 1960s and the subsequent elimination of the accumulated backlog of demand. The volume of sales was determined by supply factors rather than demand. On the demand side, relative prices have increased rather than fallen since 1964[28] and changes in car sales were negatively correlated with income changes.* As the remaining imports are replaced and the backlog of demand eliminated,

---

*The partial correlation coefficient relating changes in car sales per inhabitant to changes in income per capita between 1962 and 1970 was -0.61.

further growth of output comes to depend increasingly on income and price changes, leading to a slower rate of expansion.

Although not as spectacular as in Argentina, the initiation of local production has had a considerable effect in Chile. The increased rate of growth of the car stock has already been mentioned. Moreover, there has also been some improvement in the age structure of the stock so that, by 1971, 42 percent of all cars were less than five years old as opposed to only 22 percent in 1959, and the number of cars over ten years of age fell from 58 to 35 percent over the same period.[29] In addition, local production replaced imports as the main source of supply in 1962, and, by the early 1970s, most cars were produced locally, although about half the supply of commercial vehicles was imported.

By 1969, the number of cars in circulation in Chile was over 80 percent of its expected level, more than double what it had been at the beginning of the decade. It seems possible that the remaining 20 percent differential could be accounted for by the extremely high price of cars in Chile, where in the period 1964-68 costs averaged 4.2 times those in the country of origin.[30] The main point to be remembered for later analysis, however, is that for the greater part of the period under consideration, demand conditions were extremely favorable and that, a priori, one would not expect competition in the market to be the most important factor explaining the development of the industry.

Mexico

Throughout the 1950s, the demand for cars in Mexico was met in almost equal proportions by imports of completely builtup vehicles and by local assembly of imported parts and components. Until 1958, a rigid quota system imposed by the government had led to the creation of considerable unsatisfied demand. The system was then liberalized somewhat and the apparent consumption of cars (that is, imports plus local assembly) rose by 31.8 percent in 1959 and by a further 26.8 percent in 1960, imports increasing somewhat more sharply than assembly. Despite the increased supply of cars in these two years, the stock of cars in Mexico in 1960 was still more than 30 percent below what would have been expected given the country's level of income.

From 1951 to 1958, prices had been subject to official control, but in practice requests from manufacturers to increase them were usually granted. As a result, prices were able to increase by about 10 percent annually, especially since luxury cars were not subject to the price control. Subsequently, a stricter system of control was introduced by which prices were to be determined on the basis of costs. In 1960, therefore, the government controlled both the price at which cars were sold and their number by means of a quota, a system that has been maintained in operation since then. Government control has permitted a steady growth in the number of cars on the road in Mexico. Between 1955 and 1960, the increase was 9.4 percent per year, in the next five-year period it was slightly higher at 9.8 percent per year, and between 1965 and 1970 there was a further rise of 9.9 percent per year.* This growth of the stock of cars has only closed the gap slightly between the actual and predicted level, since per capita income and population both have grown rapidly over the same period.

As a result of the quota system and the control of prices, Mexico has not seen a situation comparable to that of Argentina in the early 1960s. There is, however, evidence to suggest that cars are not as easy to sell as they once were in Mexico. The car dealers association, Asociación Mexicana de Distribuidores de Automóviles (ANDA), has been making alarmist noises. At the 23rd Annual Convention, there were complaints that more cars were available than the market could absorb, and, since the mid-1960s, ANDA has been complaining in its publications that dealers are being squeezed between a market that is becoming saturated and the demands of the manufacturers. Such statements have to be discounted as a common grievance among intermediaries such as car dealers, but nevertheless they do contain a kernel of truth. There does appear to have been a tendency for their profits to be squeezed. Dealers' net profits on invested capital fell from 7.3 percent in 1965 to 6.1 percent in 1968 and 5.1 percent in 1971, although profits did recover somewhat to 5.7 percent in 1972.[31] Moreover, the pressure from the manufacturers is understandable when it is remembered that they have also been squeezed by rising costs and government price control measures.

The market is still a seller's market, however, in the sense that total output is determined by the government's production quotas rather than by demand. Since quotas refer to the model year beginning at the end of November and sales figures to the calendar year, it is not possible to make an exact comparison of the two. It seems to be the case, however, that in 1969 all firms, apart from VAM and FANASA, filled or almost filled their quota and that total output

---

*Statistics of the number of cars in circulation are published by the Departamento General de Estadisticas of the Secretaría de Industria y Commercio and by the Asociación Mexicana de la Industria Automotriz. The figures are not identical, so the official government figures are used here.

was thus constrained. (FANASA was on the verge of ceasing production altogether in any case.) It should be mentioned here that only
the basic quota is set by the government and that the firms can
increase their quota by exporting, increasing local content, or maintaining low prices. Thus, for firms that have export possibilities,
for example, the full utilization of quotas may not necessarily mean
that they cannot produce more but simply that it is not profitable
for them to do so given the state of the market and the cost of exports.

On the other hand, it is not a seller's market in the sense that
all firms can sell their vehicles regardless of quality, credit terms,
advertising, and so on. As far as credit goes, about 31 percent of
cars are sold with a repayment period of more than a year, between
21 and 27 percent (depending on the size of the car) with credit for
three to twelve months, and 42 to 48 percent for cash (1968 figures).[32]
As mentioned before, not all firms have filled their quota. VAM,
for instance, deliberately has kept production below the quota limit
in order to avoid sales problems, and Automex began to suffer sales
difficulties in the late 1960s. Contrary to the assertions of ANDA,
advertising has not played a major role in maintaining the level of
demand. Between 1960 and 1968, advertising expenditure as a
percentage of the total value of production and per car produced has
remained more or less constant, which would seem to contradict
the picture of the Mexican car market as one which is approaching
saturation point.

An attempt was made to estimate a statistical demand function
for cars similar to that obtained for Argentina. The available data
go back to 1950, so that the equation of the form

$$DX_t = g + aDP_t + bDY_t + cDS_{t-1}$$

was estimated for t = 1951 to t = 1970. Unlike the Argentinian case,
better results were obtained using absolute rather than per capita
data, but even so the equation gave an R^2 of only 0.56 as opposed
to 0.79 for Argentina. The inclusion of a dummy variable RP,
set at 1 up to 1960 and 0 subsequently, increased R^2 to 0.63 and
gave the following equation.

$$DX_t = -14,060 - 864DP_t + 1.47DY_t - 0.001DS_{t-1} + 962ORP \quad R^2 = 0.63$$
$$\quad\quad (7,990) \quad (380) \quad\quad (0.58) \quad\quad (0.017) \quad\quad\quad (5,550)$$

As well as giving a lower R^2 than was obtained in the Argentinian case, it was also found that the existing number of vehicles
in circulation was not a significant explanatory variable. Both
income and price were significant explanatory variables with the
income elasticity of demand in the region of 3.5 and price elasticity

around -1.2 at the mean values of the variables. Nevertheless, this still left a large part of the growth of demand unexplained.

A second attempt to obtain more satisfactory results was made for the period 1960-70 without any dummy variable.

$$DX_t = -10,530 - 103DP_t + 1.67DY_t + 0.006DS_{t-1} \quad R^2 = 0.71$$
$$(6,390) \quad (720) \quad (0.53) \quad (0.014)$$

As can be seen, this gave a slightly better result in terms of R^2, which was 0.71 for absolute values and 0.64 for per capita values. Here, however, only the income coefficient proved to be significantly different from zero, with an elasticity of 3.8. The term for vehicles in circulation in the previous period has the wrong sign (that is, is positive) in the case of absolute values.

The failure to derive a meaningful statistical demand function for cars is not surprising in view of the control exercised by the government over both prices and output. The use of the quota system in Mexico meant that there was no period of rapid growth of car production followed by a period of relative stagnation, as was the case in Argentina. As Table 6.7 shows, output grew steadily through the 1960s, but in the early 1970s the growth rate fell, and in 1972 and 1973 was only slightly greater than the growth of GDP. This may indeed be an indication that the Mexican car market is now approaching the saturation point.

CONCLUSION

This chapter has shown that the automotive industry in an underdeveloped country enjoys particularly favorable demand conditions during the early years of its development as a result of the accumulated backlog of demand created during a previous period of constrained supply. This manifested itself in a rapid growth of output during the early 1960s in Argentina and in a seller's market in both Chile and Mexico throughout the greater part of the 1960s. Once the backlog has been eliminated, demand conditions begin to change as occurred in Argentina in the mid-1960s, with an increase in consumer credit, greater depreciation on used cars, and so forth. Further growth then depends on the normal parameters of a demand function, income, and price. As was seen in the Argentinian case, however, the income elasticity of demand for cars is less than in the United States, and the price elasticity is not significantly different from zero. Moreover, the unequal income distribution means that the potential market is limited to only a fraction of the population. Thus, after a short period of growth, the industry is likely to lose its dynamic impetus.

TABLE 6.7

Growth of Car Output and Gross Domestic
Product in Mexico, 1960-73

	Cars (percent)	GDP (percent)	Cars/GDP
1961	26.9	4.9	5.5
1962	4.6	4.7	1.0
1963	19.8	8.0	2.5
1964	24.3	11.7	2.1
1965	9.2	6.5	1.4
1966	21.3	6.9	3.1
1967	7.5	6.3	1.2
1968	17.0	8.1	2.1
1969	12.4	6.3	2.0
1970	15.8	6.9	2.3
1971	11.8	3.7	3.2
1972	10.2	7.3	1.4
1973	8.9	7.6	1.2

Sources: AMIA, La Industria Automotriz de México en Cifras
1971 (Mexico City: 1972), p. 53; AMIA, La Industria Automotriz
de México en Cifras 1973 (Mexico City: 1974), p. 62; Banco de México,
S.A., Informe Anual, 1974 (Mexico City: 1975), Statistical Appendix,
Table 1; own elaboration.

In the following chapter the way in which the different demand
conditions observed in each of the three countries interacted with
changing supply conditions to bring about changes in the structure
of the industry is discussed. These demand conditions have also
influenced the form that interfirm competition has taken at different
times and in different countries, as will be seen in Chapter 8.

NOTES

1. See, for example, C. F. Roos and V. von Szeliski,
"Factors Governing Changes in Domestic Automobile Demand," in
The Dynamics of Automobile Demand (New York: General Motors
Corporation, 1939); G. C. Chow, Demand for Automobiles in the
United States (Amsterdam: North-Holland Publishing, 1957);
D. P. Suits, "The Demand for New Automobiles in the United States,
1929-56," REStat. 11 (1958): 273-80.
2. See D. Llarena and R. Trovarelli, Demanda de Automóviles
en el Peru (Lima: Universidad Nacional "Federico Villarreal,"

Centro de Investigaciones Económicas y Sociales, 1971), pp. 7-14, for a discussion of the macro- and microeconomic variables influencing the demand for cars.

3. Suits, for example, has a term to measure credit facilities (op. cit.).

4. For a long time, consumer demand theory has remained within a static framework, but some attempts have been made to develop a dynamic theory of secular demand growth. See R. Marris, The Economic Theory of "Managerial" Capitalism (New York: Macmillan, 1967), pp. 133-203, and J. Duesenberry, Income, Saving and the Theory of Consumer Demand (Cambridge, Mass.: Harvard University Press, 1949).

5. Quoted by A. G. Nowicki, Automobile Demand in Developing Countries, UNIDO (ID/WG, 13/23), 1968, pp. 18-19.

6. A discussion of Pareto's law can be found in J. Pen, Income Distribution, trans. T. S. Preston (London: Allen Lane, 1971).

7. See Nowicki, op. cit., pp. 11-12.

8. D. G. Rhys, The Motor Industry: An Economic Survey (London: Butterworths, 1972), p. 238.

9. On this point see C. Diaz-Alejandro, Essays on the Economic History of the Argentine Republic (New Haven, Conn.: Yale University Press, 1970), p. 317.

10. Nowicki, op. cit., pp. 7-13.

11. Ibid., p. 28.

12. Industrias Kaiser Argentina S. A., División Planificación Comercial, La Industria Automotriz Argentina, vol. 1, unpublished (1963), pp. 97-98.

13. Consejo Nacional de Desarrollo (CONADE), La Industria Automotriz (Análisis Preliminar) (Buenos Aires, 1966), Table 2.

14. Ibid., Table 2; and Banque Francaise et Italienne pour l'Amérique du Sud, "L'Industrie Automobile en Amérique Latine," Etudes Economique, no. 3 (1972), p. 12.

15. Camara Argentina de Fabricantes de Automotores, Significación Económica de la Industria Automotriz, 1963 (Buenos Aires, 1963).

16. Industrias Kaiser Argentina, op. cit., p. 114.

17. Ibid., p. 134.

18. Asociación de Concesionarios de Automotores de la República Argentina (ACARA), El Concesionario de Automotores en la Argentina. Examen de Su Situación Jurídica, Impositiva y Económico-Financiera (Mar del Plata, 1965), p. 144.

19. L. J. White, The Automobile Industry Since 1945 (Cambridge, Mass.: Harvard University Press, 1971), Table 7.2.

20. Suits, op. cit.

21. Corporación de Fomento (CORFO), División de Planificación Industrial, Desarrollo del Consumo Interno de Automotores, Publicación No. 13a/69, 1969, p. 5.

22. Ministerio de Economía, Rol Industrial.

23. Ibid.

24. CORFO, op. cit., pp. 3-4; Instituto de Costos, op. cit., Chap. I.

25. Rol Industrial.

26. Centro de Investigaciones Económicas de la Universidad Católica de Chile, "Efectos Económicos de la Industria Automotriz," Asociación de Industriales Metalúrgicos, Primer Seminario Nacional de la Industria Automotriz (Santiago: 1969), pp. 101-03.

27. Instituto de Costos, op. cit., Tables 73 and 74; own investigations.

28. Instituto de Costos, op. cit., Table 81.

29. ASIMET, Anexo 5; own calculation on the basis of data provided by the Comisión Automotriz.

30. Instituto de Costos, op. cit., Chap. II. 2b.

31. Héctor Vazquez Tercero, "Análisis Financiero del Sector Distribuidor, 1971 y 1972," in Estudio de Comercialización (Mexico City: Asociación Mexicana de Distribuidores de Automóviles, 1973).

32. J. Foncerrada Moreno and H. Vázquez Tercero, Informe Económico (Mexico City: Asociación Nacional de Distribuidores de Automóviles, 1969), p. 84.

7

CONCENTRATION AND DENATIONALIZATION IN THE AUTOMOTIVE INDUSTRY

In the last two chapters it has been seen that a number of the conditions that were assumed in the model presented in Chapter 4 were in fact fulfilled in the Argentinian, Chilean, and Mexican automotive industries during the 1960s. The model predicted that there would be a tendency for concentration within the industry, and that this would take the specific form of denationalization, that is to say, the elimination of locally owned firms. In this chapter, the overall developments in the industrial structure of the three countries are first examined in order to verify the extent to which the predictions of the model were realized. In the second part, more detailed attention is given to the experience of individual firms in order to adduce additional evidence on the advantages enjoyed by foreign subsidiaries over their domestic competitors.

CHANGES IN THE INDUSTRIAL STRUCTURE

The traditional analysis of concentration applied in the developed countries sees increases in concentration mainly as a function of the optimum size of plant or firm rising at a faster rate than the growth of the market, and the desire of firms to restrict competition, or what has been called "monopolization considerations."[1] In the case of the Latin American automotive industry increases in local content have played the same role as that attributed to technical progress in the advanced countries by causing the minimum optimum scale of plant and the initial capital requirement to rise, or by increasing the amount of working capital needed to finance suppliers. The Latin American experience differs from that of the developed countries in that changes in local content requirements make themselves

144

felt much more rapidly than technological changes, although the latter may also lead to sharply discontinuous changes in the minimum scale of production.

In measuring industrial concentration, two fundamental choices have to be made: the variable to be considered and the measurement of concentration to be used. The first is largely governed by considerations of data availability, and for this reason the number of vehicles produced or sold has been used for Argentina and Mexico, whereas the value of production has been used for Chile. It could be argued that the use of units rather than values underestimates the importance of companies producing trucks or the larger, more expensive cars and overestimates the market share of medium and small car producers. As far as the measurement of concentration is concerned, there is no reason to believe that the two will differ greatly, and in any case there is no a priori reason for supposing that the share of the market in value terms is a better indicator of monopoly than the share in volume terms.

In measuring concentration, one wishes to throw up two dimensions of the problem, the inequality of size distribution and the total number of firms. It is easy to see that neither of these measures on its own gives a satisfactory measure of concentration. The first fails to distinguish between the situation where the market is shared between two firms of equal size and the case where it is divided equally by 1,000 firms. The second fails to distinguish between an industry in which 1,000 firms share the market equally and one where one firm has 50 percent of the market, leaving the remaining 50 percent to be distributed between 999 firms.

An interesting attempt to incorporate both these factors in a single measure is the Herfindhal index.[2] An alternative measure frequently used is the percentage of the market accounted for by the largest three, four, or eight firms, or the number of firms to account for, say, 80 percent of the market. In the following analysis of the automotive industry in Argentina, Chile, and Mexico, three indicators of concentration have been used, the absolute number of firms, the Herfindhal index, and the market share of the four leading firms.

The most striking evidence of increased concentration in the Argentinian automotive industry is the reduction in the total number of firms in operation from 21 in 1960 to 10 at present (see Table 7.1). Most of the exits from the industry occurred during the first half of the decade and, already by 1964, the number of firms had fallen to 13. The other two indices calculated both indicate a sharp rise in concentration during the recovery from the 1964 recession. Since the mid-1960s, concentration has remained more or less constant, as indicated by the four-firm concentration ratio, although

TABLE 7.1

Indices of Concentration in the Argentinian
Automotive Industry, 1960-73

	Number of Firms	Herfindhal Index	Four Firm Concentration (percent)
1960	21	0.1839	67.6
1961	20	0.1428	61.1
1962	18	0.1429	60.1
1963	15	0.1398	61.5
1964	13	0.1631	71.9
1965	13	0.1623	72.5
1966	12	0.1491	71.5
1967	11	0.1566	73.4
1968	10	0.1535	71.2
1969	11	0.1447	68.7
1970	10	0.1441	66.8
1971	10	0.1513	69.6
1972	10	0.1500	68.1
1973	10	0.1547	69.7

Source: Appendix Table B.13.

there was a slight fall in 1969 and 1970 as a result of a continuing
decline in the market share of IKA-Renault not being offset by an
increasing share of the other three leading firms. The Herfindhal
index also declined somewhat during the late 1960s, indicating the
faster growth of the medium-sized firms, which offset the elimination of some of the smaller firms.

It is, of course, somewhat misleading to treat vehicles as a
homogeneous product since cars and trucks are not close substitutes
and even small and large cars may not be directly competitive.
Since the same firms are involved in producing different kinds of
vehicles, it is difficult to determine what the "industry" is for the
purpose of analyzing concentration. A more detailed breakdown by
category of vehicle indicates that concentration increased during
the early 1960s in all categories except large cars, where the late
entry of the U.S. Big Three reduced concentration.[3]

Perhaps more significant than the quantitative increase in
concentration has been the change in the ownership of the Argentinian
automotive industry that this process has involved. Of the 21 firms
in operation in 1960, only 4—Fiat, Ford, General Motors, and
Mercedes-Benz—were under majority foreign ownership, the remain-

der being either entirely or majority Argentinian owned and producing under license from a foreign firm. In 1963, locally owned firms accounted for more than 50 percent of total production, and as late as 1965, 6 of the 13 firms in operation were locally owned. The threat to their existence was recognized in 1964, and plans were presented to the government for a merger between the five local companies (excluding IKA) in order to form a company able to hold its own against foreign competition. These plans came to nothing, however, and at present there only remains the state-owned IME under local control. Some of these Argentinian firms, such as Siam di Tella, Isard, and Metalmecanica, which had no foreign capital participation, were driven out of the industry by competitive pressures. Others, like IKA and IAFA, were taken over by multinational corporations under whose license they had previously operated. In no case, however, was a foreign-controlled firm driven out of the industry.

During the early 1960s, the Chilean automotive industry was even more fragmented than that of Argentina. In 1962, there were a total of 20 firms, the leading 4 of which accounted for only just over half of the value of output. Some of these firms led a very unstable existence, producing 20 or 30 cars a year, and suspending production entirely in some years. Thus, the total number of firms fell from 20 in 1962 to 14 in 1963, recovering again to 18 in 1964 (see Table 7.2). By 1970, there had been a substantial increase in concentration with the number of firms being cut by half, the share of output accounted for by the four largest firms increasing by almost 20 percent and the Herfindhal index going from 0.1017 to 0.1491. The Unidad Popular government reduced the number of firms even further as part of its policy to rationalize the automotive industry. By 1973, four firms accounted for nearly the whole of Chile's production.

A detailed examination of Table 7.2 indicates a sharp upsurge in concentration in 1966 when a number of firms, including Indauto (Renault), EMSSA (BMC), and Nissan Motor Chile, were forced to suspend production because they were unable to meet the increase in local content from 41.1 to 50.0 percent required in that year. This was followed by a reduction in concentration during the next two years when these firms began production again, but further concentration in the last two years of the decade reestablished the peak of 1966. It should be noted in this context that it was the conscious policy of the Frei government to bring about increased levels of concentration in the industry through the control of prices and increasing local integration requirements.[4] Subsequently, the Allende government used more direct measures to increase concentration to a much higher level.

TABLE 7.2

Indices of Concentration in the Chilean
Automotive Industry, 1962–73

	Number of Firms	Herfindhal Index	Four Firm Concentration (percent)
1962	20	0.1017	53.2
1963	14	0.1173	60.6
1964	18	0.0842	49.1
1965	18	0.0817	44.5
1966	10	0.1551	70.2
1967	12	0.1397	67.1
1968	12	0.1203	59.0
1969	11	0.1415	68.4
1970	10	0.1491	71.9
1971	9	0.2159	82.8
1972	7	0.3966	93.4
1973	6	0.3132	96.4

Source: Appendix Table B.14.

As in Argentina, concentration has been accompanied by
increasing foreign ownership in the industry. In the early years,
only Fiat and Nissan of the world's major car companies invested
their own capital in the Chilean automotive industry. In 1963,
Citroen took an 80 percent shareholding in Importadora e Industrial
José Lhorente y Cia. Ltda., which had run into financial difficulties.
Other firms followed suit, with Ford taking a 50 percent holding in
Chilemotores in 1965, Renault a majority holding in Indauto in 1967,
and British Leyland and Peugeot majority holdings in EMSSA and
San Cristobal, respectively, in 1969. At the same time, both
General Motors and Ford replaced their local licensees, Indumotora
del Pacifico and Chilemotores, by wholly owned subsidiaries. Con-
currently, a number of locally owned firms, such as Federic and
Importsur, were being driven out of the industry. Thus, of the nine
firms remaining at the end of 1970, when the Allende government
assumed power, five were entirely foreign owned—Citroen, Fiat,
Ford, General Motors, and Nissan—two were majority foreign owned—
Automotores Franco-Chilena (Renault and Peugeot) and British
Leyland Automotores de Chile—and two were entirely locally owned,
producing under license—Nun y German (Chrysler) and Imcode
(Skoda).

In 1971, Ford and General Motors withdrew from Chile as a direct result of the political change and U.S. hostility to the Unidad Popular government, and, in 1972, Imcoda, which had produced on a very small scale, closed down.

A somewhat different picture emerges in Mexico from that in the other two countries studied. If one looks at the pattern since 1963 (see Table 7.3), the year in which the Mexican automotive program began to take effect, it can be seen that there has been little change in the level of concentration. The four-firm concentration ratio, in fact, fell slightly from 76.8 to 76.6 percent, while the Herfindhal index increased slightly. There was also a reduction in the total number of firms in the industry, but this could hardly be regarded as significant.*

Not only has concentration been less pronounced but so, too, has the elimination of locally owned firms. During the assembly

TABLE 7.3

Indices of Concentration in the Mexican
Automotive Industry, 1963-71

	Number of Firms	Herfindhal Index	Four Firm Concentration (percent)
1963	10	0.1731	76.8
1964	10	0.1867	80.1
1965	10	0.1888	81.5
1966	9	0.1850	82.2
1967	9	0.1725	78.3
1968	10	0.1619	75.9
1969	10	0.1616	74.5
1970	10	0.1615	74.2
1971	9	0.1646	74.9
1972	9	0.1667	74.8
1973	9	0.1750	76.6

Source: Appendix Table B.15.

---

*Of course, if one were to look back to the earlier period of car assembly, a significant increase in concentration would indeed emerge, since the number of firms producing cars alone, without taking into account commercial vehicles, was 17 in 1960. This fell to seven by 1973, while the share of the four largest car firms increased from around two thirds to three quarters of the total market.

period, most of the firms were either wholly or majority Mexican owned. Thus, for example, of the 12 assembly plants in operation in mid-1961, only 3 (Ford, General Motors, and International Harvester) were entirely foreign owned, the remainder having complete or majority Mexican ownership. Of the companies that began manufacturing cars under the government's local content decree, four—Ford, General Motors, Volkswagen, and Nissan—were entirely foreign owned, two—Automex (Chrysler) and VAM (American Motors)— were joint ventures with Mexican capital having the major share, and two—DINA and FANASA—were entirely Mexican owned. FANASA, which was an attempt to set up a completely Mexican car company independent of foreign licenses, by buying the Borgward plant after the failure of that company in Germany, eventually closed down in 1970 without ever really having got off the ground. Furthermore, in 1971, Automex, the most important of the Mexican-owned firms, was taken over by Chrysler, which increased its shareholding from 45 to 90.5 percent.

The market share of Mexican-owned firms fell from 38.3 percent in 1963 to 14 percent in 1973, and the only remaining locally owned firms are the state-owned companies Vehiculos Automotores Mexicanos and Diesel Nacional, and Trailers de Monterrey with a small output of commercial vehicles. Nevertheless, this is still a more significant local participation than exists in either of the other two countries considered.

The explanation for the lack of concentration in the Mexican automotive industry is to be found in the quota system imposed by the government on all firms that benefit from the legislation to promote the development of the industry. Each firm is granted a basic quota on the basis of the requests of the companies, their market penetration, an estimate of market potential, and the degree of local integration and volume of sales in the previous year. The basic quota has remained frozen since 1967.

Firms are able to increase their quota above the basic quota set in three ways. The most widely used method is through exports. Firms are permitted to import additional parts to a value equal to their exports from Mexico and to increase their quota correspondingly. This system has been used extensively by both Ford and Volkswagen in order to increase their output. In 1969, for the industry as a whole, about 10 percent of the total quota was accounted for by the export quota. The second most important method of increasing the quota is to raise local integration above the 60 percent minimum required by the 1962 decree. An additional 500 units is granted for each percentage point increase in local content, but, generally speaking, this has not proved such an attractive incentive as that for exporting owing to the increasing costs of local production.

Finally, additional quotas are granted for maintaining or reducing prices below the official prices set for vehicles. This has been of little importance, since the companies have complained frequently that official prices are set too low to permit them to obtain a reasonable profit.

Such a quota system has provided a degree of protection for the smaller producers from the larger firms, which are not able to expand their market shares at the former's expense. This is clearly seen by all the parties concerned. The foreign companies put pressure on the Mexican government to remove the quotas, while the Mexican firms argued that they were necessary to protect them against the greater financial strength of the multinational corporations. The minister of industry and commerce supported this latter view of the usefulness of the quota system.[5] The attitude of the government toward the smaller producers is in marked contrast to the complete lack of concern shown by the Argentinian and Chilean governments, no doubt partly as a result of the fact that two of these firms are controlled by government agencies.

Had the quota system been completely rigid, market shares would have been determined directly, and since prices were controlled by the government, cost differentials would lead to differences in profits without the possibility of being reflected in higher rates of investment and more rapid growth. As has just been seen, however, a degree of flexibility is introduced into the quota system as a result of the additional quotas authorized in return for exports, increased local content, or price reductions. Once this is the case, firms are able to increase their market share by undertaking to comply with one of these three alternatives.

In the previous model, the investment decision of foreign subsidiaries was based on their own profit rate and the ease with which market shares could be expanded. This latter was a function of the cost advantage enjoyed by foreign firms and the rate of profit of local firms. Now it is clear that the Mexican quota system imposes an additional cost (assuming that firms would not do any of the three things otherwise) on those firms desirous of expanding their market shares. Thus, for any given rate of profit of foreign and domestic firms, and differential cost advantage, foreign firms will increase their market share and eliminate local firms at a slower rate in the presence of this kind of quota system.

In the absence of a quota system, the increase in capital requirements in the Mexican automotive industry, which was observed in the period 1963-65 (see Chapter 5), would have resulted in a process of concentration and denationalization similar to that observed in Argentina during the first half of the 1960s. In fact, however, as the analysis of the previous paragraph would suggest, the process has been much less spectacular in Mexico.

In 1969, the Mexican government introduced new legislation that would eventually render the quota system obsolete. (In 1972, these measures were consolidated in a new decree, which replaced that of 1962.) In view of the continued outflow of foreign exchange to which the automotive industry gave rise, the government decided that the industry should no longer be a net foreign exchange loser. The intention was that all imports of parts and components for the automotive industry should be matched by exports of automotive products within ten years. This was to be achieved by gradually increasing the percentage of the imports of parts required for each firm's basic quota, which had to be covered by exports from 5 percent in 1970, 15 percent in 1971, 25 percent in 1972, and so on. As the free foreign exchange available to the industry is reduced through time, the significance of the basic quota diminishes, as does the protection the quota system affords to the smaller firms. At the same time, these firms are likely to experience relatively more difficulty in expanding exports than are the foreign subsidiaries. Consequently, the outlook for the Mexican automotive industry is likely to be further denationalization.

THE MECHANISMS OF CONCENTRATION
AND DENATIONALIZATION

In this section, the experience of a number of individual firms in the countries studied will be examined in order to illustrate the way in which the general tendencies of concentration and denationalization worked themselves out in specific cases. It will be seen that the model presented in Chapter 4 operated in its purest form in Argentina, whereas in both Chile and Mexico, government intervention assumed much greater significance.

Argentina

In Chapter 6, it was seen that during the first few years of the 1960s, say, up to 1963, the automotive industry in Argentina enjoyed very favorable demand conditions, it being essentially a seller's market. The same period up to 1963 also saw a very significant rise in the capital intensity of production as a result of the increase in local content requirements from 40 percent in 1960 to 90 percent by 1964 (see Chapter 5). Furthermore, as has just been indicated in the preceding section, these developments were accompanied by a significant reduction in the number of firms operating in the industry. This section will interpret the Argentinian experience and the cases of particular firms in the light of the model developed previously.

It was indicated in Chapter 4 that considerations of risk and lack of information in operating in an unfamiliar environment enter into the multinational corporation's investment decision, so that in the early stages it tends to keep its capital commitment as low as possible. This leads to the use of joint ventures and licensing arrangements and raising of loan capital locally.

There is considerable evidence of this phenomenon in the Argentinian case. Of the total amount invested in the Argentinian automotive industry between 1960 and 1962, only 17.3 percent was financed from foreign sources, the remaining 82.7 percent being raised locally.[6] Even those firms that set up wholly owned subsidiaries kept their actual cash investment to a minimum. General Motors is a case in point. By Decree 11625/59, it was authorized to make an investment of $20 million in order to manufacture trucks and diesel engines. This was to be divided into $6 million of local expenditure financed from reinvestment of profits earned by General Motors in Argentina and $14 million in machinery, equipment, and special tools provided by General Motors from Detroit. The fact that the parent company did not have to make any cash contribution was a crucial factor in deciding to go ahead with the investment.

> It was our expectation that the investment in expanded
> plant facilities could be accomplished without any con-
> siderable dollar outflow from the U.S. relying, in part,
> upon earnings generated within Argentina, and in part,
> upon the shipment of machinery and equipment from our
> U.S. operations in return for capital stock of the Argen-
> tine subsidiary.[7]

Similarly, Ford, by decrees in 1959 and 1961 (to manufacture trucks and cars, respectively), was authorized to invest $74.3 million, of which less than half was provided by Ford (U.S.).

Other firms chose to enter the market initially in joint ventures with locally owned companies. Chrysler, for example, formed a joint venture with the local firm of Fevre y Basset, a national dealer organization. Citroen, too, was initially a joint venture. A number of other firms chose to make no direct investment, preferring to operate through a local license. These included BMC, Peugeot, and BMW, which concluded licensing agreements with Siam di Tella, IAFA, and Metalmecanica, respectively.

A further indication of the desire not to commit too much capital initially was the decision of the three American companies not to produce cars, concentrating their efforts on truck production.

If anything, truck production was less risky than car production. There was a well-established market, whereas the exact size of the future car market was rather difficult to predict following the long period of import restrictions. (The U.S. companies also followed a policy of investing first in trucks and then in cars in Brazil.)

Over time, the foreign firms increased their participation in the joint ventures until they obtained almost complete ownership, while local licensees either ceased production or were taken over. These developments can be attributed to two basic factors. First, the takeover of local licensees by their foreign technology suppliers or joint-venture partners can be explained in part by the strategies pursued by the latter in order to minimize their risk during the initial stages of the industry's development. Second, the changes in supply and demand conditions described previously have acted to the detriment of locally owned firms in the ways suggested in Chapter 4.

The changes that have been described in both supply and demand conditions during the early 1960s led to a cost-price squeeze especially in the period 1961-62 (see Table 7.4). This tendency was reflected in a fall in profit rates for almost all companies in 1962 or 1963.*

The mechanisms at work can be best illustrated by looking at the experience of some of the nationally owned companies in order to see how the model described above operated in practice. Siam di Tella was one of Argentina's leading firms, producing domestic appliances, electrical machinery, and a variety of industrial equipment from bread- and spaghetti-making machines to equipment for the oil industry.[8] The company decided to enter into car production in response to the government's promotional decree of 1959, and obtained a license from BMC. Initially, the only serious competition faced by the new company, Siam di Tella Automotores, came from Industrias Kaiser Argentina and Fiat, but 1961 saw the entry into the market of General Motors, Ford, and Chrysler with larger more powerful cars.

In 1962, Siam di Tella approached BMC to try and get it interested in investing in the company, offering up to a 50 percent share in the equity, and discussions between the two firms dragged on for several years. The difficulties faced by the company had a

---

*Of course, this was partly attributable to the general recession in 1963. This illustrates the difficulty of distinguishing between secular and cyclical changes, especially since the total time period being considered is so short.

TABLE 7.4

Income–Cost Relation in the Automotive Industry
(1961 = 100)

	1960	1961	1962	1st half 1963	2nd half 1963
Price of vehicles	92.9	100.0	115.8	133.5	134.9
Unit costs	92.9	100.0	131.9	152.5	157.9
Local supplies	90.8	100.0	132.6	156.2	162.8
Foreign supplies	100.0	100.0	137.4	162.5	165.9
Labor	86.5	100.0	110.3	113.5	118.3
Transfers to government	91.9	100.0	134.5	153.8	159.3
Income/cost	100.4	100.0	87.8	87.5	85.4

Source: Cámara Argentina de Fabricantes de Automotores (CAFA), Significación Económica de la Industria Automotriz (Buenos Aires, 1963), Table 2.

number of causes, but all derived basically from a shortage of financial resources. Initially, Siam had financed itself in part by buying components on credit and paying suppliers at 90 or 180 days. Ford and General Motors came in and started paying suppliers cash down, which created problems for Siam.

At the same time as this source of credit was being cut off, there was an increasing need for installment finance in order to place cars in the market. In fact, even as early as 1961, sales were being limited by lack of more ample finance to the public.[9] The difficulties of sales financing are illustrated by the fact that the ratio of net sales to credit for the company was 4.97 in 1964, compared to 2.03, 1.91, and 3.23 for three foreign firms in the same year.[10] Not only was Siam able to offer less credit than its competitors but it also did so on less favorable terms.[11] As a result, the company found its market share declining after 1961 and was unable to achieve anything like full utilization of capacity.

On the supply side, Siam had obtained suppliers' credit from Britain, the United States, and West Germany to finance the company's imports of machinery and equipment, including a credit of $4.2 million from the Ex-Im Bank. These credits imposed a significant burden on the company in terms of financial charges, which was accentuated by devaluation since they were denominated in foreign currency. By 1963, interest charges were absorbing almost 5 percent of the total value of sales; and by the time the company was taken over by IKA, the monthly interest charges were running at over m$n 70 million,* while the gross profit of producing 50 cars a day (almost as much as the highest rate ever attained) before paying interest was only m$n 30 million.[12] The company, therefore, was caught in a vicious circle, whereby it was unable to cover its interest charges without expanding output and unable to expand output without consumer credit, which further worsened the firm's debt position. Thus, a program of expanded production in 1965 did not achieve the anticipated results because of a lack of credit lines.

Royalty payments do not appear to have played a crucial part in the difficulties of Siam. Although these were calculated as a percentage of the value of the vehicle produced locally, and hence tended to rise as local content increased from 49 percent in 1960 to 78 percent in 1963,[13] payments were suspended from 1962 onward. Thus, the financial difficulties appear to have been more important in this context. In 1965, Siam had heavy losses, and in the following year it was taken over by Industrias Kaiser Argentina.

---

*The expression "m$n" refers to "pesos monedanacional," the Argentinian currency at the time, which was later replaced by "pesos ley" at the rate of m$n 100 = 1 peso ley.

Another firm that was almost entirely locally owned and went out of business was Industria Automotriz Santa Fe, which produced under license from DKW, the latter also having a minority share-holding as a result of a $1 million investment. In addition, IASF obtained credit from the Banco Industrial de la República Argentina, the Banco de la Provincia de Santa Fe, the Deutsch Sudamerikanische Bank, and the Bank fur Gemeinwirtschaft en Alemania at rates of interest varying between 9.5 and 12 percent.[14] The firm enjoyed very favorable demand conditions for its car, the Auto Union 1000, and operated virtually without a stock of cars, the customer having to pay in advance of delivery. IASF was able to do this because of its low sales, which were only around 6,000 in the company's peak year. A policy of low production meant a saving on sales financing, but also involved a considerable underutilization of the plant's capacity of 14,000 units a year working two shifts.

It is interesting to compare the strategy adopted by IASF with that of Siam. The former, by accepting high unit costs of production, was able to economize on finance for consumer credit and hence achieve a low level equilibrium with considerable excess capacity. The latter attempted to push its demand curve outward through offering hire purchase facilities in order to reach a high level equilibrium point with low production costs, since capacity would be fully utilized, but with high financial charges. Figure 7.1 shows this strategy in a diagram.

The Siam strategy proved unviable, since the company did not have sufficient financial resources to arrive at the high level equilibrium point. In reality, so, too, did the IASF strategy, the problem being that, over time, competition from other firms was pushing the demand curve inward so that it became necessary to run in order to stand still. Moreover, despite the policy of low output, rising material costs following the 1962 devaluation led to a shortage of working capital, which, owing to the collapse of the stock market at the same time, it was impossible to obtain. By 1964, interest charges were running at 4 percent of the total value of sales. The problems of the company were further accen-tuated by a relatively high royalty charge of 5 percent on sales.

IASF's difficulties arose not merely from its problems within the Argentinian automotive industry but also from developments in the international industry.* In 1964, Daimler-Benz sold its majority shareholding in Auto Union, from whom IASF held the DKW license, to Volkswagen. The latter stopped making the Auto Union 1000,

---

*This illustrates the importance of an international perspective when analyzing the industry in Latin America.

FIGURE 7.1

Alternative Production and Marketing Strategies

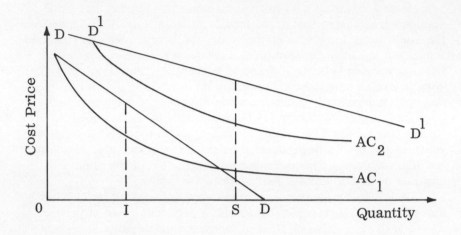

Source: Compiled by the author.

which meant an end to any technical evolution in the model. It has been suggested that since Volkswagen's major interest in Latin America was in Brazil, it wanted to use IASF to make parts for Brazil, which would explain why it refused to grant IASF rights to produce a new Auto Union model.

The final collapse of the company came about at the end of 1968 when it had debts reaching 3 billion pesos, the major creditors being the Argentinian government and Volkswagen, which were owed m$n 1 billion and m$n 700 million, respectively. It was widely expected that Volkswagen would take over the company and use it as a way of getting into the Argentinian market, but it was preempted by Fiat, which bought the company, mainly it seems, to exclude Volkswagen and converted the factory to tractor production.

Industrias Kaiser Argentina, despite large foreign share-holdings (mainly by Kaiser, but also by American Motors and Renault), could in many respects be regarded as a local firm in the early 1960s, since it did not comprise an integrated part of a multinational car company. It also had its shares quoted on the Buenos Aires stock exchange. Until 1967, when it was overtaken by Fiat, IKA was the largest firm in the industry in terms of units produced, although its relative position had been declining since 1964. The company's most successful year was 1965 when output reached 56,625 cars and light commercial vehicles.

During the early 1960s, IKA had been able to operate with negligible sales credit, but as the market tightened, this became more and more imperative. In the 1960-61 financial year, the ratio of sales to sales credit was more than 25:1, but it declined considerably to less than 5:1 during 1962-63.* Nevertheless, as in the case of Siam di Tella, IKA was unable to achieve such a low ratio of sales to credit as the foreign subsidiaries. This was reflected in the less favorable credit terms that the company was able to offer its customers.[15]

The difficulties of the company were accentuated during the 1965-66 financial year, however, as tighter government monetary policy led to a curtailment of consumer credit for IKA vehicles. Problems continued in the following year with a general recession in the demand for vehicles and increasing sales difficulties, despite the introduction of the Torino, especially designed for IKA by Pinanfarina, at the end of 1966. As a result, output fell to 40,085 in 1966 and 37,226 in 1967, and the company's market share declined from 29.1 percent in 1965 to 22.3 percent in 1966 and 21.2 percent in 1967, a decline that continued until 1970.

One consequence of these developments was the growing burden of interest charges. These had risen gradually during the first half of the 1960s and then rose sharply to 4.3 percent of the value of sales in the financial year 1966-67, increasing further to more than 7 percent by the early 1970s. If one examines the deterioration in IKA's performance in 1966-67, it can be seen that the rise in interest payments was only part of the problem. More important than this, however, was the drop in the gross profit margin, which resulted from a fall in the value of sales of m$n 3 billion, while there was no substantial change in the costs of products sold. A squeezing of the gross profit margin was, of course, to be expected as a result of the fall in output that reduced capacity utilization from 84 percent in 1965 to 60 percent in 1966 and 55 percent in 1967.

The company's position was further worsened by the takeover of Siam di Tella, which led to a loss of over m$n 1.4 billion in 1966-67. At the end of that year it was announced that Renault would take over control of the company.

The losses incurred in the bankruptcy of Siam were more than covered by the sale of Transax to Ford. The new management

----

*For the growth of consumer credit in response to changing market conditions, see above Chapter 6.

attempted to deal with the more fundamental problems facing the
company through a program of investment to modernize and rationalize the firm's production capacity, and by issuing new stock in
December 1967, which was taken up by the firm's majority shareholders in order to reinforce the company's financial structure.
This latter move was intended to reduce the firm's burden of financial
charges, but these continued to rise into the early 1970s. In 1972,
the company capitalized debts of U.S. $40 million with Renault in
order to reduce interest payments. Renault also succeeded in
reducing the ratio of sales to sales credit below 4:1 after taking
over the company, but despite these moves and Renault's intention
of using the company as the center of its Latin American operations,
IKA's position is still somewhat precarious.

Chile

It has been pointed out in previous chapters that the automotive
industry in Chile remained largely an assembly industry, buying the
greater part of its components and parts either locally or from
foreign associates or parent companies throughout the period under
consideration. The explanation given for concentration and denationalization in Argentina, therefore, does not fit the Chilean case,
insofar as it rests on the increased quantity of fixed capital required
for manufacturing production as opposed to assembly and the greater
dependence on foreign technology that this also implies.

As was seen in Chapter 5, however, there was a substantial
increase in working capital employed in the Chilean automotive
industry that would have similar effects to the increase in fixed
capital. In order to explain this increase, it is necessary to consider
the relationship that exists between the terminal industry in Chile
and its parts suppliers.

It has been estimated that about 29 percent of the value of
Chilean cars is made up of locally produced parts, that is, parts
not produced by the automotive manufacturers themselves.[16] The
parts industry, however, is still relatively underdeveloped. By
the late 1960s, the Register of Manufacturers of National Parts of
the Ministry of Economics contained around 250 firms, although
this probably overestimates the number of firms actually producing
parts for the industry. The parts produced tend to be technologically
unsophisticated and are produced not by specialist firms, but by
companies that manufacture a whole range of parts. Out of 230
locally produced parts and pieces classified by the Instituto de
Costos, only 19 were considered to embody a high technological
content, while 148 were classified as low technology parts.[17] In

the late 1960s and early 1970s, however, more specialized producers began to set up, such as Wobron producing clutches, Rockwell Standard producing springs, and Conjuntos Mecanicos Los Andes producing gear boxes. As well as lacking technological sophistication, the firms that comprise the local parts industry tend to be extremely small. According to the Fourth Census of Manufacturing (1967), the average number employed per enterprise was only 8.3.

The small size and relative financial weakness of the firms that produce parts have made it necessary for the terminal firms to supply them with credit facilities if they are to be able to meet the latter's demands. It is usual for suppliers to require 50 percent or more in cash in advance. One firm estimated that about 70 percent of its suppliers had to be paid 50 percent or more in cash, as much as four or five months in advance in some cases,[18] while another company cited payments of as much as 80 percent in advance of delivery.[19] This is reflected in a predominance of short-term credits in the balance sheets of the terminal firms. A. Aguilera found that the largest single use of funds made by these firms in the period 1965-68 was in short-term loans to nonfinancial enterprises, which accounted for 42 percent of the total uses of funds over the period.[20]

As well as requiring finance from the terminal producers, the low level of development of the parts industry in Chile led some firms in the late 1960s and early 1970s to begin production of parts themselves. Between 1968 and 1970, Citroen invested $6 million in Chile in order to produce parts locally. Similarly, Renault and Peugeot formed a joint venture with the Corporación de Fomento (CORFO), Conjuntos Mecánicos Los Andes, involving an investment of $12 million. Fiat, through its subsidiary, Agrotécnica, produced about a quarter of its requirements of Chilean parts internally.* Moreover, in 1970, Fiat took an 80 percent holding in the Chilean firm Fundición Cassali. Thus, while during the greater part of the 1960s, the capital requirements of the terminal producers were mainly for working capital in order to be able to finance suppliers, by the end of the decade investment in fixed assets was becoming increasingly important (see Chapter 5).

The growing requirements of working capital were not, however, the main reason underlying concentration and denationalization in the Chilean automotive industry. A more important factor was the increasing of the local content requirement, from 30 percent

---

*In 1969, Agrotécnica supplied 13.9 of the 52.9 percent of Chilean parts for the Fiat 600 and 9.3 of the 40.4 percent for the Fiat 1500 according to the Comisión Automotriz breakdown.

in 1963 to 57.9 percent five years later, coupled with a particular feature of Chile's policy toward the industry, namely, the special treatment accorded to parts imported from other LAFTA countries. Law 14,824 of 1962 permitted such parts to be considered national if they were compensated for by an equal value of parts exports from Chile; and by a subsequent decree in 1967, import duties on such parts were eliminated. Exchanges of parts and pieces under this legislation were started with Argentina in 1965 and followed by Mexico in 1968. As a result, a considerable volume of trade in vehicle parts has been generated, mainly between Chile and Argentina. (See Table 7.5.)

As a result of these exchanges, a large part of the legally required local content is not produced in Chile at all. Thus, in 1969, out of a required local content of 58 percent, and an achieved content slightly above this (59.1 percent), parts imported from LAFTA under compensation agreements accounted for 13.7 percent.[21] This average hides considerable variations between firms and models, as Table 7.6 shows.

Under these conditions, the response of most companies to a higher required local content was to increase imports of parts from Argentina rather than to produce new parts in Chile. This made it difficult for those firms that produced models and makes not manufactured elsewhere in Latin America to meet the content requirements and remain competitive. A number of firms did in fact go out of business because they were unable to meet the entire

TABLE 7.5

Chilean Trade with LAFTA Countries Under
Compensation Arrangements, 1965-73
(thousands of dollars FOB)

	Imports	Exports
1965	752.1	32.1
1966	3,548.0	689.0
1967	7,107.9	1,370.7
1968	7,446.7	5,572.0
1969	7,765.2	9,243.5
1970	5,733.7	8,443.7
1971	7,808.7	4,477.7
1972	4,692.0	4,121.1
1973	2,135.3	3,131.6

Source: Comisión Automotriz (unpublished data).

TABLE 7.6

Breakdown of Local Content, 1972
(percent)

	Chilean	LAFTA	Total
Citroen AX-H	53	15	68
Fiat 600/E	65	*	65
Renault R4S	44	21	65
Peugeot 404	48	18	66
Fiat 125/S	59	7	66
Nissan Datsun	43	22	65

*Parts for the Fiat 600 are imported from Argentina but these are not compensated for by exports.

Source: Comisión Automotriz (unpublished data).

local content requirement from Chilean parts. Importsur, which assembled Volvo cars, found it impossible to continue after 1966 since the make was not produced elsewhere in Latin America.22 Similar problems were faced by Federic, which assembled the NSU Prinz and went out of business in 1968. By 1970, the only firms that met the entire local content requirements with Chilean parts were British Leyland and Imcoda. The former was able to do so by producing a fiberglass body locally, while the latter was experiencing considerable difficulties.

For those firms whose models were produced in other LAFTA countries, a new problem arose from the nature of the compensation operation itself. The basic difficulty is caused by the fact that the prices of Chilean-produced parts are significantly higher than those of Argentina, with which most of the relevant exchanges take place. Given a price differential of this sort, it is possible for such interchanges to be valued in one of three different ways.

1. At the price of the part in the country of origin of the model, independently of the prices in Argentina or Chile

2. At the prices in the country with which the interchange takes place, that is, at Argentinian prices

3. At the prices of the producing country, that is, Chilean exports at Chilean prices and imports at Argentinian prices*

*A further logical possibility is that exchanges occur at Chilean prices, but this method has not apparently been used.

The different alternatives can be analyzed in a number of stages. The first is the direct way in which it appears in the accounts of the terminal company in each country. Thus, where exchange occurs at prices below the ruling prices in the country under consideration, the company will register a loss on the transaction because it must buy the parts that are to be exported at a higher price from local suppliers. That is to say, if the export was not matched by an import, it could be said unequivocally that the company had made a loss. As a second step, however it is necessary to look at the compensating import to see if this, too, does not take place at prices that are below the market prices of the exporting country. Finally, the price paid for the imported product must be compared with the price that would have had to have been paid in order to buy it locally (that is, in the importing country).

In order to clarify what this means, it is worth taking a simple numerical example. Suppose that the parts that are exported from Argentina to Chile have a price inefficiency with respect to the country of origin of 1.5, while the same parts in Chile have an inefficiency of 3.0. Similarly, suppose that the parts that are exported from Chile to Argentina have an inefficiency of 2.5, while the same parts in Argentina have an inefficiency of 2.0. Let us now consider the situations listed.

Case 1. Argentina exports to Chile $100 worth of parts valued at prices in the country of origin. The terminal firm in Argentina buys these parts from a local parts producer paying $150 (or the peso equivalent) and hence loses $50 on making the export to Chile. In Chile, $100 worth of parts for export to Argentina costs the firm $250 to buy locally, so that it makes a loss on the transaction of $150. However, it is receiving parts from Argentina at $50 below the cost to the Argentinian firm so that the net loss is only $100. On these terms, therefore, there would appear to be a transfer of $100 to Argentina. If, however, one compares what the Chilean firm pays for Argentinian parts with what it would have had to pay to buy them locally, that is, $300, then it makes a gain of $200 on the operation ($300 less $100) and a net gain, after subtracting the loss on its own exports of $50. Thus, the gains are equally divided, with Argentina also saving $50 compared to the situation had it produced the parts locally.

Case 2. Argentina exports to Chile $150 worth of parts, valued this time at Argentinian prices (and representing, therefore, the same volume of parts as in the previous example) and receives a similar value of exports from Chile, also valued at Argentinian prices (representing only $75 worth at prices ruling in the country of origin). The Argentinian company obviously makes no losses or gains from the operation. The Chilean company sells $150 of parts to Argentina but it costs $187.50 to buy them in Chile and it therefore makes a loss of $37.50 on the transaction. Since Argentina sells to Chile at cost, it receives no subsidy from Argentina so that the net loss is $37.50. Compared to purchasing the parts locally however, which would have cost $300, there is a net gain of $112.50 ($150 less $37.50) for Chile.

Case 3. If Argentina again exports to Chile $150 worth of parts valued at Argentinian prices, it now receives $150 of Chilean parts valued at Chilean prices (that is, $60 of parts valued at international prices). Neither company makes a loss on its export transaction since both take place at existing prices. Argentina could have bought the same parts locally, however, for $120 and so makes a loss of $30, while it would have cost Chile $300 to make the same parts and so it gains $150 with no offsetting loss since it sells at cost.*

It can be seen from these analyses that there has been some confusion among writers on the complementation arrangements between Chile and Argentina concerning its exact effects. It is frequently argued in Chile[23] that the higher cost of parts in that country means that it makes a loss as a result of the exchange in each of the three situations, although case 3 is the least unfavorable. One can see how this misconception arises if one fails to compare the amount paid by the Chilean company for imports from Argentina with the amount that would have had to have been paid if the parts had been bought locally. In case 1 there appears to be a loss of $100 and in case 2 a loss of $37.50. In fact, however, as the example shows, in case 1 both Argentina and Chile gain from the arrangement, in case 2 Chile gains, while Argentina is unaffected, and in case 3 Chile gains at the expense of Argentina.

The significant point, however, is that different policies with regard to the prices at which transactions are made will involve different distributions of the gains between Argentina and Chile. If the two firms involved are both wholly owned subsidiaries of the same multinational corporation, it will not matter how the gains

---

*This discussion is logically equivalent to the theory of comparative advantage in international trade, with the difference that in the latter case the international price ratio must, it is assumed, come between the two extremes represented by the national price ratios. The discussion has been purely static and has assumed constant returns to scale in order to concentrate on the effects of different pricing arrangements.

are distributed.* If, however, one firm is a subsidiary and the other a local firm producing under license, then the parent company will wish to see that profits are realized in the country in which the subsidiary operates and this may become a source of conflict. General Motors, Ford, Peugeot, and Chrysler all had licensed producers in Chile and subsidiaries in Argentina, and were therefore in a situation that could generate this kind of conflict.

It is also interesting to note that only with two wholly owned subsidiaries would it be possible to operate the third type of system, which imposes an absolute loss on one or other of the parties. Were the producers independent of each other, it would pay one to break the arrangement in exactly the same way as the theory of comparative advantage indicates that mutually advantageous trade will occur at prices that lie between the relative price ratios in the two countries concerned, and that if prices lie outside this limit, trade will not occur. It is not surprising, therefore, to find that only those multinational companies that have wholly owned subsidiaries in Chile have used this third system.24

It is possible to identify two reasons why, given this situation, a move toward wholly owned subsidiaries would be expected. First, none of the three arrangements discussed enables all the benefits of complementation to be realized in Argentina. Thus, by having a licensee in Chile rather than a wholly owned subsidiary, the parent company loses some of the benefits of its multinationalism. Second, the takeover of the licensee might be seen as a way of resolving conflict in the same way as taking over local shareholders in a joint venture is often necessary.

It is not surprising, therefore, that during the late 1960s, Ford, General Motors, and Peugeot all took over their local licensees. In each of these cases, it was foreseen that the replacement of a licensee by a subsidiary would ease the operation of LAFTA complementation arrangements. Both in the cases of Industria Automotores del Pacífico the General Motors licensee, and of Automotores San Cristobal, the Peugeot licensee, the advantages from the point of view of these exchanges were mentioned specifically as the major factor leading to the takeover by the licensor.25 In the case of the Ford licensee, Industrias Chilenas de Automotores, LAFTA exchanges were made at international prices up to the end

---

*This should not be taken to imply that the parent company will necessarily be indifferent to which of the two countries its profits will be realized in. Tax and other considerations may well mean that it prefers to realize its profits in one country or the other. The distribution of profit will not be a source of tension, however.

of 1966, this being the most advantageous arrangement from the point of view of Ford, which had a wholly owned subsidiary in Argentina. This led to a considerable accounting loss on Chilean exports in the 1966-67 financial year, and from 1967 on, exchanges were made at commercial prices.[26] Subsequently, in 1969, Ford acquired all the company's shares, having held 50 percent since 1965, and put it into liquidation. The only company with a subsidiary in Argentina that still had a licensee in Chile by the early 1970s was Chrysler. Here, too, there had been conflict between the local company, Nun y German, and Chrysler over the prices at which complementation exchanges were made, and generally they occurred at Argentinian prices.[27]

Mexico

As was seen in the first section of this chapter, the quota system enforced by the Mexican government played an important part during the 1960s in limiting the extent of concentration and denationalization in the automotive industry. Despite this, there have been some developments that parallel those in Argentina and Chile, as can be seen from a more detailed examination of the experience of individual companies.

The most striking evidence to support the hypothesis that the same underlying forces were at work in Mexico as in the other two countries is the case of Fábricas Automex, which was set up in 1939 to assemble vehicles under license for Chrysler. At the time of the government decree that initiated manufacturing of vehicles in Mexico, Chrysler held 33 percent of the company's shares. The company's declared profitability has been low since then, and has tended to deteriorate over time. In the two years 1970 and 1971, the company had losses amounting to 180 million pesos, while its share capital came to only 300 million pesos. At the same time, Automex became increasingly indebted to the Chrysler group. In 1968, it had short-term debts to Chrysler of over 260 million pesos and in 1969 of 350 million pesos. In 1969, too, it contracted a long-term debt of 73 million pesos, which rose to a further 191 million in 1970. In 1970, Chrysler increased its participation in the company from 33 to 45 percent, and in December 1971 invested a further U.S. $14.5 million to hold 90.5 percent of the company's share capital, at which point it became a consolidated subsidiary.[28] This pattern of increasing indebtedness to the foreign corporations whose license is held, leading to a takeover, is a fairly typical mechanism for the denationalization of locally owned firms.[29]

The main problem lying behind these difficulties appears to have been the company's falling market share, which declined from 29 percent of the vehicle market in 1965 to 17 percent in 1971. In 1968, the company opened a new industrial complex in Toluca, with an assembly plant capacity of 126,000 units, that has been utilized at levels far below this potential maximum. Although Automex has fully utilized its quota, it appears to have had difficulty in selling all its production (see Chapter 6). In terms of the analysis carried out, the firm had built an optimum scale plant, but then not had sufficient financial resources to shift its demand curve to the required position. The financial problems of the firm are further indicated by the fact that the debt-equity ratio rose considerably from 1.5 in 1968 to 2.1 in 1969 and 3.4 in 1970.[30]

The difficulties of the company during the late 1960s were only one reason for the change of ownership at the end of 1971. Equally important was the new government policy, introduced in 1969, requiring firms to cover all their parts imports with exports by the end of a ten-year period (see above). The possibilities of exporting are obviously far greater for the wholly owned subsidiary, which is part of an integrated international operation, as was seen in the Chilean case. The multinational companies can concentrate the production of certain parts in a particular country in order that the subsidiary in that country can benefit from the government's legislation. Licensors may be unwilling to do this, and it has been widely predicted in Mexico that the new policy will make it particularly difficult for the local firms to continue production.[31] Despite the fact that, until 1970, Automex was one of the leading exporters among the Mexican automotive manufacturers, the need to increase these exports substantially has been mentioned as an important factor in the Chrysler takeover.

Another interesting case to analyze is that of the only other joint venture between Mexican and foreign capital, Vehículos Automotores Mexicanos. The firm was set up in 1946 as Willys Mexicana to import assembled Jeeps and distribute them in Mexico. In the late 1940s, the company began to have its vehicles assembled locally in the Armadora Automotriz (Nash) factory, and as demand for the company's cars continued to grow, it decided to build its own assembly plant in 1953. Between 1953 and 1964, the firm assembled cars of many different makes, including Austin, Datsun, Peugeot, and Rambler. Following the 1962 decree, the company set up a joint venture in which U.S. firms Kaiser Jeep and American Motors had a minority participation, and changed its name from Willys Mexicana to Vehículos Automotores Mexicanos.

Unlike Automex, the company has chosen not to build a large plant and has not filled its production quota. Until 1969, the plant had an estimated annual capacity of only just over 15,000 (working two shifts) and in 1970 it was increased to almost 20,000. As a result, the firm was able to enjoy relatively high levels of capacity utilization, reaching 74 percent in 1969 and 70 percent in 1971. Moreover, the decision not to utilize the company's production quota fully was a deliberate one in order to avoid running the company into sales difficulties. This enabled VAM to operate with very little sales financing, which was reflected in a very high ratio of net sales to credit to dealers. In the 1971-72 financial year, this was 34:1, much higher than the ratio found for Chrysler, the only other firm for which comparable data were available, 11:1 in the same year.

In analytical terms, this case is similar to that of Industria Automotriz Santa Fe in Argentina in that the company deliberately pursued a policy of small-scale production without massive install-ment financing. It differs, however, in that the financial constraint on VAM was not as stringent as that on IASF, since the Mexican government, through the Sociedad Mexicana de Crédito Industrial (SOMEX), was the majority shareholder in the company. It also differs from the Argentinian case because of the quota, which pre-vented the foreign firms from taking advantage of their large scale to drive the company out of the market. Despite this, VAM has been subject to a squeeze that reduced its pretax profits on capital plus reserves from 22.8 percent in 1964-65 to only 2.9 percent in 1970-71.

Before closing this section, it is worth mentioning briefly the case of FANASA, which bought the Borgward plant in West Germany and set it up in Mexico. The firm was 100 percent Mexican owned but signed a technical assistance contract with a Spanish firm in order to set up and operate the plant.[32] Despite official government encouragement, the firm was never able to get off the ground, al-though it started production in 1967. In 1969, the firm was taken over by the government, since it was in financial difficulties, and subsequently put into liquidation. Nothing came of the suggestion that all the majority Mexican-owned companies should be joined together to form one company capable of resisting the competition of the multinational corporations. Thus, by 1972, there were only two firms remaining in the Mexican automotive industry under local ownership, the majority-owned VAM and the wholly owned DINA. Significantly, both of these were government-controlled companies.

CONCLUSION

It has been shown in this chapter that there has been a tendency for production in the Latin American automotive industries considered to become increasingly concentrated in the hands of a limited number

of firms, and that this has taken the specific form of denationalization, that is, the elimination or takeover of locally owned firms.
The form and extent of the process have differed between countries,
mainly as a result of the different legal and institutional framework
within which it has taken place. Thus, in Argentina, developments
have taken place virtually free from government intervention, whereas
in Mexico, the quota system and government ownership of two of the
local companies have played a determining role. In Chile, the form
of integration within LAFTA through complementation agreements
has given additional advantages to the multinational companies.
Despite these differences, the underlying trend has been in the same
direction in all three countries, and none has been able to resist the
growing penetration of the international firms. Neither in Argentina
nor in Mexico (with its much more favorable nationalistic policies)
were suggestions for a merger of the major local companies, to
combat the competitive strength of the foreign subsidiaries, taken
up. The result in Argentina was the demise of all the companies
concerned, and the same fate is a distinct possibility for the remaining Mexican companies.

NOTES

1. See, for example, J. Bain, Industrial Organization, 2nd ed.
(New York: Wiley, 1968), pp. 81-92; and K. D. George, Industrial
Organization: Competition, Growth, and Structural Change in Britain
(London: Allen & Unwin, 1971), pp. 81-92. In addition, Bain
mentions financial considerations promoting mergers and George
discusses the growth motivation of managers, but both these may
lead to diversification rather than concentration.

2. This is the sum of the squares of each firm's market share.
See C. Rosenbluth, Concentration in Canadian Manufacturing Industry,
National Bureau of Economic Research, General Series No. 61
(Princeton, N.J.: Princeton University Press, 1957), pp. 11-13.

3. See Jorge L. Remes Lenicov, "Algunos Resulutdos de la
Política Desarollista (1958-64); El Caso de la Industria Automotriz,"
Económica 19, no. 3 (1973): 305-10.

4. See the statement of Herman Lacalle, undersecretary of
economics at the Asociación de Industriales Metalúrgicos (ASIMET)
seminar, Primer Seminario Nacional de la Industria Automotriz
(Santiago: ASIMET, 1969), pp. 195-96.

5. See the statement of the minister of industry and commerce
at the time of the 1962 decree: "Se esablecio, empero el sistema de
quotas de producción, a fin de dar igual oportunidad a empresas con
diferentes capacidades financieras, las poderosas, hubiesen absor-

bido desde un principio una parte muy apreciable del mercado."
Quoted in Jorge Orvananos Lascurain, "Aspectos de la Demanda y
Oferta Automotriz" (professional thesis, Instituto Tecnológico
Autonóme de México, 1967), Chap. 5.

6. C. M. Jiménez, "Contribución al Estudio Crítica Sobre
la Política de Radicación de Capitales en la República Argentina:
La Industria Automotriz" (Thesis, Universidad de Buenos Aires,
1964), Table 26.

7. F. G. Donner, The World-wide Industrial Enterprise:
Its Challenge and Promises (New York: McGraw-Hill, 1967), p. 66.

8. For a history of Siam, see T. C. Cochran and R. E. Reina,
Entrepreneurship in Argentine Culture: Torcuato di Tella and
S.I.A.M. (Philadelphia: University of Pennsylvania Press, 1962).

9. Siam de Tella, Memoria (Buenos Aires: 1961).

10. Company accounts.

11. Inverview with Guido di Tella.

12. J. F. McCloud, "Prologue," Documentos Referentes a la
Compra de Acciones de Siam di Tella Automotores (Industrias
Kaiser Argentina: n.d.).

13. Memoria, 1963.

14. Memoria, 1961.

15. See "The Argentine Motor Industry," Economist Intelligence
Unit, Motor Business, no. 38 (1964): 42-55.

16. Felix Gil Mitjans, "Un Modelo de Programación de la
Industria Automotriz Chilena" (professional thesis, Universidad
de Chile, 1969), Chap. 2.

17. Gamma Ingenieros, Estudio de la Industria Automotriz
Chilena, UNIDO (ID/WG 76/6), 1970, p. 78.

18. Interview with Sr. Patricio Salas (Nun y German).

19. Interview with Sr. Orlando Canales (General Motors).

20. Asociación de Industriales Metalúrgicos (ASIMET), pp.
58-75. It seems probable in view of what has been said that this
item consists mainly of financing to suppliers rather than consumers.

21. Gil Mitjans, op. cit.

22. Importsur, Memoria, 1966.

23. See, for example, Instituto de Costos, op. cit., Chap. II 3a.
The point was also made to the author during interviews with company
executives in Chile.

24. Instituto de Costos, op. cit., Chap. II. 3a.

25. Industria Automotora del Pacífico, 13 Memoria (1968).
Automotores San Cristobal, 8th Memoria (October 1, 1968-
December 31, 1969). Problems concerning LAFTA exchanges were
also frequently referred to in interviews with executives of the
various companies undertaken by the author in January-March 1972.

26. Industrias Chilenas de Automotores, Estados Financieros July 1, 1966–June 30, 1967 and July 1, 1967–June 30, 1968.

27. Interview with Patricio Salas.

28. From annual reports of Automex and Chrysler.

29. A. G. Frank, J. D. Cockroft, and D. L. Johnson, Dependence and Underdevelopment: Latin America's Political Economy (New York: Doubleday, 1972).

30. Automex annual reports.

31. See Manuel Franco Rosas, "Problemas y Perspectivas de la Industria Automotriz en México (professional thesis, Universidad Nacional Autónoma de México, 1971), Chap. 3b.

32. M. Wionczek, G. Bueno, and J. E. Navarrette, "La Transferencia Internacional de Tecnología al Nivel de Empresa: El Caso de México," mimeographed (Mexico: Fondo de Cultura Económica, 1974), p. 85.

8

THE PATTERN
OF DEPENDENT
INDUSTRIALIZATION
IN THE AUTOMOTIVE
INDUSTRY

It is now possible to discuss the implications of the pattern of dependent industrial development that has been described in the last three chapters. Critical studies of the impact of multinational corporations on underdeveloped countries have tended to concentrate on the repatriation of profits from these countries. This, however, is only a part of the effect of penetration by international firms on the local economy. Equally important, in terms of the prospects for development, are the effects on the industrial structure, the forms of competition, and the consequences for cost and prices.

This chapter presents some evidence to suggest that there is a significant outflow of profits from the Latin American automotive industry. It concentrates mainly on the other effects that have tended to be neglected in the literature. The first part of the chapter extends the theoretical model of Chapter 4 to the situation where all locally owned firms have been eliminated and the industry is dominated by foreign subsidiaries. In the following sections, the main effects of this pattern of development will be analyzed in Argentina, Chile, and Mexico.

A MODEL OF THE DEPENDENT SECTOR
OF PRODUCTION

In Chapter 4 a model was presented in which significant cost differentials between foreign and nationally owned companies led to local firms becoming the marginal producers in the industry under consideration. Over time, a process of denationalization and concentration occurs, leading to the elimination of all locally owned firms. Once these firms have been driven out of the industry,

174   DEPENDENT INDUSTRIALIZATION IN LATIN AMERICA

the cost differential between firms is narrowed considerably and,
at the same time, becomes a less important parameter in the competitive process, since all firms now have the backing of much
larger parent corporations. These two factors are characteristic
of monopolistic industries in Steindl's terminology.[1] In this chapter,
we shall develop some of the implications of substituting a monopolistic structure of foreign-owned firms for a competitive structure
(again in the Steindlian sense) composed of both foreign subsidiaries
and national firms.

The main characteristic of the monopolistic type of industry
(indeed, one might say its defining characteristic) is the fact that
surplus capacity is not eliminated through price-cutting. The logic
of this in the case of an industry dominated by foreign subsidiaries
is easy to understand. The particular subsidiary of a multinational
corporation in, say, Argentina represents a relatively small proportion of its total global sales and profits, and losses there cannot
threaten the existence of the corporation as a whole. Having once
made a commitment to a particular market, companies tend to be
reluctant to abandon that market to their competitors, and since
the parent company's existence cannot be threatened come what
may, there is no mechanism that will force it to abandon the market.*
This is not to say that companies cannot be forced out of a particular
market by persistent price-cutting, but that the costs of doing so
for the successful firm are likely to be so high as to act as a severe
disincentive to such behavior.

Figure 8.1 illustrates this concept in a diagram similar to
Figure 4.2. After the elimination of all locally owned firms, there
is no longer a sharp discontinuity in the industry cost curve HL,
although there may still be some differences in costs because of
the different scales of operation of the various firms. Immediately
after the elimination of all local firms, price AQ will be above the
costs of the marginal firm AH as a result of the discontinuity in
costs between local and foreign firms. It will still be possible for
some firms to eliminate others by cutting prices from AQ to AR.

As in the case analyzed in Chapter 4, this will lead to the
elimination of the firms whose output is represented by the segment
AP on the horizontal axis and the expansion of those firms on PC
to PM. There is little incentive to do this, however, since the
additional profit from an expansion of output (area UELV minus

---

*If Ford had given away all the vehicles it produced in Argentina
in that year, the rate of return of the parent company before tax
would only have been reduced from 21.3 to 17.3 percent in 1969.

FIGURE 8.1

Intraindustry Competition in a
Foreign-Dominated Sector

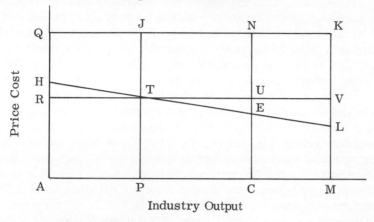

Source: Compiled by the author.

area JNUT) is small compared to the gain where there are local
firms in the industry (see Figure 4.2) and may even be negative.
Thus, in a monopolistic industry, supply is not likely to be adjusted
to demand through exits from the industry. It must therefore be
adjusted through changes in the capacity utilization of existing firms.

This rigidity is an important feature of a monopolistic market
structure dominated by foreign firms. Entry to and exit from the
industry are both extremely rare. Competition no longer operates
to reduce the number of firms to a level that would make it possible
for each firm to have an optimal scale of plant. Further rationalization of the industry in the peripheral country depends on developments
at the international level, such as mergers between two multinational
corporations or some kind of less formal cooperative agreement (for
example, the Renault-Peugeot linkup) rather than on developments
internal to that country itself.

Entry is also rendered difficult for both economic and institutional reasons. With increasing local content requirements, the
initial investment to start production increased considerably (see
Chapter 5), acting as a barrier to entry at least to local firms if
not to multinational corporations with their far greater financial
capacity. Moreover, the need to meet this content requirement
within a very short time span imposes additional costs. New investment requires government approval in most cases, and there may
be an increasing reluctance to grant this to latecomers, which are

in a weaker bargaining position in that they cannot accuse the government of discrimination if they themselves passed up the opportunity of entering the market initially.*

The rigidity of the market structure and its relative fragmentation, compared to the advanced countries where most companies were locally owned and there were few if any foreign subsidiaries at a similar stage in the industry's development, have meant uneconomic scales of production and high costs. This is an especially important factor in industries such as automotive manufacturing where economies of scale are so significant. With a given market size, a larger number of firms implies either a higher level of costs at a determined level of local integration or a lower level of local integration if a certain level of costs is taken as the objective. Market size, of course, need not be given. Thus, high costs lead to a high price for the product, which restricts the domestic market to certain income groups and makes it extremely difficult to achieve exports except under special arrangements.

Different economic (and social) structures will result in different rates and forms of capital accumulation. Monopolistic structures, it has been argued, are less favorable to accumulation than competitive structures.[2] At the macroeconomic level, this can be related to the effect of such structures on income distribution and the appropriation of the gains from technical progress and the effect that these in turn have on demand and hence on the incentive to invest. (See Chapter 10 for further details.) At the industry level, the emergence of excess capacity acts to dampen the rate of accumulation. Since capacity is no longer eliminated in the downswing through bankruptcies and so on, new investment in the upswing tends to be less as unused capacity can be brought back into production. In addition, the normal restraints on competition implicit in oligopolistic situations will tend to limit the extent to which firms will invest in order to expand their market shares. On the other hand, measures to increase capacity utilization through advertising, the extension of consumer credit, and so forth will be stimulated. Thus nonprice competition tends to assume particular significance in oligopolistic industries.

A further consequence of this model relates to the outflow of funds from the peripheral economy. The tendency over time is for the profit rates in the industry to increase relatively to the oppor-

---

*This is illustrated by the commitment Fiat had to make to the Brazilian government, to export a substantial portion of its output, in order to be able to enter the Brazilian automotive industry in 1973.

tunities for new investment. This phenomenon is a familiar argument in Marxist writings on imperialism[3] and more recent writings on capitalist development.[4] As we have seen, the oligopolistic market structure tends to reduce the opportunities for new investment, either through collusion in the form of cartels or through tacit understandings. Profits continue to be generated, however, and these are in excess of reinvestment requirements. The theories of imperialism see the export of capital as an outlet for the investment of these profits. Another alternative, from the point of view of the individual firm, is diversification into other industries within the same country. In the case of a peripheral economy, the two alternatives present themselves as repatriation of profits or diversification locally.

It has been observed in the context of regional economics that a large corporation is more likely to respond to investment opportunities in its traditional activity in new locations than to investment opportunities in unrelated industries at existing locations.[5] This point seems relevant in considering the possibilities of foreign subsidiaries diversifying into new industries in underdeveloped countries. On the whole, they will prefer to limit their investment to those industries that are already familiar to the parent company; indeed, in some cases, they may be prevented from diversifying by host country policies (for example, the Mexican legislation preventing the terminal firms in the automotive industry from investing in parts production). Diversification in underdeveloped countries is also inhibited by the unequal income distribution and the interdependence of firm reactions, even in different industries, because of the small size of the total market.[6]

Unfortunately, there are no available studies on the extent of diversification by foreign subsidiaries in underdeveloped countries, but a priori theorizing suggests that subsidiaries will be less diversified than their parents. Faced with these limitations, it will not be long before a foreign firm finds itself with more profitable opportunities for investment elsewhere in the world, and starts to transfer funds either indirectly through the parent company or directly to other affiliates. Thus, even if in the initial years of development of an industry there is a net inflow of funds to the country concerned, this soon becomes negative once the scope for expansion has been restricted.

It is worth noting here the comment of General Motors vice-president T. A. Murphy.

General Motors has relied on overseas capital markets to augment earnings retained for investment overseas. This has been our standard practice for the past 25 years. It has also been our policy to remit overseas earnings

promptly, retaining overseas only those resources necessary to maintaining and expanding the subsidiary as an
effective competitor.[7]

The impact of foreign investment in terms of employment
creation, both within the industry under consideration and on the
economy as a whole, must also be examined. It is important to
remember that capital accumulation has a dual effect on employment.
It displaces labor through the incorporation of more advanced techniques of production, on the one hand, while absorbing labor through
the expansion of the market, on the other. The balance struck
between displacement and absorption depends on the competitive
or monopolistic structures within which these mechansims operate.
Competition tends to favor the expansion of the base of accumulation
and the absorption of labor.[8] The rate of growth of employment
depends on the rate of accumulation and the rate of growth of capital
per man. As already seen, the rate of accumulation tends to be
lower in the case of monopolistic structures, so that, unless technological advance embodied in the new investment was less, then
the employment generation effects would be less. Monopoly tends
to accentuate technological discontinuities, thus weakening the
mechanisms for reabsorbing labor.[9] This is particularly true in
peripheral economies where technology is exogeneously generated*
and there is a substantial difference between the capital intensity
of imported technology and indigenous technology. Therefore, it
is to be expected that the employment effects of capital accumulation
in an industry in a peripheral economy will be negative where it
competes with existing industries and only limited when it replaces
previously imported products.

CAPITAL FLOWS

One of the major implications to come out of the model
described is that, as an industry develops over time, the accumulation of funds from profits tends to exceed the outlets for new investment. In the context of a metropolitan economy, this, it has been
argued, is likely to lead to either foreign investment or diversification or both. In the case of a peripheral economy where the industry
is dominated by foreign subsidiaries, the probable effect is an outflow

---

*At least if one thinks in terms of the national economy. It
is, of course, endogenous if one thinks of the peripheral economy
as integrated into the world economy.

of funds from the country. This is the equivalent at the industry
level of what has become known as the drain of investable surplus
from the underdeveloped countries at the macrolevel.

Unfortunately, it is not easy to obtain data on the total outflow
of funds in profits, royalties, and overpricing of intermediate inputs
either for entire economies or for particular industries. The figures
that will be presented in this section, therefore, are incomplete and
represent only rough orders of magnitude. In Argentina it has been
estimated that between 1958 and 1964, that is, the period during
which most of the foreign investment in the automotive industry was
made, the inflow of $33 million into the industry was exceeded by
the outflow of dividend payments that amounted to $52.3 million.[10]
This is a truly remarkable figure if, as it suggests, foreign firms
were able to recoup their investment in such a short period without
even including royalty payments and overpricing of intermediates
in the calculation.

In the second half of the 1960s, the balance between new inflows
of foreign investment and outflows of dividends and technology payments was even less favorable to the Argentinian economy. The
total amount of investment approved by the government between
1965 and 1970 came to U.S. $15.5 million, whereas data for the
period 1968 to 1970 suggest that in each of these years profit remissions were at least U.S. $15 million. If technology payments are
added to profit remissions, then the total outflow between 1968 and
1970 amounted to U.S. $83.9 million.[11] In the period 1971-72, it
is estimated that a further U.S. $37.4 million was paid in royalty,
technical assistance, dividend, and other payments.[12] There is,
moreover, reason to believe that these figures underestimate the
amounts actually transferred under the heading of technology payments.

According to this study, technology payments by eight firms
in 1970 amounted to U.S. $10.7 million. A survey of contracts
in the Registro Nacional de Contratos de Licencias y Transferencia
de Tecnología indicated that royalty payments by the automotive
industry came to U.S. $26 million, or 37 percent of the total
royalties paid by Argentina, in 1970.[13] Of this total, more than
U.S. $8 million was accounted for by the parts industry and at
least U.S. $18 million by the seven terminal firms included. If
the other three important automotive manufacturers are added, the
total outflow could be more than U.S. $20 million, or twice the level
indicated by the D.G.I. study. Data for 1973 indicate that the eight
major foreign firms paid more than U.S. $18 million in royalties
in that year, despite the introduction of measures by the government
to restrict such payments.

It appears, therefore, that during the late 1960s and early
1970s, the annual payments of both dividends and royalties were at

least as great as the total amount of new foreign capital authorized
in the automotive industry during the six years from 1965 to 1970.
Moreover, these figures take no account of any overpricing of
intermediate inputs that may have occurred on imports by Argentinian
automotive manufacturers from their parent companies. In the early
years of the industry's development, the relatively low local content
of the vehicles produced gave considerable scope for such overpricing
with imports running at over U.S. $100 million a year.[14] Even in
the late 1960s and early 1970s, imports were between U.S. $50
million and U.S. $100 million a year, a high enough level to have
acted as a significant channel for profit remissions.[15] That this
is not simply a theoretical possibility is indicated by the decision
of the Argentinian supreme court that a part of deferred payments
made by the local Ford subsidiary to the parent company for imported
parts represented profit remissions.[16]

In Chile, dividend payments have not been an important form
of surplus transfer, since it is only locally owned companies that
have tended to pay dividends. Royalties have been more significant.
Estimates derived from the Ministry of Economics' Rol Industrial
suggest that, in 1968, the total amount paid by the automotive manufacturers in royalties came to around U.S. $650,000.[17]

More important than direct license and technical assistance
payments are the possibilities of overpricing mentioned in Chapter 7.
The Censo de Regalías made by the Corporación de Fomento (CORFO)
estimated that total payments from firms located in Chile to licensers
abroad in the transport equipment sector, the main component of
which is the automotive industry, came to $3,479,800 in 1968.[18]
An alternative estimate is to take the total imports of the terminal
firms of $23,940,000 in 1968 and assume that 20 percent of this
represented overpricing, so that the outflow under this heading
comes to $4,788,000, and add to it the previous estimate for royalty
payments, giving an approximate total outflow of U.S. $5,433,000.
Even if only 10 percent of the total value of imports was overpricing,
the total outflow would still be somewhat in excess of U.S. $3 million.
As was noted, all these calculations give only a rough order of
magnitude.

A comparative indication of this magnitude is obtained when
one finds that the total inflow of foreign capital into the transport
equipment sector over the period 1960-69 came to only $3,038,740,[19]
that is, less than our estimate of the outflow in a single year, 1968.*

---

*Between 1961 and 1966, no new inflow of foreign investment
into the automotive industry took place, all investment presumably
being reinvestment of profits by existing firms.

Over the three-year period 1967-69, during which all the above investment in the automotive industry was made, the outflow of payments for licenses and technical assistance alone came to almost $2 million, and had complete data been available for the period 1961-66, royalty payments would probably have exceeded the total inflow over the whole period.

Two general studies of foreign investment in Mexico have estimated the outflow of currency on capital account by industrial sector, taking the difference between new inflows of capital and remittances of profits, royalties, technical assistance, and other payments. Both studies present data on the transport equipment sector of which an important, but not the only, component is the terminal automotive industry. B. Sepulveda and A. Chumacero found that in 1967 new investment in the sector amounted to almost U.S. $25 million, while the capital outflow was U.S. $8,250,000, giving a favorable balance of U.S. $16,660,000.[20] By 1970, however, the situation had been dramatically reversed with new investment at U.S. $4,282,000 and remissions reaching U.S. $20,888,000, giving a net outflow of U.S. $16,600,000. The second study, by F. Fajnzylber and T. Martinez, gives a somewhat lower estimate of the outflow in 1970, the only year for which data are presented, of slightly over U.S. $10 million.[21] This clearly bears out the point that during the early phase of an industry's development there is a net inflow of capital as the initial investment is made, but subsequently investment falls off substantially or is financed by retained profits, while profit and other remissions increase, giving rise to a deficit on capital account.

As was seen earlier, the excess price charged for imported components should be added to the outflow of capital. If 10 percent of the total value of imported inputs represented overpricing (that is, if imported parts were overpriced by 11 percent), there would have been an outflow under this head in 1971 of about U.S. $17.1 million. This is greater than the total royalty and technical assistance payments made by the terminal automotive industry in the same year, which was estimated at U.S. $11.2 million (based on AMIA data on imports of parts).

MARKET STRUCTURE AND THE FORMS
OF COMPETITION

It has been argued that the domination of an industry by foreign subsidiaries tended to lead to a certain rigidity in its structure. This can be seen most clearly in the case of Argentina where the process of concentration and denationalization has been underway for the longest period of time. With the elimination of the last remaining national firm, Industria Automotriz Santa Fe, the number of firms in the industry has been stabilized, in marked contrast to the sharp fall from 21 in 1960 to 13 in 1965. Although it has not gone so far, and there are still two government-controlled firms in the industry, the same process can also be seen in Mexico, while prior to the election of Allende as president in 1970, Chile, too, was following the same path.

That competition will not continue to reduce the number of firms even further appears to be supported at least by developments in Argentina. This phenomenon, which is characteristic of the Latin American automotive industry, will be referred to as premature oligopolization, the main features of which are the importance of nonprice forms of competition, and few cases of either entries to or exits from the industry, while firms are still small relative to the optimum scale of plant, and the market is fragmented between a number of producers.

Argentina

This section seeks to show that competition in the Argentinian automotive industry has not taken the form of price-cutting, lower costs, and increased output, but rather the typical forms of nonprice competition characteristic of oligopolistic industries, such as advertising, consumer credit, model diversification, and so forth.

The pattern of competition in the automotive industry of developed countries, such as Britain and the United States, has been described as one of model-price competition. Companies direct their vehicles at particular segments of the market, and within these segments, price differentials are of no great significance. It seems probable that the same pattern of behavior has been carried over to the Argentinian market. One would expect, therefore, that in dividing the market up into segments, price differentials between competing models would be relatively small.

The segments identified in Table 8.1 correspond roughly with a division of the market according to engine capacity, the cutoff points being 1,100 cc, 1,500 cc, and 2,000 cc. The two segments described as U.S. compacts and U.S. standard are the cheapest and most expensive vehicles, respectively, produced in each line. Market segments are not, however, necessarily defined in technological terms, since what is relevant is which models the firms themselves and their customers see as competing. Thus, despite having a much smaller cc rating than other models, the Citroen Ami 8 has been included in the intermediate category since this

TABLE 8.1

Prices of Argentinian Cars by Market Segment, 1971
(pesos ley)

Small		Intermediate		European Compacts	
Fiat 600	12,440	Fiat 128	16,950	Fiat 1500	20,250
Citroen 2CV	11,500	Renault R6	15,600	Fiat 1600	20,250
Citroen 3CV	12,850	Renault R12	17,600	Peugeot 404	20,180
Renault R4L	11,900	Citroen Ami 8	14,950	Peugeot 504	23,305
Renault R4S	13,100	Dodge 1500	17,550		

U.S. Compacts		U.S. Standard	
Rambler Custom	24,590	Rambler Ambassador	35,900
Torino L	23,200	Torino GS	34,800
Ford Falcon	24,639	Ford Fairlane LTD	31,129
Chevrolet Special	20,740	Chevrolet SS Coupe	32,124
Dodge 4	21,234	Dodge GTX	32,764

Source: Fiat (unpublished data).

seems to be the sector of the market at which it is aimed in terms
of price and quality. That price is not the only consideration determining market segments can be seen from the fact that European
compacts are competitive in price, but since they are such different
products, they have been considered separately.

In Table 8.2, the coefficient of variation of prices has been
calculated for each of the market segments that has been identified
(based on Table 8.1). In no case does this coefficient come to over
10 percent, indicating little dispersion within each group, despite
the fact that the average price of the most expensive cars on the
market is almost three times that of the cheapest cars. This suggests
that firms follow a policy of aiming a model at a particular section
of the market and setting its price with reference to similar models,
that is, model-price competition.

Another indication of the lack of price competition in the automotive industry is obtained if one looks at the path of prices over
time. The data seem to indicate that prices for competing models
have tended to move more or less in step, increasing with increases
in the rate of taxation and increases in local costs and with devaluations. A detailed study of the years from 1960 to 1963 indicated
that, "the increases—even if not simultaneous—occurred on each
occasion within a period of two or three months for all firms, and
moreover by a similar amount in each case."[22] What competition
there was on prices took the form of delaying price increases for
as long as possible, given the inflationary climate, in order to avoid
losing market shares. This pattern appears to have applied equally
to more recent years. It is worth noting here that most prices were
stabilized, in money terms, for a period of two or three years in
the late 1960s, despite a continued rise in the internal price level.

TABLE 8.2

Average Price and Dispersion by
Market Segment

	Small	Intermediate	European Compacts
Mean	12,358	16,530	20,996
Standard deviation	661	1,196	1,540
Coefficient of variation	5.35	7.24	7.33

	U.S. Compacts	U.S. Standard
Mean	22,881	33,343
Standard deviation	1,831	1,961
Coefficient of variation	8	5.88

As just seen, price competition has not been particularly significant in the Argentinian automotive industry. It seems, therefore, that what competition there may have been has taken other forms, which it is known are important in developed countries, such as advertising, the use of consumer credit, and model changes and diversity.

Table 8.3 gives the total advertising expenditure of the terminal firms in the Argentinian automotive industry. As can be seen, advertising has tended to increase, whether measured as a percentage of total sales (column 2) or as advertising per car (columns 3 and 4). It is to be expected that the Argentinian car market would show much lower levels of advertising than the more mature U.S. and U.K. markets. In fact, although the level is higher in the United States, the difference is small, while British firms spend a lower percentage on advertising than their Argentinian counterparts.

The average advertising expenditure by U.S. car manufacturers was about $40 per car in 1967, while the advertising expenditure of the Big Three, as a percentage of their worldwide sales, came to 0.9 percent for General Motors, 1.0 percent for Ford, and 1.3 percent for Chrysler.[23] (An almost equal amount of advertising per car in Argentina is translated into a lower ratio of advertising to sales because of the higher price of cars in that country.) Compared to Britain, where the ratio of advertising to sales in the automotive industry was only 0.5 percent in 1963,[24] advertising expenditures in Argentina were relatively heavy. Data for individual firms indicated advertising expenditures varying between 0.6 and 1.6 percent of sales, with a tendency for U.S. subsidiaries to show a higher level of advertising than the European firms.

It is not only the manufacturing firms that spend on advertising but also the dealers. A higher proportion of advertising expenditure by the former in Argentina might occur as a result of institutional arrangements that meant that dealers had to support a lesser part of the total expenditure than in developed countries. In fact, however, it appears that advertising by dealers is at least as great in relation to turnover as in the United States, being between 0.8 and 1.25 percent in Argentina compared to 0.88 percent in the United States in 1964.[25]

A second feature of competition within the industry has been the proliferation of models produced by the various firms. Taking the nine most important car producers, their range of models increased from 10 in 1960 to 48 in 1974, and the total number of models produced in Argentina increased from 22 in 1960, despite the reduction in the number of firms during the same period. As far as can be seen from the data, model diversity increased in a number of steps. The first was in 1962, as a result of Industrias

TABLE 8.3

Advertising in the Argentinian Automotive Industry, 1964–73

(millions of m$n)

| | Advertising (1) | Advertising/Sales Percent (2) | Advertising per Car | |
			m$n (3)	U.S. (4)
1964	750	0.65	4,505	29.9
1965	900	0.50	4,626	24.5
1966	1,300	0.64	7,244	29.3
1967	1,700	0.66	9,697	29.1
1968	2,200	0.79	12,156	34.7
1969	2,600	0.73	11,894	34.0
1970	3,350	0.93	15,255	38.1
1971	3,600	0.71	14,193	35.5
1972	6,500	0.81	24,200	29.1
1973	11,700	0.86	39,831	39.9

Source: ADEFA, Informe Estadistico, no. 588 (August 28, 1974), Table 4, and own investigation.

Kaiser Argentina and the Big Three from the United States starting production of large cars—Rambler, Falcon, Chevrolet, and Valiant.

A second significant increase occurred in 1966, again mainly as a result of IKA adding several variations of the Torino to its line and diversifying the production of Siam di Tella which it had taken over. In 1969, the number of models again increased, with Ford introducing the Fairlane line and General Motors introducing several new models, while, in the early 1970s, Chrysler led the U.S. firms into the medium-sized market with the Dodge 1500. The success of this model led Ford and General Motors to begin production of their Taunus and Opel medium-sized cars in 1974. Despite this increase in diversity, the average production of each model has increased from less than 2,000 in 1960 to 4,418 in 1974, although compared to the United States, where average production per model was 20,700 in 1967,[26] this figure is still extremely small.

Not surprisingly, the extent of model changes and model diversity is associated with its prevalence in the parent company. Thus, the firms that have most models and have changed them most often tend to be the subsidiaries of the U.S. companies and Fiat, known in Europe for its model policy, while Citroen and SAFRAR (Peugeot), like their parents, have had much less change and diversity.

Looking particularly at the large car section of the market, the models introduced in the early 1960s remained unchanged until the mid-1960s when General Motors, Chrysler, and Ford changed their models between 1965 and 1967 and IKA supplemented its range by introducing the Torino. Then, again in 1969 and 1970, Chrysler, General Motors, and IKA changed their models and Ford introduced the Fairlane. In other segments of the market, Fiat has had three basic model changes with the replacement of the 1100 by the 1500 in 1963, the 1500 by the 1600 in 1969, and the 1600 by the 125 in 1972.

Other firms have tended to introduce new models while keeping on the old ones for several years after, as did SAFRAR with the 404 in 1962 and the 504 in 1968 and IKA with the Renault 4 in 1963. As a result, model runs have tended to be extremely short in Argentina. Only one model has been reproduced in more than 100,000 units, namely, the Fiat 600, which reached 205,159 between 1960 and 1973. This was followed by a number of models with output of between 60,000 and 100,000. (See Table 8.4.) The problems of scale, owing to the small size of the market and the large number of producers, have been further aggravated by the diversity of models and the short life cycle of the majority of them.*

*See below, pp. 206-08, for a discussion of the effect of model diversity and model changes on costs of production.

TABLE 8.4

Total Output of Most Popular Argentinian Cars,
1959-73

Model	Total Output	Period
Fiat 600	205,159	1960-73
Peugeot 404	98,644	1962-73
Fiat 1500 Berlina	78,346	1963-69
Ford Falcon de Lujo	69,705	1967-73
Peugeot 504	61,561	1969-73
Fiat 128	60,970	1971-73

Source: ADEFA, Informe Estadistico, no. 577 (May 31, 1974):
3-6.

A further aspect of competition in the automotive industry
(previously discussed in a different context in Chapter 6) is the use
of installment finance. It was indicated that increasing use of hire
purchase arrangements came to be made as the market for cars
tightened. The use of consumer credit is by now widespread, and
the terms offered are generous with relatively small downpayments
and a long repayment period. As would be expected in an oligopolistic

TABLE 8.5

Examples of Credit Terms Offered to the
Consumer, 1971

	U.S. Compacts			
	IKA	Ford	General Motors	Chrysler
Cash (percent)	30 to 35	30 to 40	40	30
Interest (monthly) (percent)	1.50 to 1.70	1.30 to 1.52	1.45 to 1.65	1.52 to 1.84
Repayments (months)	9 to 36	12 to 40	12 to 36	12 to 30

	Intermediate		
	IKA	Fiat	Citroen
Cash (percent)	30 to 35	29 to 39	30
Interest (monthly) (percent)	1.50 to 1.60	1.46 to 1.87	1.50 to 1.70
Repayment (months)	9 to 36	12 to 36	9 to 36

Source: Industrias Kaiser Argentina (unpublished data).

situation, the credit terms offered by different firms do not vary
greatly (see Table 8.5). This is in marked contrast to the situation
in earlier years, when foreign subsidiaries made use of their preferential access to capital in order to compete with local firms by
offering more favorable credit terms (see Chapter 7).

Chile

Since 1966, vehicle prices in Chile have been subject to government control. Prices to the public are fixed by the Dirección de
Industria y Comercio (DIRINCO) of the ministry of economics using
one of two methods (this refers to the situation in 1970). For vehicles
that make up the entire local content requirement from Chilean parts,
the price is calculated by multiplying the FOB price of a complete
vehicle by a coefficient 5.4, determined by the Comisión Automotriz.
Vehicles that have a local content partly made up of parts imported
from other LAFTA countries have their prices calculated directly
on the basis of a study of costs made by the Cost Department of
DIRINCO.

Because of the very favorable demand conditions in Chile
throughout most of the 1960s, there has been no incentive for firms
to sell at below the official prices. In fact, prices have tended to
rise in real terms, and between 1964 and 1968 they increased by
20 percent.[27] Similarly, there was little incentive for firms to
resort to any other type of competitive behavior in order to improve
their market position. It was only in the last years of the period
that the situation changed significantly (see Chapter 6).

Table 8.6 shows the price of cars by market segments. The
market segments that can be identified in Chile are small cars (less
than 1,100 cc), medium (1,100 to 2,000 cc), and U.S. compacts
(over 2,000 cc). Unlike Argentina, cars in the intermediate category and larger U.S. models were not produced in Chile in 1970.
Table 8.7 (based on Table 8.6) shows that, apart from the case
of U.S. compacts, all of which are very similarly priced, there
is more price dispersion within each market segment in Chile than
there was in Argentina. This is not surprising, however, if one
remembers that prices are in fact controlled by the government
and, therefore, firms are not free to take account of the prices
being charged by other companies.

It has not been possible to obtain global figures for advertising
expenditure in the Chilean automotive industry. Data for individual
firms do not appear to be very different from the figures found for
Argentina. Thus, in 1970 Fiat's advertising expenditure was 0.83
percent of its total turnover and Citroen's was 0.92 percent. In

TABLE 8.6

Prices of Chilean Cars by Market Segment, July 1970
(escudos)

Small		Medium		U.S. Compacts	
Austin Mini	57,617	Datsun 1300	78,364	Chevrolet II Nova	118,198
Citroen AZAM	42,731	Fiat 1500	81,680	Dodge Dart 290	116,090
Citroen AZU	40,260	Peugeot 404	95,146	Ford Falcon	118,198
Fiat 600	48,198	Skoda Combi	74,595	Acadian	120,584
Renault 4L	51,879				

Source: Comisión Automotriz (unpublished data).

190

TABLE 8.7

Average Price and Dispersion by
Market Segment
(escudos)

	Small	Medium	U.S. Compacts
Mean	48,137	82,446	118,268
Standard deviation	6,985	8,948	1,836
Coefficient of variation	14.5%	10.85%	1.55%

terms of advertising per car produced, this came to $38.3 and $25.3, respectively. As the figures for Fiat indicate (see Table 8.8), however, high levels of advertising occurred during the late 1960s and early 1970s when demand conditions were unfavorable. Subsequently, the emergence of excess demand once more under the Unidad Popular led to a reduction in the level of advertising.

Similarly, the other forms of competition observed in Argentina were not very important in Chile throughout the greater part of the 1960s. Model diversification, for example, has been extremely limited. Almost all firms produce one or at most two basic models, usually one car and one commercial vehicle, as in the case of

TABLE 8.8

Fiat Advertising Expenditure, 1965-73
(escudos)

	Total Advertising	Percent of Sales	Advertising per Car (U.S. dollars)
1965	6,231	0.03	1.8
1966	15,444	0.04	2.1
1967	66,526	0.14	9.1
1968	619,116	0.50	18.9
1969	1,637,000	0.78	26.5
1970	2,911,000	0.83	38.3
1971	6,628,493	1.31	n.a.
1972	7,610,000	0.75	n.a.
1973	7,229,792	0.24	n.a.

*Converted at free market exchange rate.
Source: Company accounts.

Citroen and General Motors. In contrast to what was observed in
Argentina, in Chile the reduction in the number of firms was accompanied by a reduction in the number of models produced from 37 in
1962 to 22 in 1970, to only 13 in 1971. Model changes have not been
used as a competitive weapon in the industry, although changes have
occurred quite frequently in response to changes in the models produced by the parent company or licensor, which it has been easy to
reproduce in Chile since bodies and other parts are imported. This
has made possible many variations that can be incorporated without
altering any of the parts produced in Chile, which need to be amor-
tized over a longer time period.

The growth of installment finance is a feature of the late 1960s
and was absent for most of the period that is being considered. As
was indicated in Chapter 6, credit to the consumer was relatively
unimportant before 1968, being extended for less than a year with
an average downpayment of 50 percent. Even in 1968, the disequilib-
rium between supply and demand meant relatively high downpayments.[28] It was only with the changing market conditions in 1969
and 1970 that credit to dealers and to the public assumed significant
proportions. There is little uniformity in the terms that are offered
to dealers, either in the length of time for which credit is extended
or in the initial downpayment. (See Table 8.9.)

Mexico

In Mexico, as in Chile, price competition in the automotive
industry has been limited by government control of prices. The
prices of foreign makes are not allowed to exceed their prices in
the country of origin by more than a certain percentage determined
by the Secretaría de Industria y Comercio. The manufacturers have
concentrated their attention on getting the price ceilings raised
rather than attempting to cut prices below the official level. If they
are to be believed, these ceilings are unreasonably low and they
certainly would not wish to cut prices further. Moreover, even
if this were not the case, they provide a convenient level for tacit
price collusion. Government incentives in terms of additional
quotas for price reductions have not proved sufficiently attractive
for them to be used widely.

What is found again in Mexico appears to be model-price
competition, although the different segments of the market are
not as clearly separated as in the other cases considered. Table
8.10 gives the four main market segments identified by AMIA, the
others not given being subcompacts, which includes only one model
(Opel), and sports cars.

TABLE 8.9

Credit Terms to Dealers in Chile

	1968–69 Cash	1968–69 Credit	October 1969 Cash	October 1969 Credit	July 1970 Cash	July 1970 Credit
Citroen	50	3 to 7	50	3	40	7
Fiat 600	55	7	45	10	60	6
Austin Mini	60	6	55	6	60	6
Renault	n.a.	n.a.	30	2	39	2
Fiat 1500	60	4	60	3	68	2
						(Fiat 125)
Peugeot	100*	—	100*	—	50	2
Datsun	50	6	50	2	n.a.	n.a.
Dart	30	6 to 8	n.a.	n.a.	40	6
Falcon	n.a.	n.a.	40	4	40	3
Chevrolet	100	—	100	—	100	—

*Advance payment made by dealer.

Note: Cash is given in percent, credit is given in months.

Sources: Instituto de Costos, Estudio Sobre la Industria Automotriz (Santiago, 1969), Table 73; and own investigation.

TABLE 8.10

Prices of Mexican Cars by
Market Segment, 1971
(pesos)

Popular		Compact	
Renault R4L	23,800	Valiant Duster	45,363
Renault R8	28,986	Dodge Dart	48,087
Renault R10	31,047	Falcon Maverick	46,215
Datsun 1500	33,203	Rambler American	44,506
Volkswagen 1500	28,825		

Standard		DeLuxe	
Rambler Classic	54,585	Dodge Monaco	80,901
Chevrolet Chevelle	56,012	Ford Galaxie	81,363
Dodge Coronet	66,150	Chevrolet Impala	76,988

Note: Four-door versions when there is a choice of two- or four-door.

Source: Nacional Financiera (unpublished data).

TABLE 8.11

Average Price and Dispersion by
Market Segment
(pesos)

	Mean	Standard Deviation	Coefficient of Variation (percent)
Popular	29,172	3,492	11.97
Compact	46,043	1,531	3.33
Standard	58,916	6,306	10.7
Deluxe	79,751	2,404	3.01

Source: Secretaría de Industria y Comercio, Dirección
General de Estadísticas, Annario Estadística de los Estados Unidos
Mexicanos, 1960-61 and . . . 1968-69 (Mexico, 1962; 1971).

As Table 8.11 (based on Table 8.10) shows, two of the four
groups considered have a very low degree of dispersion, tending
to confirm the hypothesis that what is observed is model-price
competition. In the case of popular cars, where the highest dispersion is observed, this can be explained by the fact that the group
includes one car, the Renault 4, which is much smaller than the
others and which would have been included in a different group in
Argentina or Chile. If this is taken into account, then the degree
of dispersion is roughly similar to that found in Argentina. Since
prices have remained virtually frozen for several years, changes
over time during the period since 1965 have been insignificant.

Advertising has been a significant feature of the Mexican
automotive industry throughout the 1960s. Both in 1960 and in
1968, advertising expenditure amounted to slightly less than 1 percent of the value of the industry's total sales, a level that was only
attained in Argentina at the end of the decade.[29] The total amount
spent by the industry in 1968 came to 57,409,000 pesos, which
represented an average expenditure per car of U.S. $31.2, slightly
less than in Argentina. Data on individual companies seem to confirm these orders of magnitude. Thus, in 1970-71, VAM's
advertising expenditure was 1.5 percent of its total turnover, while
that of Automex was about 1 percent (figures based on author's
investigations).

As with advertising, model diversity has been a feature of
the Mexican automotive industry throughout the decade. It has
already been indicated that when the Mexican automotive industry

was essentially an assembly industry, a large number of different makes were available locally and an even greater number of different models. The number of firms was considerably reduced when manufacturing operations were begun, but each firm still produced a large number of different models, facilitated incidentally by the decision not to enforce local production of the major body stampings.

The number of different models of cars being produced in Mexico has fluctuated around 40 since 1965. This meant, in 1973, an average production of 4,950 units per model, almost the same as the corresponding figure for Argentina. The only model to be produced on a reasonably large scale in 1973 was the Volkswagen with an output of 62,914. Otherwise, the only models to have an output of more than 10,000 a year was the Datsun 1500 with 16,391 and the Chrysler Valiant Duster with 10,822. When comparing these figures with Argentina, one should bear in mind that small scale is likely to have less effect on costs in Mexico because of the higher import content.

The same considerations apply when one looks at model changes over time. In Argentina the high cost of dies for body stamping makes it necessary to maintain a basic model unchanged for a minimum of five years in order to amortize the investment, while in Mexico some firms make annual model changes. One must distinguish here between European and Japanese cars, which have a longer model life both in their country of origin and in Mexico, and the U.S. cars, which change annually. Of the former, Datsun, with a drastic model change in 1968, has used this as a weapon to increase market penetration, with considerable success, and DINA, in 1971, replaced the Renault 10 by the Renault 12. The producers of U.S. cars have a model year beginning slightly later than the U.S. model year in order to use U.S. parts and follow the U.S. model changes. As a result, the Volkswagen 113 sedan is the only car to have achieved a model run in excess of 100,000, with 291,941 being produced between 1965 and 1973.

As has already been indicated in Chapter 6, hire purchase facilities had come to be quite widely used in the sale of cars by the late 1960s. Generally speaking, the tendency has been for sales to the dealers to be made on a cash basis and for the dealers themselves to finance sales to the public from their own resources with the aid of financial institutions. Some firms do tend to provide assistance to their dealers and all tend to do so at the end of the model year. Renault only makes 30 percent of its sales to the dealers on a cash basis. Automex gave credit to dealers until about 1970, but the scheme has since been discontinued, while Ford sells to its dealers for cash, but intercedes with a local financial institution to provide credit for sales to the public.

TABLE 8.12

Distribution of Sales by Dealers According to
Length of Credit Granted, 1968
(percent)

Months	Small	Compact	Standard
0	48.0	42.8	41.9
0 to 12	21.9	25.6	26.7
12 to 24	29.6	30.8	30.5
24+	0.5	0.8	0.9

Source: J. Foncerrada Moreno and H. Vazquez Tercero,
Informe Económico (Mexico City: Asociacion Nacional de Distribuidores de Automóviles, 1969), p. 84.

As can be seen from Table 8.12, sales on credit vary from
52 to 58 percent of total sales, and over 30 percent of sales are
repayable over a period of more than a year. This does not indicate
the minimum downpayments involved, which tend to vary from firm
to firm. In the small car section of the market, deposits are low,
with Datsun requiring only 18 percent cash down and Volkswagen
introducing a similar plan with a cash payment of 21 percent in
1969. Renault, in the early 1970s, was selling for 20 to 25 percent
down. Thus, it appears that in at least one section of the market,
installment finance has reached substantial proportions. Significantly, this is a sector in which competition has been particularly
intense and where a supply shortage during the 1960s has been
rectified.

A Comparison of Competition in the
Three Countries

It is useful at this point to compare the forms of competition
that have been observed in each of the three countries, relating
them to the different demand and supply conditions in each case.
The most striking common characteristic of the industry in the
three countries is the lack of price competition and the tendency
of firms to follow the model-price competition pattern characteristic
of the developed countries, giving rise to well-defined market
segments in each country. As a result, the nonprice forms of competition characteristic of the developed countries have been transferred to Latin America to a greater or lesser extent depending on
market conditions in the host country concerned.

Here the most significant difference is that which marks Chile
off from Argentina and Mexico. For most of the period, demand
conditions were extremely favorable for the Chilean automotive
industry, and as a result nonprice competition did not become significant until the end of the 1960s. Advertising expenditure did not
acquire substantial proportions until 1968, while model diversity
and model changes did not play the same role as in Argentina and
Mexico. Similarly, hire purchase facilities were much less developed
in Chile even at their peak. For example, the Renault 4, which was
sold in Argentina for a minimum deposit of 30 percent and a maximum
repayment period of 30 months, and in Mexico for a downpayment of
25 to 30 percent and a repayment period of 24 months, required 56
percent cash and the remainder in 12 monthly quotas in Chile. The
Peugeot 404, which was sold for 45 percent cash in Argentina with
a repayment period of up to 36 months, needed a 47.3 percent deposit
with only a 12-month payback period in Chile.

MARKET FRAGMENTATION AND
LOCAL COSTS

One of the features of what has been called here premature
oligopolization in the Latin American automotive industry is that
concentration has ceased to increase while firms are still below the
optimal size from the point of view of economies of scale in production. The genesis of market fragmentation in the Latin American
automotive industry and the failure of competition to rationalize
market structures have already been analyzed. In this section, the
consequences of the existing market structure for production costs
in Argentina, Chile, and Mexico will be analyzed.

In this context the key concept is that of economies of scale.*
It must be emphasized, however, that scale economies are not
simply a technological relationship but also an economic one, since
the cost curves from which they are derived assume certain factor
prices. This implies that it is not possible to make universally
valid statements about the minimum optimum scale of production,
or the disadvantages of small-scale production, in a particular
industry. Such statements are only meaningful when they refer to
a particular economy at a given moment in time. It is not, therefore, possible to use the estimates of economies of scale referred
to previously in discussing the automotive industry in the advanced

---

*See Appendix A for a discussion of the origins of economies
of scale in production.

industrial countries (see Chapter 2 and Appendix A) when analyzing the Latin American automotive industry. Rather, each case must be considered on its own merit. This conclusion is reinforced when it is remembered that costs in the automotive industry depend not only on output but also on the number of models being produced, the length of life of these models, and the level of local integration.

There are two aspects of the level of output that are important from the point of view of economies of scale: the total market for the industry as a whole and the level of output for each individual firm.[30] The former determines the scale of production for certain standardized components that are generally bought out, while the latter determines the scale for engines and the main body parts that give the vehicle its distinctive characteristics and are generally produced by the terminal manufacturer itself, as well as for final assembly. The need to distinguish between these two aspects of output has been mentioned in the literature on the Latin American automotive industry,[31] but little has been done by way of analyzing the contribution made by each of these two factors to diseconomies of scale in the industry. Indeed, the implicit assumption of much of the work on regional integration is that it is the small size of industry output that is responsible for the high cost of vehicles.[32]

In Argentina the total market for vehicles in 1971 was over 250,000 units, while the average output per firm was only 25,000. Until 1970, the average output per firm was less than 20,000, a figure that compared with several hundred thousands in the advanced industrial countries. Since Argentina had achieved a high level of local content during the 1960s, it is to be expected that such low volumes of production would lead to high costs. In fact, Argentinian car prices are about twice as high as those of the same car in its country of origin.[33]

The Argentinian automotive industry has been the subject of a detailed study of the factors that contribute to the high prices of vehicles. This study, undertaken by the Comisión de Estudios Económicos de la Industria Automotriz,[34] involved a minute breakdown of all the factors that contributed to the excess cost of Argentinian vehicles. It concluded that the average Argentinian car in 1967 cost 122 percent more than in the country of origin. Fifty-seven percent, or almost half of this excess cost, could be accounted for by the low scale of production in Argentina, and this could be further broken down into 44 percent accounted for by differences in scale economies in the terminal industry and 13 percent by differences in the parts industry.[35]

One defect of the study is the fact that the excess cost attributable to a lack of scale economies was calculated using data from the advanced industrial countries, and not from an examination of the

Argentinian automotive industry itself. There are two reasons for supposing that this has not led to large errors in the estimate of the cost penalty due to small-scale production. First, the study was able to account for all but 2 percent of the total excess cost, which suggests that the effect of economies of scale could not have been greatly underestimated or overestimated. Second, the effect of different factor prices is not likely to have distorted the results a great deal since the capital-labor ratio does not change much with increases of output at scales above 25,000 cars a year.[36]

It is by no means surprising that this study concludes that the greater part of the price inefficiency of the Argentinian automotive industry is accounted for by the low volumes of production in the terminal industry, and that only a secondary role is attributed to the parts industry. The relevant scale of production from the point of view of the terminal industry is that of the individual firm for virtually all purposes. A fully integrated plant producing 25,000 vehicles a year has excess costs of more than 100 percent for machining, stamping, foundry, and forge operations.[37] Thus, if it is assumed that the average plant in Argentina produced at this level, with an in-plant content of 45 percent of the total vehicle and an average excess cost of 100 percent for all operations, the contribution made to the increased price by a lack of economies of scale in the terminal sector would be almost exactly the same as that calculated by the Comisión de Estudios Económicos de la Industria Automotriz.

In terms of the earlier discussion, the relevance of the distinction between those costs that arise in the terminal sector and those that arise in the parts sector is that the former are clearly a consequence of the fragmentation of the market between a large number of firms. The fact that costs of production are so high among the terminal firms is due not to the small absolute size of the Argentinian market but to its division between ten firms. Nor can the entire contribution made by the lack of economies of scale in the auxiliary industry be attributed to the low volume of total production. The parts industry is also highly fragmented with a number of firms producing the same parts and components.[38] This is at least partly because of the desire of the terminal producers to set up "captive" suppliers.[39] Even where the number of suppliers is not excessive, the terminal producers may demand different specifications from their suppliers. Thus the fragmentation of the terminal industry contributes directly to the lack of economies of scale in the parts industry.

It can be concluded, therefore, that the most important factor accounting for the high prices of vehicles in Argentina is the loss of economies of scale as a result of the fragmentation of the market, while the small size of the total market has merely been a secondary factor.* This goes a long way to explain why Sweden, with a total production in 1971 of around 317,000 vehicles, has one of the most internationally competitive automotive industries in the world, while Argentina, with an output of only 60,000 less in the same year, has one of the highest cost industries. In Sweden there are only two firms, Volvo and Saab-Scania, whereas in Argentina there are ten.

Like that of Argentina, the Chilean automotive industry is also characterized by a high degree of market fragmentation between a large number of firms. Despite a considerable reduction in the number of firms and an increase in local production, average output was still less than 3,000 vehicles per firm in 1971. It has been seen previously in Chapter 7 how the Chilean government used local content requirements and price control to bring about increased levels of concentration in the industry. By the late 1960s, the limits of this policy had virtually been reached, with almost all of the remaining firms having well over the required local content or being able to increase it through imports from other LAFTA countries.[40]

The breakdown of costs given in Table 8.13 indicates that the main factor accounting for the high costs of vehicles in Chile, relative to the countries from which they originate, is the high duties paid on parts imported from third countries (that is, countries outside LAFTA). These consisted of a specific duty of $1.50 oro per kilo net of parts imported, an ad valorem duty of 17 percent, and an additional tax of 100 percent on the CIF value of all parts except the engine, for which the duty is only 5 percent. Thus, custom duties come to about twice the FOB price of parts imported and that imported parts have the highest ratio of Chilean price relative to the price in the country of origin.

If these duties are eliminated, Chilean vehicles have an excess cost of 152.1 percent. Of this, 56.6 percent arises in the parts industry and 51.6 percent in final assembly, the remainder being attributable to freight and insurance charges, the inefficiency of parts imported from other LAFTA countries relative to the country of origin, and any overpricing of imported parts that takes place. Some of the excess cost that arises both in parts production and in final assembly can be attributed to small scales of production as a

---

*The other important factors in explaining the high price of local vehicles were the high prices of certain raw materials, import duties, taxes, and distribution costs. The last mentioned could be a result of diseconomies of scale in distribution stemming from a large number of terminal firms each operating their own distribution systems.

TABLE 8.13

Structure of Costs in the Chilean
Automotive Industry, 1969

Item (1)	Percent Despiece (2)	Excess Cost Factor (3)	Inefficiency (4)	(2) × (4) (percent) (5)
Imported	40.9	Custom duties	2.00	81.8
parts		CIF costs	0.25	10.2
		Overpricing	0.22	9.0
LAFTA	13.7	Custom duties	0.19	2.6
exchanges		CIF costs	1.10	15.1
		Exchange loss	0.59	8.0
Local	40.4	Economies of		
parts		scale	0.42	17.0
		Other	0.99	39.6
Production	5.0	Economies of		
costs		scale	2.00	10.0
		Other	8.32	41.6
				233.9

Source: Own elaboration based on F. Gil Mitjans, "Un Modelo de Programación de la Industria Automotriz Chilena" (professional thesis, Universidad de Chile, 1969).

result of the fragmentation of the market between a large number of firms.

In the case of parts, it has been estimated that Chilean parts are 2.41 times as expensive as the FOB price of the same parts in the country of origin (see Table 8.13). It has also been shown that an increase in the scale of output from 1,000 to 8,000 cars a year would reduce the cost of parts to the assembler by about 17.5 percent[41] to a level just under twice the FOB price. Since the cost calculations have been made on the basis of existing technologies, whereas larger volumes of output would make possible the use of new technologies in some cases, 17.5 percent is an underestimate of the reduction in costs as a result of an increase in production to 8,000 cars a year. It should be noticed also that a large part of the remaining inefficiency (classified under other in the table) is due to the loss of economies of scale even at the higher level of production,[42] rather than to distortions such as the high price of raw materials. The relevance of the 17.5 percent figure is that it represents a scale of production that could have been achieved with a more rational productive structure during the late 1960s.

The highest level of inefficiency is found in production costs, that is, the costs of assembly, and the overheads of the terminal firm. This derives in part from the fact that the despiece value of vehicles has been taken as the base for comparison. This allows only 5 percent for the costs of final assembly, and so on, which, judging by most estimates, seems to be on the low side.[43]   Other factors tending to contribute to the high excess cost of this section may be inefficient management, high profit rates, low capacity utilization, and, of course, economies of scale. It has already been argued that economies of scale are less significant in assembly than in the other processes involved in the production of vehicles, so that the cost disadvantage of small scale will be less in Chile where the engine and body are imported than in Argentina.

It is difficult to obtain estimates of assembly costs for volumes of output as low as 1,000 vehicles per year. Table 8.14 indicates that projecting backward, one may obtain an estimate of costs for final assembly of 1,000 units that would be somewhere in the region of twice what could be obtained at volumes of 10,000 units. Unfortunately, no other estimates are known that isolate assembly costs at low volumes of output against which this can be checked.

On the basis of these data, an increase in the average production by Chilean firms from 1,000 to 8,000 to 10,000 cars a year would only reduce the excess cost of Chilean vehicles by about 11 percent (27/234) and the excess cost excluding import duties by 18 percent (27/152). Obviously, increases to the level of production of 40,000+ per model, planned for 1980 under the Unidad Popular's program for the automotive industry, would lead to much greater cost reduction. This brings out the point that in Chile, unlike Argentina, the small size of the total market, as well as its fragmentation between a number of firms, are important factors accounting for the high level of local costs.

A more rational structure of production, although bringing about some reduction in costs, would still leave them considerably higher than in the country of origin, and the only hope of attaining efficient scales of production would be through regional integration as proposed, for example, within the Andean Pact. A more rational structure and regional integration would both make possible a further reduction in costs as a result of the elimination of some of the tariffs on imports of parts. Larger volumes of output per firm would make higher levels of local content economic, while the proposed regional integration of the industry within the Andean Pact would both give rise to further economies of scale and reduce the incidence of customs duties in the cost of the vehicle.[44]

In order to arrive from the cost figures given above to the price to the public, it is necessary to add the profit of the producer

TABLE 8.14

Index of Costs in the Assembly of Vehicles
(300,000 = 100)

3,500	300
5,000	245
10,000	215
25,000	185
50,000	155
100,000	122
200,000	103

Source: C. Sicard, Les Relations Cout-Volume dans l'Industrie Automobile, UNIDO (ID/WG 76/17), 1970.

and the dealer and also the sales tax. Taking the factory cost as 100, the profit of the producer was 7.7 and the dealer's (gross) profit 18.3, while the sales tax (9.4 percent of the price to the public) came to 13.1.[45] Thus, the final price to the public comes to 139.1, a markup of almost 40 percent on the cost of production. This does not seem to be significantly different from the markup normally found in the country of origin of the models produced,[46] so that the ratio of Chilean prices to prices in the country of origin is roughly equal to the ratio of Chilean costs to FOB costs in the country of origin. This, however, means higher absolute levels per car produced in Chile because of the higher level of cost.

A rationalization of production would reduce these costs, not only indirectly by reducing the base on which they are calculated but also directly by a corresponding rationalization of the distribution system. Thus, one can see that the high margins of dealers, relative to those in the country of origin in absolute terms, is a function partly of the high cost of local production, which means that stocks of vehicles and parts are more expensive to hold, and credit requirements greater, partly of the low average sales volumes. Thus, in the latter half of the 1960s, around 300 dealers made sales that varied between 10,000 and 20,000 vehicles. Data for 1968 indicate that some dealers managed to sell only one car (the Ford and Nun y German dealers in the province of Cautin and the Austin dealer in Valdivia).[47]

Insofar as there are economies of scale in the distribution of cars, then a reduction in the number of firms could reduce the dealer margin in Chile. It has been estimated[48] that distribution costs per unit fall from 130 with annual sales of cars of 100 a year to 100 at a volume of 600 a year. Since some Chilean dealers sell the vehicles of more than one firm, the total number of different dealers is 240. Sales in 1969 were a little over 22,000, giving an average per dealer of 92 units. A reduction in the number of dealers to around 40 would reduce the total costs of distribution by more than 20 percent.*

The Mexican automotive industry also displays a considerable degree of market fragmentation with an average output per firm of only 17,570 in 1971. Prices of cars in Mexico are higher than in the country of origin by between 30 and 65 percent, depending on the segment of the market.[49] These represent lower levels of excess cost than are found in most other Latin American countries.

Table 8.15 shows that in Mexico by far the most important factor behind the high cost of local vehicles is the high cost of local materials, which accounts for 36 percent of the total excess cost of 42 percent. It has not been possible to calculate how far the excess price of local parts is owing to a lack of scale economies in the industry. One survey of a number of parts producers suggests that it may be significant since 77 percent of the firms interviewed mentioned the size of the market as one of the factors accounting for the high price of their product.[50] This, however, does not indicate the quantitative importance of small scale, especially since all the firms studied mentioned the cost of locally produced inputs as a factor making for high costs. Other factors also mentioned were the cost of working capital, the cost of imported inputs, labor costs, the costs of technology, and the incidence of taxes.

Since the major body parts, which are subject to large-scale economies, are imported to Mexico, one would expect the excess cost of local production to be less than in Argentina. There are two studies available that attempt to measure the impact of scale on costs in the Mexican automotive industry, taking account of the particular local content requirements. The Wassink study[51] uses the Maxcy and Silberston[52] data suitably adjusted to take account of the less advanced industrial structure, lower wage rates, and 40 percent import content in Mexico, while that of Martinez[53] is the increase in price of a Renault Dauphine (excluding the body) at different levels of output. If one takes the average output per firm of the late 1960s as around 12,500, then it appears that a large part of the excess cost of Mexican production is due to the fragmentation of the market. Orvananos has estimated, using Wassink's data,

_____

*Owing to different factor prices in Chile, the shape of the cost curve may, of course, be different from that estimated by Pashigan.

TABLE 8.15

Direct Cost Structure in the Mexican
Automotive Industry, Late 1960s

Item	Local Costs (percent)	Country of Origin Costs (percent)	Inefficiency (percent)
Foreign materials	35.05	45.97	1.08
Local materials	51.70	36.71	1.99
Fuel, auxiliary materials	1.48	0.77	2.73
Electric energy	0.37	0.19	2.77
Wages and salaries	5.13	6.34	1.15
Other direct costs	2.12	6.05	0.50
Depreciation and amortization	4.15	3.97	1.48
Total	100	100	1.42

Source: Own elaboration based on R. Viscaino Velasco,
"La Industria Automotriz Mexicana: Análisis, Evaluación y Perspectivas" (professional thesis Escuela Superior de Economía, 1969).

that a reduction in the number of firms so that one company produced 120,000 vehicles would reduce costs by around 34 percent,
or more than three quarters of the total excess.[54] If one takes
Martinez's data, the cost reduction of an increase in output to
100,000 units would be of the order of 21 percent, that is, half of
the total excess cost. (See Table 8.16.)

As in the case of Argentina, therefore, it can be concluded
that the fragmentation of the Mexican automotive industry has been
a much more important factor in explaining the high price of locally
produced vehicles than the small absolute size of the market. This
finding contradicts the usual argument that what is needed is regional
integration in order to obtain larger markets.[55] While this is true
for the countries of the Andean Pact, the main requirement for
reducing costs in Argentina and Mexico is a rationalization of the
structure of production.

This, however, will not come about, as some writers projecting from the experience of the new developed countries suppose,
by the operation of the market mechanism.* The implications of

---

*Munk, discussing the large number of producers in Latin
American countries, states that, "If the American experience is

TABLE 8.16

Economies of Scale in the Mexican
Automotive Industry
(Import = 100)

	A	B
8,000	153	n.a.
12,500	144	122
20,000	n.a.	117
25,000	130	n.a.
50,000	112	108
100,000	n.a.	101

Sources: Line A: D. Wassink, "Commercial Policy and
Development: A Study of the Automobile Industry in Developing
Countries" (Ph.D. thesis, Stanford University, 1968; Line B:
Constantino Martinez Tamayo, "La Mexicanización de la Industria
Automotriz: 'Caso Diesel Nacional, S. A.'" (professional thesis,
Universidad Nacional Autónoma de México, 1963).

continued market fragmentation are twofold. First, as was seen in
Chapter 6, the high prices that result in the domestic market confirm the demand for cars to a relatively limited high income group,
preventing the development of a mass market. Second, as will be
discussed, it makes it difficult to expand through penetration of
foreign markets.

In the discussion so far, attention has been concentrated on
two factors, the size of the overall market and the average firm
size. As was indicated previously, these are only two aspects of
the scale problem; it is also necessary to take account of the diversity of models and the frequency of model changes. An increase in
the number of models produced by a firm will certainly increase its
costs.* It results in shorter production runs for those parts that
are not common to all models, more detailed planning of product
flows within the plant, and larger inventories of parts and components.

---

used as a guide, such fragmentation is unlikely to persist."[56] This
overlooks the fact that the American experience cannot be used as
a guide to developments in dependent economies.

*It was with good reason that Henry Ford said, referring to
the Model T, "They can have any color they like as long as it's
black."

Pratten indicates that in Britain the costs of production of a firm producing three basic bodies and five basic engines would be more than 25 percent greater than that of a firm producing only one model, at a level of output of 100,000 vehicles a year.[57]

Some of these additional costs would not have to be borne by a subsidiary in an underdeveloped country since they include the initial research and development costs of developing a number of models. The cost penalty of model diversity will also reflect the level of local integration. The costs of producing a number of models are likely to be greater in Argentina, because the major body parts are stamped there, than in Mexico or Chile. Nevertheless, even in cases where there is only a limited local content, costs will increase as a result of diversity.[58] Thus, the form of competition observed in the last section, which led to a proliferation of models especially in Argentina and Mexico, is likely to have increased further the level of costs in those industries.

The length of life of models is a further important factor in determining production costs. Unlike model diversity, it has little effect on assembly costs, so that for plants with low levels of local content there is little incentive to keep models in production over a long time period.[59] The period over which a model is kept in production becomes much more significant at high levels of integration, especially when the major body stampings are produced locally. It has been estimated that extending a model's life from two to ten years reduces the cost of the body by about 30 percent at an output of 25,000 units a year.[60] Other estimates suggest an even greater saving in body costs as a result of freezing models over a number of years.[61] Savings can also be made in engine manufacture by spreading tooling costs over a longer time period. But because engines are changed less often than bodies and a lot of the machinery used can be adapted to produce different engines, these savings are likely to be less significant than those in stamping.

It is not surprising, therefore, that model changes tended to be less frequent in Argentina than in Chile or Mexico. Nevertheless, as was observed in the previous section, production runs have been relatively short in Argentina, and only one model had been produced in more than 100,000 units by 1970. In Mexico, an official study in 1960 that recommended that the government should develop an automotive manufacturing industry emphasized the need to freeze models for a minimum of five years in order to amortize tooling, since it considered that a total output of 100,000 over the period would be required for production to be economic.[62]

The conclusion of this section, therefore, must be that the nature of oligopolistic competition in the international automotive industry, which has led to a fragmentation of Latin American markets between a large number of producers, has been a major factor contributing to the high cost of cars, especially in Argentina and Mexico. These costs also have been raised by the forms of competition employed by the multinational corporations in these markets, which have emphasized model diversity and model changes rather than longer production runs and cost reductions.

THE UTILIZATION OF CAPACITY

It was indicated earlier that the main characteristic of a monopolistic industry, in the sense in which the term has been used here, is that excess capacity is not eliminated by some firms being driven out of the industry. It is to be expected, therefore, that those industries that are dominated by foreign subsidiaries will be characterized by a low level of capacity utilization. The concept of full capacity is a tricky one that is often difficult to measure accurately. In this context, it will be taken as the level of output at which costs begin to rise sharply.[63]

There are problems of measurement, however, where different machines or production processes within a plant have different output capacities.[64] There are also difficulties in determining the number of shifts on the basis of which capacity output should be calculated. For example, if demand conditions are such that only one shift is worked, a firm may not know whether it would be technically feasible to operate three daily shifts, and would certainly not have a very precise notion of the output that could be obtained with a three-shift schedule.

In what follows, estimates made by the terminal firms themselves have been used for the calculation of capacity utilization rates. These may tend to exaggerate the potential increase in output that could be obtained for the industry as a whole by operating at full capacity, since bottlenecks may appear in the parts industry if all firms expand output simultaneously.

During the early years of the development of the Argentinian automotive industry, in 1960 and 1961, the backlog of demand ensured that capacity was more or less fully utilized.[65] The rate of construction of new capacity far exceeded the growth of output, however, so that utilization fell to about 65 to 70 percent in 1962 and to 42 percent in the recession of 1963. Although the recovery brought about an increase in utilization, as did the elimination of some of the locally owned firms during the mid-1960s, only 61 percent of capacity was used in 1967, rising slightly to 63 percent in 1970 and about 70 percent in 1973.

Despite the fact that it has risen somewhat in the last few years, capacity utilization in the Argentinian automotive industry still has not regained the high levels of the early 1960s. It is significant that the automotive industry has one of the highest levels of excess capacity among Argentinian industries. An ECLA study of 15 industries in 1964 showed only four sectors with capacity utilization of less than the 53 percent that we estimated for the automotive industry in that year, and all were within 5 percent of that figure.[66] The level of utilization also compares unfavorably with that found in the same industry in the developed countries.[67]

It has been suggested by A. O. Hirschman[68] that excess capacity in import-substituting industries is a result of overoptimistic projections of market demand. Two reasons why this might occur are suggested. First, the higher price of the domestic article compared to the imported one tends to lower demand; second, import statistics tend to overestimate the market for the new domestic industry because they include some speciality products that the latter cannot supply. Neither of these arguments is applicable to the case of the Argentinian automotive industry since imports before the initiation of local production could provide no guide to market potential. The only direct information on what firms saw as the market potential in the early 1960s is a study by Industrias Kaiser Argentina,[69] which estimated the total market for vehicles in 1970 at between 135,000 and 159,000, depending on the assumptions made. Since production in 1970 reached almost 220,000 units, this seems to suggest that firms were unduly pessimistic rather than the reverse.

Nevertheless, even if firms did not overestimate the total market, it is quite possible that each firm overestimated its expected share of that market, and since investment decisions are taken on the basis of this, excess capacity may have been created. Even where firms are not unduly optimistic about their future market shares, they may deliberately "build ahead of demand." Steindl explains at some length how, under oligopolistic market conditions, indivisibilities of plant, and economies of scale, this tendency will appear.[70] Fajnzylber suggests that this is a typical form of operation for international firms that have the finance available to build a larger plant than is justified by the existing size of the market.[71]

As has already been seen, scale economies and indivisibilities are particularly important in the automotive industry, and although the size of plant found in Argentina is far below what would be considered the minimal optimum scale in developed countries, there is evidence to suggest that foreign corporations investing in Argentina tended to build plants with a capacity far in excess of the initial demand for their products. Both Ford and General Motors built plants with a capacity of over 30,000 a year, although they did not achieve an output of 30,000 until 1965 and 1969, respectively.

The result of this process was that considerable excess capacity was created once all the plants were completed. Since this occurred in 1963 and coincided with a downturn in the overall level of activity, the fall in utilization was spectacular. The elimination of some firms meant that total capacity fell somewhat around the mid-1960s so that utilization figures improved but were still relatively low in the early 1970s. The period during which capacity appears to have been reduced as a result of exits from the industry was short-lived and any further increase in capacity utilization would appear to have to come from increased output. This is rendered more difficult by the fact that firms with high utilization figures, such as Fiat, are continuously expanding their capacity so that total capacity also has been increasing.

The same pattern is also evident in the case of Mexico. Since 1965, capacity utilization has fluctuated between 40 and 60 percent, suggesting that utilization in Mexico is even lower than in Argentina. This refers only to assembly operations, however; if engine manufacture is considered, there is even greater excess capacity. Thus, in 1965, there were six engine plants in Mexico with a total capacity of 400,000 units, operating at only 25 percent of full capacity. Despite this, by 1967, the number of plants had increased to ten and the total capacity to more than 600,000 engines.[72]

A comparison with other Mexican industries also suggests that excess capacity in the automotive industry is extremely high. A survey of 92 manufacturing enterprises in 1968 indicated that the industry was one of those in which a number of firms with low levels of utilization were found.[73] Perhaps even more significant was the fact that only 7.6 percent of the firms had levels of utilization below 50 percent, and that the modal class was between 80 and 90 percent, whereas utilization in vehicle assembly was only 45 percent in that year.

In the Mexican automotive industry, as in the Argentinian, there is a market structure that prevents this vast excess capacity from being eliminated. Here, however, it is reinforced by the quota system, which prevents some firms from fully utilizing their capacity and from driving out competitors that have less favorable demand conditions. The phenomenon of building ahead of demand observed in Argentina can be seen here on an even greater scale.[74] This is particularly evident in the case of engine plants where both Ford and Volkswagen built plants in the mid-1960s with a capacity of 100,000 engine blocks and heads a year, working two shifts. By 1971, the firms still did not produce enough vehicles to justify more than one shift working.

The fact that the Chilean automotive industry is essentially an assembly operation makes the estimation of the extent of capacity utilization rather difficult. Generally speaking, at low levels of technology with little investment in machinery and equipment, the concept of capacity tends to become meaningless since operations are not machine paced and capacity can be easily increased by employing more labor. This is particularly true of the early years of the industry's development in Chile; however, it is possible to arrive at some estimate of capacity for the late 1960s and early 1970s. The Instituto de Costos' study[75] put capacity at 36,000 in 1969, giving a degree of utilization of over 60 percent, but it should be noted that a one-shift schedule is the rule. Capacity was increased somewhat in the early 1970s to 44,250 in 1973, according to ODEPLAN estimates. The fall in production in that year gave rise to a very low level of capacity utilization of less than 40 percent.

Excess capacity in the Chilean automotive industry has not been a consequence of foreign firms building up capacity ahead of demand. The leading foreign firms had plants with one-shift capacity of only 3,000 to 6,000 cars in the late 1960s.[76] The plans to build new plants in the early 1970s by Renault, Peugeot, and General Motors may have indicated the beginnings of such a phenomenon had other firms followed suit, but the Unidad Popular's policy of restructuring the industry prevented further developments. Excess capacity, rather, must be explained by problems of supply, references to which abound in the literature on the Chilean automotive industry.[77] This applies not only to the quality and quantity of local parts supplied to the terminal industry and the difficulty of increasing exchanges with other LAFTA countries but also to the availability of skilled labor. The firms themselves almost invariably cite difficulties in meeting local content requirements as a result of the inadequacy of local parts production as the main factor accounting for underutilization of capacity.

The low levels of capacity utilization in these industries involve an immense waste of resources. It appears paradoxical that in economies that are conventionally regarded as being short of capital, a significant part of the productive capacity that has been constructed is lying idle. In addition, underutilization of capacity is a further factor contributing to high costs in the industry. In Argentina it was estimated that full utilization of capacity in 1968 could have reduced car prices by 10 percent.[78] Relative to the cost penalties imposed by a lack of economies of scale, this is small, but it must be remembered that it is when excess capacity exceeds 40 percent that costs begin to rise sharply in the automotive industry. In Mexico it was estimated that costs were 7 percent higher than at full capacity with excess capacity of 40 and 16 percent higher if excess capacity was 60 percent.

THE POSSIBILITIES OF DEVELOPING EXPORTS

Foreign domination of the Latin American automotive industry has made it difficult to develop exports for two basic reasons. First, as just seen, one of the consequences of the presence of multinational corporations has been to raise local production costs through market fragmentation and capacity underutilization, which means that exports are not competitive in third markets. Second, foreign firms may impose export restrictions on their subsidiaries or on the licensees with which they have contractual agreements in order to prevent them competing with the parent company or another affiliate in third countries. This is particularly prevalent in the case of locally owned licensees, whereas with wholly owned subsidiaries, control may be exercised directly through ownership.[79]

There is considerable evidence of such contractual limitations on exports in the Latin American automotive industry, although the extent of participation by wholly owned subsidiaries limits the degree to which explicit restrictions are used. The most detailed survey has been carried out in Argentina where it was found that only 3.4 percent of the contracts studied in the terminal automotive industry and the parts industry explicitly permitted exports.[80] On the other hand, 31.7 percent of the contracts required the permission of the licensor for exports to be made, and 29.1 percent permitted exports of parts incorporated in Argentinian vehicles (but this was more of a restriction than an authorization since exports of completed vehicles are so limited). Another method of discriminating against exports found in a number of contracts was a higher royalty charge on exports than on products destined for the domestic market.

In Chile there has been no in-depth study of contractual arrangements in the automotive industry, but a general study of licensing contracts in Chilean industry found that of the six cases examined in the automotive industry, half explicitly restricted exports through absolute prohibition, limitation to certain areas, or by requiring the written permission of the licenser.[81]

In Mexico a similar pattern emerges. Out of 16 contracts between terminal automotive manufacturers and foreign firms, only 5 were free from any export restrictions. Of the remainder, three required the permission of the licenser for exports to be made, three permitted parts to be exported only if they were incorporated in terminated vehicles, three permitted exports only when made via the licenser, and two restricted exports to a certain area.

As Table 8.17 shows, Argentinian exports of completed vehicles were negligible up to 1971, and despite a rapid expansion between 1972 and 1974 reaching a value of U.S. $71 million, less than 5 percent of the vehicles produced in Argentina were sold abroad

TABLE 8.17

Exports by the Argentinian Automotive
Industry, 1965-74
(thousands of U.S. dollars)

	Completed Units		Parts	Total
	Number	Value	Parts	Total
1965	88	189	817	1,006
1966	35	113	3,648	3,761
1967	58	112	6,796	6,908
1968	76	216	6,396	6,612
1969	459	2,675	7,312	9,987
1970	884	3,444	7,405	10,849
1971	601	3,329	13,667	16,996
1972	3,493	17,791	21,014	38,806
1973	11,214	53,300	40,285	93,586
1974	15,132	71,131	60,207	131,339

Sources: Asosiación de Fabricas de Automotores (ADEFA),
"Informe Estadistico," no. 611 (February 5, 1975), no. 622 (May 7,
1975), Table 1; 1974 Industria Automotriz Argentina (Buenos Aires:
1975).

in that year. The rapid growth of vehicle exports in recent years
is directly attributable to government policy, which has attempted
to increase exports using both carrot and stick. The stick in this
case is Decree 680/73, which only permits firms to increase their
car sales in Argentina by 8 percent a year if certain export quotas
are met. Thus, in 1974, firms must make exports equal to 15
percent of their sales in 1973, and this percentage is increased
each year to reach 100 percent by 1978. Firms that fail to meet
the required level of exports will have their domestic sales reduced
accordingly. This decree applies only to cars and there is no such
requirement for commercial vehicles. As a result, in 1974, the
first year in which the decree was in force, exports of cars more
than doubled while those of commercial vehicles increased only
marginally.

The carrot, which has also played a part in export promotion,
is a whole series of incentives, subsidies, and drawbacks provided
by the government. The most important of these are a subsidy of
35 percent for cars and 40 percent for commercial vehicles on the
FOB value, established by Decree 3864/72, and the repayment of
taxes paid on earlier stages of production. This latter is estimated

at about 11 percent of the FOB price for cars and over 18 percent for a heavy truck. Taken together with a number of other smaller incentives, such as those for exporting tires, the repayment of freight and insurance charges (Decree 2864/72), and the incentive for exports to new markets (Decree 2863/72), the total payments received by an exporting company can amount to almost 60 percent of the export price for cars and 75 percent for heavy trucks. To this must be added a number of financial incentives provided by the Central Bank for pre- and postsales financing, which give a further subsidy of more than 5 percent of the price of the vehicle. Moreover, some exports made by the industry are financed by loans from the Argentinian government, such as the much publicized exports to Cuba.

Although these subsidies, together with substantial devaluations in 1971 and 1972, made exports profitable in late 1972 and early 1973, internal cost increases, which were not compensated for by devaluations, eroded this position. The oil crisis and the downturn in demand for cars worldwide have also made it more difficult for Argentina to find markets for its vehicles. There are signs that commercial vehicle exports are already declining, while it is only the need to export in order to maintain a share of the domestic market that is keeping up car exports.

Until 1973, exports of parts were more important than those of built-up vehicles, but the rapid growth of the latter has reversed the situation. During the 1960s, exports of parts were almost entirely to Chile under the LAFTA complementation agreement between the two countries, but the expansion of these exports was limited by the restrictions placed by the Argentinian legislation on imports from Chile, which cannot exceed 6 percent of the FOB value of production of each firm. The small size of the Chilean market and that country's desire to expand its own parts industry were also factors limiting the growth of exports. Since 1970, so-called pure exports of parts, not under complementation agreements, have acquired a certain significance, and by 1974 accounted for about two thirds of the value of exported parts in that year. These have also benefited from government subsidies, although to a lesser extent than completed vehicles, since the subsidy established by Decree 3804/72 is only 20 percent for parts compared to 35 percent on cars and 40 percent on trucks.*

---

*Exports of CKD packs that contain more than 50 percent of the total parts can, however, be counted as complete vehicles for the purpose of the subsidy.

TABLE 8.18

Exports of Parts from Chile, 1965-73
(thousands of U.S. dollars)

	To Argentina	Total
1965	32.1	32.1
1966	689.0	689.0
1967	1,370.7	1,370.7
1968	5,572.0	5,572.0
1969	8,531.2	9,243.5
1970	7,040.9	8,443.7
1971	3,902.2	4,477.7
1972	n.a.	4,121.1
1973	n.a.	3,131.6

Source: Comisión Automotriz (unpublished data).

Not surprisingly, considering the high price of locally produced
vehicles, even compared with Argentina, Chile does not export any
completed vehicles. The late 1960s did, however, see a significant
development of exports of parts, mainly to Argentina (see Table 8.18).
The main factor behind the growth of Chilean exports of parts has
been the government's policy of increasing local content requirements, which has led to local firms undertaking exchanges under
the special complementation arrangements discussed above in order
to avoid having to invest in Chile or develop Chilean suppliers.[82]
In the absence of such arrangements, Chilean parts exports would
have been negligible. In any case, the major Chilean exports are
low technology parts, such as springs, radiators, and wheels, in
contrast to the high technology parts that are imported.

Mexican exports of finished vehicles have grown spectacularly
from 11 units in 1970 to 20,141 in 1973 (see Table 8.19). An examination of the figures, however, reveals that this is almost entirely
due to one firm, Volkswagen, exporting one model, the Safari 181,
to the United States. This is a novelty model not produced elsewhere
and therefore represents something of a special case, although it
does indicate the possibility of certain countries specializing in the
production of particular models. Compared to Argentina there is
a greater emphasis on the export of parts from Mexico than of
assembled vehicles. Thus, 1973 was the first year during which
completed vehicles accounted for more than 10 percent of the
industry's exports.

TABLE 8.19

Exports by the Mexican Automotive Industry, 1967-73
(thousands of U.S. dollars)

	Completed Units Number	Value	Parts	Total
1967	31	82.1	9,040.0	9,122.1
1968	12	18.5	10,720.0	10,738.5
1969	33	511.1	20,880.0	21,391.1
1970	11	224.6	36,480.0	36,704.6
1971	244	1,565.0	50,240.0	51,805.0
1972	2,212	5,728.8	75,871.2	81,600.0
1973*	20,141	40,415.5	112,195.2	152,610.7

*Preliminary.

Source: AMIA on the basis of Anuario Estadistica del Comercio Exterior; Informe Estadistico, no. 100 (April 15, 1974), p. 2.

216

As in the case of Argentina, the growth of exports is largely a consequence of government policy. As mentioned previously, since 1969, the terminal producers have been obliged to cover an increasing proportion of their import requirements with exports. The Decree of October 24, 1972, which at present regulates the industry, set the proportion of import requirements that must be covered by exports at 40 percent for 1974 and this is programmed to reach 100 percent by 1979. Exports have also been promoted through a tax drawback of 11 percent of the value of exports, which, although not on the massive scale found in Argentina, has provided an additional stimulus to growth since 1972.

Further factors have been the relatively low prices of parts in Mexico compared to other Latin American countries and the proximity to the U.S. market. Mexico, thus, has been able to make use of the inherent advantages that multinational corporations have in developing export markets. The most important parts being exported in 1973 were engines and parts for the engine and transmission, each accounting for more than U.S. $20 million in export earnings. This indicates the possibility for some countries favorably placed of specializing in particular parts for export. However, as has been seen, the government's policy already has contributed to further denationalization of the Mexican automotive industry.

CAPITAL ACCUMULATION AND
EMPLOYMENT CREATION

As discussed in Chapter 5, the automotive industry in the countries under consideration passed through a rather short-lived period of heavy investment associated with increases in local content requirements imposed by the host country governments. Otherwise, as the model put forward in the first section of this chapter implies, the oligopolistic structure of the industry has tended to keep investment low. This, together with the tendency for capital intensity to increase considerably in the industry,* has meant that employment creation has been rather limited. Since automotive manufacturing has been an import-substituting industry in these countries, it has not had a major effect in displacing workers in other sectors. Thus, in the following discussion, attention will be focused on the extent to which additional employment has been created within the industry.

---

*See Chapter 5 on the increase in the capital-output ratio. This has been accompanied by an increase in the capital-labor ratio, which is the relevant variable in this context.

New sources of employment obviously have been created by
the development of the automotive industry, but the extent to which
this has occurred is often exaggerated. In Argentina, for example,
the industry trade association, ADEFA, claims that over 1.75 million
people are directly or indirectly related to the industry. However,
the terminal and parts industries employed directly 112,800 people
in 1973, only slightly more than 1 percent of the economically active
population. The remainder were employed in sales, repair and
maintenance, petroleum refining, service stations, insurance, road
works, and transport services, none of which can be said to depend
on a local industry for its existence.* It should be pointed out,
moreover, that not all of these 112,800 jobs can be credited to the
development of a local manufacturing industry since there already
existed a well-developed parts industry, producing for the replacement market, before 1959. Unfortunately, it is impossible to
estimate exactly what proportion of these jobs would have existed
in the absence of a local terminal industry. Comparison of the
1964 National Economic Census with the Industrial Census of 1954
indicates a growth of employment in the automotive industry and
related sectors from just under 90,000 to over 120,000.

Although the classification is different for the two years, the
groups taken broadly cover the same area of vehicle and parts
production and repair. The fact that over this ten-year period, in
which a domestic automotive industry was effectively created,
employment appears to have increased by only 33,000 suggests that
industry sources' claims as to employment generation have been
exaggerated.

In Chile, the automotive industry is relatively insignificant
as a source of employment because of its small weight (in terms
of value added) within the manufacturing sector. Thus, although
employment in parts production and assembly increased more than
tenfold between the 1957 and 1967 census, this merely reflects the
low base from which the industry started in the earlier year. Thus,
total employment in 1967 was only 7,063 compared to total employment in industry in the same year of 580,000. This total was divided
roughly equally between the parts industry and the terminal industry.
In 1968, employment in the terminal industry was estimated at
3,952, while five years later in 1973 it had increased to 4,550.

---

*It should be noted, however, that in the absence of a local
industry the total number of vehicles in circulation might well have
been considerably less, thus reducing the demand for gasoline,
service stations, and so on. On the other hand, the greater average
age of the vehicle stock under such conditions might increase the
demand for repair and maintenance.

The limited employment in the auxiliary industry is an indication of the latter's underdevelopment and the fact that a large proportion of the parts used by the terminals still comes from abroad.

Estimates of employment in the terminal automotive industry in Mexico are available from both the industry trade association, AMIA, and the Ministry of Industry and Commerce (SIC). The estimates made by the latter are considerably lower than those of the firms themselves. For example, in 1965, SIC census data gave a figure of only 13,838, compared to the 19,308 claimed by AMIA, and, in 1969, the corresponding figures were 21,937 and 29,091. If one takes the AMIA estimates, employment in the terminal industry increased more than fourfold between 1960 and 1970, mainly between 1963 and 1966. If employment in parts production is put at around 10,000 in 1960, this has grown even more spectacularly to reach 56,309 in 1970.[83] Again, however, most of the growth took place before 1966 when employment in the auxiliary industry was already about 52,000.[84]

Thus, one can estimate that total employment in the parts and terminal industries together increased more than four times between 1960 and 1966 and by only some 16 percent between 1966 and 1970. As has already been indicated, official government statistics suggest that employment creation in the industry was substantially less. Thus, according to the 1960 census, total employment in the production of vehicles and parts (including tires) was 18,488; by the time of the 1965 census it had reached only 40,018, which was substantially less than the figures of over 74,000 given by industry sources for the following year. It appears to be the case, therefore, that, although the development of the automotive industry generated considerable additional employment in the first half of the 1960s, this has been overestimated in unofficial statistics, and in the second half of the decade, there has been relatively little further growth. As a result, the automotive industry in 1970 employed less than 0.5 percent of the economically active population, even on the basis of the AMIA figures.[85]

CONCLUSION

This chapter has indicated that a number of features that were earlier identified as being characteristic of the Latin American automotive industry can be explained, at least in part, by the operations of the multinational corporations in that industry. The manner of operations was discussed, and it was found that, to a greater or lesser degree, the tendency was for the same forms of nonprice competition to be used as are current in the developed countries. This, together with the market fragmentation that has resulted from the nature of international competition in the automotive industry analyzed in Chapter 2, has led to high costs of production, high prices, low capacity utilization, an inability to develop exports, and only limited employment creation. Chapter 9 discusses how government policy has contributed to, or failed to avoid, these problems.

NOTES

1. Josef Steindl, Maturity and Stagnation in American Capitalism (Oxford: Blackwell, 1952).

2. P. Sylos-Labini, Oligopoly and Technical Progress (Cambridge, Mass.: Harvard University Press, 1962), pp. 103-31.

3. See, for example, R. Hilferding, El Capital Financiero, trans. V. Romano Garcia (Madrid: Editorial Tecnos, 1963); V. I. Lenin, Imperialism, the Highest Stage of Capitalism (Moscow: Progress Publishers, 1968); and N. Bukharin, Imperialism and World Economy (London: Merlin Press, 1972).

4. For example, Steindl, op. cit., and P. Baran and P. Sweezy, Monopoly Capital, An Essay on the American Economic and Social Order (London: Penguin, 1968).

5. B. Chinitz, "Contrasts in Agglomeration: New York and Pittsburgh," AER Papers and Proceedings 51 (1961), pp. 279-89.

6. See M. Merhav, Technological Dependence, Monopoly and Growth (Oxford: Pergamon Press, 1969), pp. 96-102, for an elaboration of these and other points.

7. U.S., Congress, Senate, Subcommittee on International Trade of the Committee on Finance, statement of General Motors Corporation, 1973.

8. P. Salama, Le Proces de Sous Développement (Paris: Maspero, 1972), pp. 95-108.

9. Sylos-Labini, op. cit., pp. 132-42.

10. E. Cimillo, E. Gastiazoro, and E. Lifschitz, "Acumulación y Centralización del Capital en la Industria Argentina" (Paper presented to the Congreso de Economía Política, Buenos Aires, November 1971), p. 16.

11. S. M. MacDonell and M. R. Lascano, La Industria Automotriz, Aspectos Económicos y Fiscales (Dirección General Impositiva, Departemento de Estudios, División Planes, June 1974), Table 40.

12. Ibid., Table 8.

13. B. C. Raddavero, "Análisis de la Transferencia de la Tecnología Externa a la Industria Argentina: El Caso de la Industria Automotriz," Económica 18 (1972): 367-88.

14. Consejo Nacional de Desarrollo (CONADE), Sector Industria y Minería, Diagnósticos Global y de Siderurgia y Métales, Fundición Ferrossa, Bienes de Capital, Industria Automotriz, Celulosa y Papel, Industria Textil, Industria Petroquímica (Buenos Aires, 1967).

15. MacDonell and Lascano, op. cit., Table 40.

16. La Opinion (May 22, 1974).

17. This is surprisingly much higher than the estimate arrived at by E. Acevedo and H. Vergara, but they used Banco Central data. E. Acevedo and H. Vergana, "Algunos Antecedentes Sobre Concentracion, Participacion Extranjera y Transferencia Tecnologica en la Industria Manufacturera en Chile" (Professional thesis, Universidad de Chile 1970).

18. Corporación de Fomento (CORFO), Censo de Regalías, in United Nations, Division of Public Finance and Financial Institutions, Arrangements for the Transfer of Operative Technology to Developing Countries: Case Study of Chile (ST/ECA/151/A), 1971, p. 64.

19. CORFO, División de Planificación Industrial, Las Inversiones Extranjeras en la Industria Chilena, 1960-69, Publicación No. 57-a/71, 1971.

20. B. Sepulveda and A. Chumacero, La Inversión Extranjera en México (Mexico City: Fondo de Cultura Económica, 1973), pp. 104-05.

21. Fernando Fajnzylber and Trinidad Martinez Tarrago, "Las Empresas Transnacionales, Expansión a Nivel Mundial y Proyección en la Industria Mexicana" (versión preliminar), mimeographed (Mexico: Centro de Investigacion y Docencia Economica, 1975), p. 517.

22. Industrias Kaiser Argentina (IKA), La Industria Automotriz Argentina (1963), p. 109.

23. L. J. White, The Automobile Industry Since 1945 (Cambridge, Mass.: Harvard University Press, 1971), pp. 222-27.

24. C. Pratten, Economies of Scale in Manufacturing Industry (Cambridge: Cambridge University Press, 1971).

25. Asociación de Concesionarios de Automotores de la República Argentina (ACARA), El Concesionario de Automotores en la Argentina. Examen de Su Situación Jurídica, Impositiva y Económico-Financiero (Mar del Plata, 1965), p. 136.

26. White, op. cit., Table 12.4.

27. Instituto de Costos, Estudio Sobre la Industria Automotriz (Santiago, 1969), Table 81. The deflator used was the consumer price index.

28. F. Cordova, L. Muxica, and G. Wagner, "Algunos Aspectos del Crédito al Consumo," Cuadernos de Economía 5 (1968): 30-50.

29. Departamento General de Estadisticas, Secretaría de Industria y Comercio.

30. This corresponds to the distinction between the optimum size of firm and optimum size of industry made by E. A. G. Robinson, The Structure of Competitive Industry, new ed. (Cambridge: Cambridge University Press, 1958), pp. 10-33, 118-26.

31. See, for example, B. Munk, "The Welfare Costs of Content Protection: The Automotive Industry in Latin America," Journal of Political Economy 77 (1969): 85-98.

32. See, for instance, J. Behrman, The Role of International Companies in Latin American Integration: Autos and Petrochemicals (Lexington, Mass.: D. C. Heath, 1972).

33. Economic Commission for Latin America (ECLA), Perspectivas y Modalidades de Integración Regional de la Industria Automotriz en America Latina, ECLA/DI/DRAFT/92, División de Desarrollo Industrial (1973), Table I.23.

34. Comisión de Estudios Económicos de la Industria Automotriz, La Industria Automotriz Argentina: Informe Económico 1969 (Buenos Aires: Asociación de Fabricas de Automotores [ADEFA], 1969).

35. A study carried out a year later came to similar conclusions. Local cars had an excess cost of 102 percent, of which 48 percent was accounted for by a lack of scale economies. Dirección Nacional de Estudios Industriales, Situación Actual y Perspectivas del Mercado de Automóviles en la Republica Argentina (Buenos Aires, 1969), pp. 41-42.

36. ECLA, op. cit., Table II.7. It is often thought that at larger volumes of output, production becomes more capital intensive as capital is substituted for labor. In the automotive industry, however, economies of scale are so important that the savings on capital costs equal or even exceed the savings on labor as output increases.

37. Ibid., pp. 128-50.

38. Comisión de Estudios Económicos de la Industria Automotriz, op. cit.

39. J. Baranson, Automotive Industries in Developing Countries, World Bank Staff Occasion Paper No. 8, 1969, p. 47.

40. On this point, see A. Aguilera Jorquera, "La Industria Automotriz Chilena y su Participación en el Sector Industrial" (professional thesis, Universidad de Chile, 1970), Chap. 8.

41. J. de Coyeneche Valdovinos, Economies of Scale in the Chilean Motor-Vehicle Industry, UNIDO (ID/WG. 76/4), 1970, p. 17.

42. ECLA estimates that parts have an excess cost due to a lack of economies of scale of 85 percent at an output of 10,000 vehicles a year. ECLA, Perspectivas, op. cit., Table II.33.

43. See, for example, Baranson, op. cit., Table 4.

44. See ECLA, op. cit., pp. 188-220, for a study of the possibilities of developing an integrated automotive industry with a limited excess cost in the Andean Pact countries. See also Junta del Acuerdo de Cartagena, Propuesta de la Junta Sobre Programa Sectorial de la Industria Automotriz (JUN/Propuesta 45, 1974).

45. F. Gil Mitjans, "Un Modelo de Programación de la Industria Automotriz Chilena" (professional thesis, Universidad de Chile, 1969), Table 2A.

46. ECLA, op. cit., Table I.25.

47. Instituto de Costos, op. cit., Anexo 40.

48. B. P. Pashigan, "The Distribution of Automobiles; An Economic Analysis of the Franchise System," in White, op. cit., pp. 144-47.

49. Data for 1970 from AMIA (unpublished data).

50. M. S. Wionczek, G. Bueno, and J. E. Navarrette, "La Transferencia Internacional de Tecnología al Nivel de Empresa: El Caso de México," mimeographed, p. 150. (New York: United Nations ESA/FF/AC2/10, 1971).

51. D. Wassink, "Commercial Policy and Development: A Study of the Automobile Industry in Developing Countries" (Ph.D. thesis, Stanford University, 1968).

52. Maxcy and Silberston, op. cit., pp. 75-98.

53. Constantino Martinez Tamayo, "La Mexicanización de la Industria Automotriz: Caso Diesel Nacional, S.A." (professional thesis, Universidad Nacional Autónoma de México, 1963).

54. J. Orvañanos Lascurain, "Aspectos de la Demanda y Oferta Automotriz" (professional thesis, Instituto Tecnológico Autónomo de México, 1967), Chap. 3b.

55. Behrman, op. cit.

56. Munk, op. cit., p. 89.

57. Pratten, op. cit., Tables 14.3 and 14.4.

58. See C. Sicard, Les Relations Cout-volume dans l'industrie Automobile, UNIDO (ID/WG 76/17), 1970, pp. 15-32.

59. Sicard estimates that increasing the life of a model from 7 to 15 years reduces assembly costs by only 5 percent and price by about 0.5 percent at a volume of production of 10,000 vehicles a year. Ibid., Table 4.

60. Pratten, op. cit., Table 14.2. The costs include tooling, materials, labor, depreciation, and other works overheads for the production of body shells.

61. ECLA, op. cit., pp. 144-46. Both the studies referred to use developed country costs. In an underdeveloped country the cost reductions are likely to be greater because the main saving is on capital, which is relatively more expensive. This would not

necessarily be the case where secondhand dies were used, but this
has not occurred widely as far as is known.

62. Nacional Financiera, op. cit., pp. 57-58. In any event,
the Mexican government preferred not to produce bodies locally and
thus continues to follow the U.S. model changes.

63. See A. Phillips, "Measuring Industrial Capacity and
Capacity Utilization in Less Developed Countries," Industrialization
and Productivity Bulletin 15 (1970): 16-21.

64. See M. Merhav, "Excess Capacity—Measurement, Causes
and Uses: A Case Study of Industry in Israel," Industrialization and
Productivity Bulletin 15 (1970): 22-48.

65. E. J. Parellada, La Industria Automotriz en la Argentina,
UNIDO (ID/WG 76/9), 1970, p. 6.

66. United Nations, Economic and Social Council, The Process
of Industrialization in Latin America, Statistical Annex (ST/ECLA/
conf.23/L.2/Add.2; E/CN 12/716/Add.2), in I. M. D. Little,
T. Scitovsky, and M. Scott, Industry and Trade in Some Developing
Countries: A Comparative Study (Oxford: Oxford University Press
for OECD, 1970), p. 93. The ECLA study does not identify the
automotive industry as a separate sector but indicates that capacity
utilization in vehicles and nonelectrical machinery was 56.6 percent,
that is, only slightly greater than our estimate for the automotive
industry.

67. In Britain, for example, capacity utilization for seven
automotive manufacturers fluctuated between a high of 88 percent
and a low of 64 percent over the period 1963-67. National Economic
Development Office (NEDO), The Effect of Government Economic
Policy on the Motor Industry (London: Her Majesty's Stationery
Office, 1968), Table 8.

68. A. O. Hirschman, "The Political Economy of Import
Substituting Industrialization," Quarterly Journal of Economics 82
(1968): 1-32.

69. IKA, op. cit., pp. 141-58, 190-203.

70. Steindl, op. cit., pp. 9-11.

71. F. Fajnzylber, Estrategia Industrial y Empresas Internacionales: Posición Relativa de América Latina y Brasil, ECLA,
UNE/CN 121 12/ (1970), pp. 280-98.

72. K. Rethwisch, "An Economic Analysis of the Mexican
System of Developing an Automotive Industry and Some Proposed
Alternatives" (Ph.D. thesis, University of Maryland, 1969), Chap. 3.

73. United Nations, Conference on Trade and Development
(UNCTAD), Major Issues Arising from the Transfer of Technology
to Developing Countries (TD/B/AC. 11/10), 1972, Add. 1, p. 34.
Others were food, electric-electronic, machinery, and metal products.

74. As in Argentina, there is no evidence to support the view that firms tend to overestimate future demand. A study made by Ford in 1960 suggested that the total market for vehicles in 1967 would be 111,000, whereas, in fact, sales in that year were over 125,000. Ford Motor Co. S.A., Estudio de la Fabricación de Automóviles en México (Mexico City, 1960).

75. Instituto de Costos, op. cit., Chap. I.

76. Gamma Ingenieros, Estudio de la Industria Automotriz Chilena, UNIDO (ID/WG 76/6), 1970, pp. 42-44.

77. See, for example, Asociacion de Industriales Metalurgicos (ASIMET), Primer Seminario Nacional de la Industria Automotriz (Santiago: 1969); and L. J. Johnson, "Problems of Import Substitution: The Chilean Automobile Industry," Economic Development and Cultural Change 15 (1967), pp. 202-16.

78. Dirección Nacional de Estudios Industriales, Situación Actual y Perspectivas del Mercado de Automóviles in la República Argentina (Buenos Aires, 1969), p. 38. The previously quoted study by the Comisión de Estudios Económicos estimates that an increase to 80 percent would reduce prices by about 2.5 percent, op. cit., pp. 178-80.

79. On the incidence of export restrictions generally, see UNCTAD, op. cit., pp. 30-35.

80. Raddavero, op. cit.

81. Acevedo and Vérgara, op. cit.

82. Citroen estimates that the complementation agreement with Argentina has saved Citroen Chilena an investment of U.S. $9 million. S.A. Automobiles Citroen, Citroen in Latin America, UNIDO (ID/WG 76/18), 1970, p. 20.

83. Banco Nacional de México, Review 17 (1971).

84. Joel Luis Prendes Bonilla, Importancia de los Estímulos Fiscales en el Desarrollo de la Industria Automotriz Terminal en México (Thesis, Universidad Nacional Autónoma de México, 1969), Chap. 3.

85. AMIA and Banco de México (unpublished data).

9

ALTERNATIVE PATTERNS
OF AUTOMOTIVE INDUSTRY
DEVELOPMENT

The purpose of this chapter is to analyze the key features of
the policies adopted by the Argentinian, Chilean, and Mexican governments to promote the development of a local automotive industry,
identifying the main weaknesses of these policies. In the opening
section, the essential features of the automotive industry policy of
each of the three countries are recapitulated. Then alternative
strategies are analyzed, taking as the starting point new policies
being adopted by certain Latin American countries in the early
1970s and the experiences of certain other countries that have
developed automotive industries in the postwar period under conditions radically different from those found in Latin America, namely,
Japan, the Soviet Union, and Eastern Europe. This chapter is not
intended to provide policy prescriptions for the Latin American
automotive industry, but merely to indicate the deficiencies of
existing policies and to suggest that in other situations it has been
possible to adopt alternatives that avoid some of these difficulties.

There are two reasons why this chapter should not be taken
as a guide to policy. First, it deals with the conditions under which
the industry is set up initially, and since these decisions already
have been taken in the countries being studied, says nothing about
the second-best solution in the existing suboptimal situation. Second,
policies for the development of the automotive industry cannot be
prescribed in a vacuum, socially and politically. One only needs
to observe the fact that a radical change in Chilean policy toward
the automotive industry had to await the election of a Marxist government.

POLICIES IN ARGENTINA, CHILE
AND MEXICO

Detailed descriptions of the policies used to develop the automotive industry in each of the three counties under study have already been given in Chapter 3. Here, only the most important features common to these policies will be identified in a brief recapitulation of the main points.

First, all three countries imposed protective tariffs as part of their policies to encourage the development of a local automotive industry. These varied from 400 to 500 percent for imports of cars to Argentina (1960),[1] to 30 to 150 percent on cars in Mexico (1962),[2] with Chile in an intermediate position. Rates of protection on commercial vehicles were much lower, being below 100 percent for all three countries.[3] These tariffs were rendered insignificant, however, by the fact that free imports were not permitted. Thus, imports of vehicles to Argentina were prohibited in 1960, while in 1962 they were removed from the list of permitted imports in Chile. In Mexico they could only be imported under license. As a result, the level of nominal tariffs gives no indication of the extent of the implicit protection afforded to the local value added in the automotive industry. This has been calculated as around 180 percent in Argentina in 1960, 393 percent in Chile in 1964, and 167 percent in Mexico in the mid-1960s.* One may notice in passing that, whereas in Argentina internal competition kept implicit protection below the nominal rate, in Chile and Mexico the protection given to value added was significantly above the nominal rates.

The second feature of these policies, in addition to the protection given from imports, was the requirement that the local content of the vehicles produced should be increased. In Argentina local content was to be increased from between 55 and 70 percent (depending on category) to 90 percent for cars and from 55 to 80 percent for commercial vehicles in the period between 1960 and 1964. Similarly, in Chile, content requirements rose from 30 percent in 1963 to 57.9 percent in 1968 for cars and from 25 percent in 1966 to 50 percent in 1969 for commercial vehicles, while in Mexico,

---

*This was calculated as the excess cost of domestic value added in the industry over that value added at international prices. The data used for Argentina were from ADEFA, for Mexico from AMIA, and for Chile from Instituto de Costos. These years were chosen because they were early years of the development of the industry in each country.

firms were required to attain 60 percent local content (including production of the engine) within two years.

These percentage requirements, however, are not comparable. Whereas both the Argentinian and Chilean systems were based on international prices, that of Mexico referred to domestic prices, so that the content requirement was only about 36 percent at international prices.[4] In Chile the national content was overestimated since local content was permitted to include parts imported from other LAFTA countries under complementation agreements, as well as Chilean parts. Nevertheless, despite these difficulties in the measurement and extent of integration, the broad pattern was the same in each country.

A third feature of the policies adopted by each of these countries was the liberal treatment accorded to foreign investors. The failure of the host government to screen the investment proposals of foreign companies and to select only a limited number to prevent excessive fragmentation of the market has already been dealt with in Chapter 3. The foreign investment legislation under which the automotive industry was set up in each of these countries also reflected the openness to foreign capital of the governments in power at that time.

Most of the investment in the Argentinian automotive industry came in, as noted, under Law 14,780, which permitted both the initial capital and profits earned to be repatriated free of any restrictions. It also accepted foreign capital in the form of goods, equipment, and capitalized know-how, not requiring any hard cash to enter the country. Similarly, in Chile, the two main regulatory devices for foreign investment, Decree 1272 and DFL 258, both permitted free withdrawal of capital and profits. There were also measures to permit tariff reductions on imports of machinery. Although the Mexican government adopted a less liberal policy toward foreign investment, requiring 51 percent Mexican capital in a number of fields, it did not enforce this requirement in the automotive industry. Although legislation included clauses to ensure greater reinvestment and less remittances by foreign companies and preferential treatment for firms with majority Mexican shareholdings, these measures seem to have remained largely a dead letter.[5]

A fourth aspect of government policy was the granting of tax concessions to firms setting up in the automotive industry. In Argentina these were confined to exemptions from tariff duties for firms that imported machinery, while the industry did not receive any relief from general taxation. In Chile, Law 13,039 of 1958 granted a 50 percent exemption from import duties for firms in Arica that produced goods not manufactured elsewhere in Chile. Firms in Arica also received a 90 percent exemption from income tax and property taxes. The most generous treatment in terms of tax exemptions was probably that in Mexico. Imports of machinery were to be exempt from tariff duties for five years and imports of raw materials and components for a period of four years. Firms were also offered a reduction of 80 percent on the federal assembly tax. The cost to the government in terms of taxes foregone was estimated at 9,161 million pesos between 1965 and 1973.[6]

The final common characteristic of these policies was the failure to give priority to commercial vehicle production over car production, as it could be argued would be desirable for an under-developed country. In some respects, commercial vehicles were granted more favorable treatment. In Argentina, for example, local content requirements for commercial vehicles were less stringent than for cars, reaching 80 percent instead of 90 percent by 1964. The duty on permitted imports for commercial vehicle production was also lower, 20 percent instead of 40 percent. These factors, however, were more than offset by the much lower duty on the finished product, which was only 35 to 40 percent as opposed to 400 to 500 percent for cars.* In Chile a program for the local incorporation of parts in cars started in 1963, whereas similar legislation for commercial vehicles was not introduced until 1966, again indicating the priority given to the development of the car sector of the industry. In Mexico, too, no special incentives were given for commercial vehicle production as opposed to cars. The results can be seen in the predominance of car production from an early state in the development of the industry in each of the three countries. By the mid-1960s, more than two thirds of local vehicle production in Argentina, Chile, and Mexico was of cars and less than a third of commercial vehicles.

NEW DEVELOPMENTS IN THE LATIN AMERICAN AUTOMOTIVE INDUSTRY

In the early 1970s, Argentina, Chile, and Mexico adopted new policies toward their local automotive industries that represented a break with the previous liberal treatment of foreign capital in the industry. These were not isolated changes, confined to these three countries and this industry alone, but part of a much wider move-ment toward a more critical view of the operations of foreign

---

*This implies a level of effective protection for commercial vehicle production of only 25 percent in 1964, but this does not take direct controls in imports into account.

companies in Latin America and a new awareness of the problems they create that was evident across the continent.[7] The Argentinian and Mexican policies, on the one hand, and the Chilean policy, on the other, represent contrasting responses to the problems faced by the automotive industry.

Argentina and Mexico: The Nationalist Response

The Argentinian response was embodied in Law No. 19135 of July 1971, the so-called "Ley de la Reconversión de la Industria Automotriz." It was part of an overall concern of the Argentinian government with the problems of foreign capital and technology transfer at this time, which was also expressed in Law 18587 of February 1970 and Law 19231 of 1971, which created the National Register of Licensing and Transfer of Technology Contracts.[8] In the second article of the law, the main problems of the Argentinian automotive industry, which have been indicated in the preceding chapters, are aptly summarized in a list of objectives.

(a) gradual reduction of the price of vehicles in the internal market to enable their acquisition by relatively low income sectors.
(b) concentration of the terminal and parts industries, obtaining a greater productive efficiency with the maximum possible economies of scale.
(c) intensive promotion of national design and technology.
(d) reduction of the outflow of foreign exchange from the country to import goods or technology for the industry, with the consequent increase in national value added.
(e) significant and permanent exports of vehicles and parts.
(f) consolidation of national capital with real decision-making powers in the parts industry.[9]

The law itself does not go to the roots of these problems, namely, the dependence of the automotive industry on foreign capital, but rather represents a series of piecemeal measures designed to ameliorate the adverse consequence of this dependence. Chapter III of the law, which deals with the terminal industry, is concerned with the fragmentation of the industry, both in terms of the number of firms producing vehicles and the number of different models they offer. Article 13 suspends the establishment of any new automotive firm, except one resulting from the fusion of existing firms, until after December 31, 1980. Since the number of terminal firms is already excessive, this move will do nothing to improve the situation, and appears to be aimed only at preventing a deterioration of the position through the entry of new firms causing further fragmentation of the market.

The whole responsibility for improving the existing situation in the terminal industry rests, therefore, on measures to reduce the proliferation of models, which, as was seen above, was a contributory factor in the high costs of production of the sector. The original plan was to set minimum quotas for each model and to withdraw from production those that did not meet the quota in any six-month period. This led to strong protests and was watered down so that firms are only required before launching a new model to show that their existing average annual output per model in production exceeds a certain volume that increases from 15,000 in 1973 to 50,000 after 1980. While, on the surface, this appears to be a sensible requirement designed to reduce the excessive variety of models, it is not clear how far it will do so in practice. The definition of a basic model and its variants includes vehicles with different engines, transmissions, two- or four-door, station wagon, and van derivatives of the body, suggesting that a number of different variants will continue to be offered and that new models could be introduced without having to meet the official requirements. In the ultimate analysis, the Ministry of Industry, Commerce and Mines decides whether a car is a version of an existing model or a different model.

The same concern with excessive fragmentation of the market is also evident in Chapter II of the law, dealing with the parts industry. The setting up of new parts factories is subject to the approval of the Ministry of Industry, Commerce and Mines, as is the production of new parts not previously produced by existing firms in the parts and terminal industries. These measures are designed to prevent the trend on the part of terminal firms to integrate backward and to set up their own captive suppliers. Like the measures regarding the terminal industry, these are likely to do little more than prevent a further deterioration in the existing situation.

The second main concern of the law, as far as the parts industry is concerned, is to grant certain advantages to national firms in order to halt the increasing domination of the sector by foreign companies. In order to be considered as national for the purpose of the law, companies have to fulfill a number of requirements, the most important of which are that they:

Have their legal domicile in Argentina
Develop their principal activities in Argentina
Have at least 51 percent of their capital in the hands of people
    domiciled in the country

Have 80 percent of the directors and 90 percent of professionals,
     experts, and executives Argentinian nationals
Do not have licenses that limit exports directly or indirectly
Do not depend directly or indirectly on foreign individuals or entities

     The benefits obtained by such firms are twofold. Article 5
gives preferential access to credit from the Banco Nacional de
Desarrollo and the Banco Central de la República Argentina, as well
as preferential treatment in the purchasing policy of the government
and firms in which the government has a majority shareholding.
Second, special export incentives are offered under Article 29,
which provides for tax repayments on exports of firms that are
considered national.
     Chapter IV of the law deals with imports and is designed to
reduce the outflow of foreign exchange, both for machinery and for
parts. Imports of dies and molds for the production of bodies require
approval from the Ministry of Industry, Commerce and Mines, which
will be granted usually for new models, where 90 percent of the total
dies and molds are produced locally or when at least 50 percent of
the production will be exported during the next five years. At the
same time, the direct outflow of foreign exchange for parts will be
reduced by a lowering of the permitted import content to 4 percent
of the FOB value for cars and 10 percent for commercial vehicles.
     Another measure designed to reduce the foreign exchange costs
of the industry is the creation of a register of license and technology
transfer contracts. Royalty payments will be limited to a maximum
of 2 percent of the total value of sales and new contracts can only
be registered when they do not impose arbitrary restrictions on the
recipient, such as tie-in clauses for equipment or materials,
restrictions on exports, and an obligation to pay royalties on licenses
not used.
     As was seen in Chapter 8, the Peronist government took further
steps to reduce the balance of payments costs imposed by the automotive industry through Decree 680/73 to promote car exports.
This decree imposed quotas for the domestic market that depended
on the firm's having a satisfactory export performance. As already
indicated, some success was achieved in expanding exports, although
the companies are likely to face increasing difficulties in meeting
the export requirements laid down.
     The Mexican decree passed in 1972 to regulate the future
development of the automotive industry was similar in many respects
to the Argentinian law of the previous year. It was essentially a
reformist measure designed to improve some of the features of the
industry without any fundamental change in structure. The declared

objectives of the law were to increase employment and exports, to develop a structure of supply that would be more appropriate to Mexico's needs and the purchasing power of the population, to increase productivity and to strengthen the participation of Mexican capital in the parts industry.

As in Argentina, an attempt is made to limit the proliferation of models in the Mexican industry. Those firms producing popular models, that is, Dina, Nissan, and Volkswagen, are not permitted to produce models in the other categories of cars, while those that produce compact, standard, and sports models, that is, Chrysler, Ford, General Motors, and VAM, are excluded from the popular car sector. A further measure to limit model diversity is that from 1974 firms producing popular cars will not be allowed to produce more than four lines with three models up to a maximum of seven models in all and the firms producing U.S. style cars can only produce three lines with three models, also providing that the total number of models is no more than seven. Although this measure might prevent further model diversification by the car companies, it did little to reduce the existing proliferation of models, since only VAM, which produced seven models in four different lines, was above the limit in 1973. Similarly, a clause that required firms that wished to produce more than one basic gasoline engine to export more than 60 percent of the new engines was not likely to have much effect because of the broad definition of a basic engine.

A major part of the decree is concerned with the promotion of exports in order to compensate for the outflow of foreign exchange incurred by the automotive industry (see Chapter 8). In line with the policy of promoting the parts industry, 40 percent of the exports required each year to compensate for imports to meet the basic quota must come from the auxiliary industry and no more than 60 percent can be produced by the terminal firms themselves. Parts manufacturers must have at least 60 percent of their share capital in the hands of Mexicans.

As has already been mentioned, there are contradictions between the different objectives being pursued by the Mexican government. The attempt to expand exports of vehicles and parts leads to a closer integration of the Mexican automotive industry with the global operations of the multinational corporations whose subsidiaries operate in the country, contributing to the denationalization of the terminal industry. It is not likely that a strong national parts industry can be built up if at the same time it depends on the foreign terminal producers for markets. Under these circumstances, it is unlikely that parts producers, which are formally in majority Mexican ownership, have much real independence.

Chile: The Socialist Response

Chile, at the time of the election of President Allende in 1970, was in one respect better placed to restructure its local automotive industry than was Argentina. As has already been pointed out, the terminal industry in Chile was still essentially an assembly industry and neither the engine nor the main body parts were produced locally. Consequently, what little investment there was in fixed assets was mainly in buildings and general-purpose tools, rather than highly specialized machinery that could only be used in the automotive industry. As a result, the Chilean government had much more room to maneuver and could, if it so wished, build up a new automotive industry from scratch without having to write off large sums of existing capital.

The objectives of the government in restructuring the automotive industry were the following:

(a) to produce commercial vehicles and cars for mass consumption.

(b) to develop the technology of national industry, especially the metal-mechanical industries, and create infrastructural conditions which permit the development of new high technology industries for export.

(c) to create, directly or indirectly, high productivity jobs.

(d) to obtain fiscal resources and appropriate economic surpluses.

(e) to compensate for the foreign exchange expenditures which satisfying the demand for cars implies.

(f) to obtain the necessary efficiency in the industry in order to be able to exchange with LAFTA and the Andean Pact without losses for the country and within the competitive margin.[10]

It was decided that the most appropriate way of achieving these ends was to open the industry to international bidding. The broad outlines of the form that the development of the industry should take was laid down in June 1971.[11] The number of models was to be restricted to one small car of less than 1,200 cc and its commercial vehicle derivative (category A), one medium-sized car between 1,300 and 2,000 cc and its commercial vehicle derivative (category B), and a chassis with diesel engine for a 6- to 8-ton truck and a bus chassis based on the same mechanical parts (category C). It was planned to produce 40,000 vehicles in 1973, rising to 100,000 by 1980, distributed as follows among the three categories:[12]

	1973	1980
Category A	20,000	45,000
Category B	15,000	40,000
Category C	5,000	15,000

The permitted import content (except parts imported under LAFTA complementation agreements) was 30 percent of the FOB price for cars and 40 percent for trucks. At the same time, the local content should include the engine, the gear box, and the differential. In the case of the engines for cars, they should have a local content of 80 percent by weight, while for the diesel engine for trucks and buses, this should be 50 percent. The vehicles are to be produced in a joint company between CORFO and the foreign company selected, in which CORFO will have a minimum of 51 percent and a maximum of 60 percent of the share capital and a majority of the directors. The contract between the two partners will be for an initial period of ten years and renewable thereafter. The contribution of the foreign partner must be mainly in the form of convertible currency, but the balance may be made up from credits for the purchase of machinery and equipment, as long as such contributions are free from any tie-in clauses. Under no circumstances can capitalized know-how form part of the contribution of the foreign partner. Finally, the Chilean government offers to guarantee a minimum post-tax return, which may be repatriated, of no more than 6.5 percent on the subscribed capital, and a maximum rate of repatriation of 12 percent of capital and reserves is imposed.

These, then, are the basic outlines of the form to be taken by the Chilean automotive industry. In the selection of projects in each of the three categories, a number of criteria were considered. First was the amount of investment required to meet the levels of output planned in the proposal, and the manpower requirements by degree of expertise. Second, a number of measures of the FOB price of the vehicle to be produced in its country of origin were considered, for example, price per horsepower and price per kilogram. Third, the extent to which exports outside the LAFTA complementation agreements were developed played an important part. Consideration was also given to the payments for technical assistance both in the setting up phase and during normal operations. (Royalty payments as a proportion of either the value or volume of production were not permitted.) The amount and terms of the contribution of the foreign firm and the credits offered to CORFO to finance its own share in the company were also considered. Finally, the lower the minimum profit guarantee and the lower the maximum repatriation accepted by the foreign company the more favorably would the project be viewed.[13]

In practice, it was found that the investment requirements involved in the different projects did not vary greatly. It was also decided that the prices of cars of similar size and quality did not differ significantly in their country of origin, so that this factor, too, did not play an important part in the final decision. The key factor, therefore, came to be the net foreign exchange costs of the various projects, that is, setting the total exports offered against the outflow of exchange to pay for parts, technical assistance fees, and profit repatriations. In determining to which firms to give preference, the net foreign exchange outflow of the different projects over the period 1973-80 was discounted at a rate of 6 percent. The main differences between the various proposals were on the side of exports proposed and credits offered to finance the investment by CORFO.

The number of firms that participated in the bidding, despite the restrictive conditions proposed by the government, such as the maximum rate of profit repatriation, is a further illustration of the workings of competition in the international automotive industry (see Chapters 2 and 3). Four companies participated in each of the three categories: British Leyland, Citroen, Fiat, and Renault in small cars; Fiat, Nissan, Peugeot, and Volvo in medium-sized cars; and Fiat, Pegaso, Fap Famos, and British Leyland in trucks. In February 1972, it was decided to hold further discussions with Citroen and Renault in category A and Fiat and Pegaso in category C. In category B none of the projects came to the required standard since they would have meant an exchange loss of at least U.S. $130 million over the period.

The bidding was seen by the Chilean authorities as only the first step in the process of bargaining with the international companies. Some of the presentations made by the firms had been extremely vague about the extent of their commitment to export from Chile and this offered scope for negotiation. For example, the original Peugeot offer only undertook to export gear boxes and back-axles, the annual value of which would be less than U.S. $2 million. Apart from this, the firm indicated its willingness to encourage exports of Chilean copper to France and to study the possibility of exporting finished vehicles to eastern Europe. (It seemed a foregone conclusion that the possibilities were negligible.)

In the contract eventually signed with Peugeot, exports were increased to U.S. $102,711,000 over an eight-year period, of which exports of automotive products accounted for more than U.S. $75 million. As a result the foreign exchange costs of the project were reduced to U.S. $3 million a year.[14] Similarly, in the case of Citroen, the firm originally offered to exports good to the value of U.S. $15 million up to 1980 and the Chilean government was able to increase this almost fourfold to U.S. $59.8 million.

The Chilean government also was able to reduce the rate of return received by the foreign company. In the case of Peugeot, the firm originally had requested a guaranteed minimum profit of 6.5 percent and a maximum return that could be repatriated of 10 percent, but eventually accepted 6.5 percent as both the minimum and maximum. Other changes led to a reduction in the internal rate of return (including payments for technical assistance) to 14 percent in the contract eventually adopted.

After a period of negotiation, the firms selected were Citroen in category A, Peugeot in category B, and Pegaso in category C. This created a political problem for the Unidad Popular government since it meant that of the four automotive centers in the country, Arica, Los Andes, Casablanca, and Rancagua, the last-named would be left without a plant. This would mean the closure of the existing Fiat plant and the loss of over 1,000 jobs. Fiat mobilized its workers to protest against this decision and, as a result of this pressure, the government reached an agreement with Nissan only four days before the military coup, by which it would produce an intermediate-sized car between the Citroen and the Peugeot models. This was accommodated by reducing Citroen's share of the cars less than 1,200 cc market to 65 percent of the total.

It is interesting to compare the terms of the contracts between CORFO and Citroen, Peugeot, and Pegaso, respectively.* As far as guaranteed profits and remittances permitted are concerned, the most favorable conditions from the point of view of the firm were those obtained by Pegaso. The company was guaranteed a return of 6.5 percent, the same as Peugeot and 1.5 percent more than Citroen, and permitted to remit up to 12 percent compared to 10 percent for Citroen and 6.5 percent for Peugeot. From the Chilean point of view, the most favorable offer of technical assistance came from Citroen, which charged only U.S. $231,000 compared to U.S. $550,000 for Pegaso and U.S. $3 million for Peugeot. It is by no means clear from the contracts why Peugeot's charges are so much greater than those of the other firms, and it can only be surmised that either the other firms are intending to transfer profits in other ways or that Peugeot found itself in a stronger bargaining position than Citroen and Pegaso.

One of the most important aspects of these agreements, from the Chilean point of view, is the undertaking by the companies to make substantial exports to offset the foreign exchange costs of the

---

*No contract was drawn up between CORFO and Nissan, only a declaration of intent, which was not sufficiently detailed to permit comparison with the other contracts.

imported parts. These exports have been estimated at about U.S. $60 million for Citroen, U.S. $100 million for Peugeot, and U.S. $240 million by Pegaso over the period 1973-80, which compares with a total of U.S. $30 million exported by the industry between 1965 and 1971. Not only is the volume of exports to be increased but this will involve exporting new products and developing new markets, such as France, Spain, Madagascar, Nigeria, and Greece.

In the case of Peugeot and Pegaso, however, not all the exports are automotive products. Peugeot will realize about 20 percent of its total exports in other nontraditional products, while 60 percent of Pegaso's exports will be nonautomotive, mainly pulp, copper products, iron ore, and saltpeter (hardly nontraditional products, it should be noted). In the case of both Citroen and Pegaso, these exports would compensate entirely for the imports of CKD material required, while, as mentioned earlier, in the case of Peugeot there would be an annual exchange cost of U.S. $3 million.

The joint ventures formed with Citroen and Peugeot used as their basis the existing affiliates of the two firms, Industria Citroen S.A. and Automotores Franco Chilena S.A. The state has a participation of 50.6 percent in the joint venture with Citroen and 60 percent in that with Peugeot as a result of an increase in the capital of both companies. Consequently, the new investment the foreign partners have to make is minimal. The initial Citroen contribution is entirely made up of the existing subsidiary, with a further U.S. $2 million over a three-year period, while Peugeot's 40 percent share comes mainly from its holdings in and loans to Automotores Franco Chilena and Cormecanica, with only U.S. $360,000 out of a total of U.S. $2,640,000 being supplied in foreign exchange.[15] The case of Pegaso is somewhat different since it is not based on an existing affiliate. CORFO has a 51 percent share in the joint venture, while Pegaso is obliged to make an investment of U.S. $9,555,000. Production was to be based at the old Ford assembly plant at Casablanca, which had been taken over by CORFO, and would provide part of the government's contribution.

The last agreement with Pegaso was much criticized within Chile. Originally, category C had been awarded to Fiat with Pegaso in second place. It is generally recognized that a Spanish government offer of U.S. $50 million credit to import grain at a time when the country was going through a grave political and economic crisis in 1972 as a result of the truck owners strike was an important consideration in signing the contract with Pegaso. It has been suggested that the vehicle that Pegaso proposed to build in Chile was not adequate for local conditions, and that there may be supply problems in the case of parts provided from Spain because of the firm's small size in that country. It is interesting to note in this context that CORFO was not able to obtain such favorable terms in the case of its agreement with Pegaso, as in the other two contracts, not for reasons specific to the automotive industry, but because of the change in Chile's general economic and political situation by the time that the contract came to be signed, which weakened the government's bargaining position.

It is impossible, at present, to analyze the consequences of the Argentinian, Mexican, and Chilean measures. The effect of the Argentinian law will depend very much on the strictness with which it is applied by the Ministry of Industry, Commerce and Mines. As has already been suggested, it seems more likely to act as a stop-gap measure to prevent further deterioration in the industry than to solve the fundamental problems that afflict it. Similar considerations apply in the case of Mexico. In Chile the military coup of September 1973 put an end to the developments initiated by the Unidad Popular. The Chilean solution, too, had its weaknesses, deriving from the low levels of output, even if those projected are achieved, and the requirement that the engine, gear box, and differential are produced locally, and the priority given to car production over commercial vehicles.* Nevertheless, the setting up of joint companies, in which CORFO had a majority holding, gave the Chilean system advantages in terms of control and of access to information.

THE JAPANESE MODEL

The Japanese case provides an interesting comparison for the Latin American automotive industry because of its relatively recent development. As late as 1957, when the first steps toward the development of a local automotive industry already had been taken in Brazil and Argentina, the Japanese automotive industry was still comparatively small with a total output of around 182,000 vehicles in that year, of which only 47,000 were passenger cars. This represents a lower level of production than is currently achieved in Argentina or Mexico. It is relevant to ask, therefore, how the Japanese automotive industry became, within a period of ten years, the second largest vehicle producer in the world after the United States. In the following sections the main characteristics of the development of the automotive industry in Japan are indicated and

----

*ECLA projections of the demand for cars and commercial vehicles in Chile in 1980 put them at 50,000 and 58,200, respectively, compared to the production planned of 85,000 and 15,000.

then the part played by the government in this development is discussed.

The development of the Japanese automotive industry during the early 1950s in many ways was similar to the early development of the industry in Latin America. The local firms were involved in collaboration agreements with foreign producers, such as those between Nissan and Austin, Isuzu and Rootes, Hino and Renault, and Mitsubishi Heavy Industries and Willys, all concluded in 1952 and 1953. Moreover, in the early years, almost all the parts were imported in the form of SKD or CKD packs. Japanese parts were gradually incorporated, with Nissan achieving full domestic production by 1956, followed in 1957 by Isuzu and a year later by Hino. Having achieved 100 percent domestic content, the Japanese firms were able to go on to develop their own models when the contracts with the foreign firms expired. The Nissan contract with Austin terminated in 1960 and the local firm introduced its own Cedric model. Similarly, the Isuzu contract with Rootes, although extended to 1965, was subsequently terminated.

The basis of the rapid expansion of the 1960s was the explosive growth of home demand. New registrations of vehicles in Japan grew ten times during the 1960s, from just over 400,000 at the beginning of the decade to more than 4 million in 1970. Although exports grew more rapidly than production for the home market and faster than the exports of any other country, they did not contribute a great deal to the overall expansion of production because of their small share of total output. This, however, increased from 4 percent in 1961 to 18 percent in 1969 and 29 percent by 1973,[16] still low in comparison to the major European producing countries. The growth of home demand was a consequence of the tremendous boom enjoyed by the Japanese economy, which experienced an average growth rate of more than 11 percent per year over the decade from 1959 to 1969, and of the low level of motorization (in terms of vehicles per inhabitant given the country's income level) at the beginning of the period. Since 1969 there appears to have been a change in the situation with exports now assuming the dominant role for the growth of the industry and the expansion of the domestic market showing signs of slowing down.

The 1960s saw a considerable concentration of production in the automotive industry. Although Toyota and Nissan had accounted for virtually all Japan's car production before the war, their position had been considerably weakened by 1960. At that time there were 12 vehicle producers in Japan, and the two leading firms held 60 percent of the market. In 1963, the Ministry of Trade and Industry (MITI) began to encourage a rationalization of the industry that led to mergers between Nissan and Prince in 1966 and Toyota and

Daihatsu Kogyo in 1967. There have also been business links between
the Big Two and other producers. Thus, the Toyota group, in addition
to Daihatsu, also includes Hino, and it seems likely that Suzuki will
join it in the near future. The Nissan group includes Fuji Heavy
Industries and the two commercial vehicle producers, Aichi Machine
Industry and Nissan Diesel. Between them, the two groups accounted
for more than 70 percent of Japanese vehicle production in 1973.
Outside these two groups there are only four remaining producers,
the independent Toyo-Kogyo and Honda and two firms linked, respectively, to Chrysler and General Motors, Mitsubishi and Isuzu.

This concentration, coupled with the rapid growth of the market,
meant a vast increase in production for the two major companies
whose output increased from just over 100,000 in 1960 to 2,692,393
for Toyota and 2,271,448 for Nissan in 1973, making them among
the largest automotive companies in the world and the second and
third largest firms in Japan. This, together with fewer versions
of basic models (for example, Toyota only offers two versions of
the Corolla 1200 compared to the ten versions of British Leyland's
1300 and seven of the Vauxhall Viva), means that the companies are
able to obtain long production runs of about 240,000 cars a year for
these models.[17]

Another characteristic of the industry has been the predominant
role played by commercial vehicles as opposed to cars. Production
of commercial vehicles exceeded that of cars until as recently as
1967. In 1951, car production accounted for only 10 percent of the
total output of the industry rising to 31 percent in 1961 and 64 percent by 1971. The predominance of commercial vehicle production
was not only a quantitative phenomenon. Whereas in the United
States and Western Europe truck production has been more or less
subordinated to car production, in Japan the reverse was true.
Thus the development of productivity and engineering techniques in
passenger car production has been based on developments in commercial vehicle production. In the early stages of the industry,
production equipment was used in common. Finally full-fledged
car production was established on the basis of capital accumulation
in the truck industry.[18] Some of the car producers, such as Isuzu
and Hino, diversified from commercial vehicle manufacture into
cars, while even the old established car firms, such as Toyota and
Nissan, produced mainly commercial vehicles during the 1950s.

Government Policy

In some respects, the policy of the Japanese government toward
the development of a local automotive industry was similar to that

adopted by the Latin American countries studied. One similarity
was the protection afforded to domestic producers against imports
of vehicles. During the early 1960s, imports reached about 1 percent of total production and since then have fallen to less than half
that amount. The protection provided took several forms. Until
1968, passenger cars were subject to an import duty of 40 percent
and commercial vehicles to a tariff of 30 percent. In the early 1950s,
when foreign imports threatened to overcome this tariff because of
the high cost and technical backwardness of locally produced cars,
foreign currency control was introduced, which provided additional
protection until removed in 1957. Passenger cars were also subject
to quota restrictions until 1965 and all motor vehicles, parts, and
components were thus controlled until 1970. Unfortunately, it is
not possible to gauge exactly how much implicit protection was
afforded to the industry by these measures taken together during
the formative stage of the industry's development.[19] It was sufficient
however, to enable the Japanese producers to earn high profits,
which were then plowed back into domestic expansion.

The key difference between the policy pursued by the Japanese
and that of the Latin American countries was that they did not exclude
the international automotive companies from participating in the
market through imports, only to let them in again as direct investors.
Before the war, both General Motors and Ford had assembled cars
in Japan. In the postwar period, however, foreign capital participation in the automotive industry was limited to 7 percent of the
share capital for an individual entity and 20 percent in total. This
measure was designed to prevent the international companies,
especially the U.S. firms, from buying into controlling positions
in Japanese companies and benefiting from the rapid growth of the
domestic market. Thus, although in the 1950s, as just seen,
Japanese companies produced under license from a number of
European firms, this did not lead to the progressive denationalization of the industry that occurred in Latin America.

Recently, the Japanese government has opened up somewhat
its automotive industry to foreign participation. This has permitted
Chrysler to take a 35 percent shareholding in Mitsubishi and for
General Motors to come to a similar agreement with Isuzu. The
extent of this liberalization is limited and has been motivated by
the importance that the United States has assumed as a market for
Japanese vehicles (about 700,000 were exported there in 1971) and
the fear that restrictive measures would be taken against Japanese
imports unless some concessions were granted.

The timing of the liberalization measure is also significant.
MITI has been preparing the ground for such a move since 1963,
encouraging the polarization of the industry around Toyota and

Nissan. This has now been largely achieved, leaving only the two
large groups and four smaller producers. As one report on the
industry summed up the situation, "Liberalization, such as it is,
has been delayed for the motor industry until the last possible moment
to maximize the home manufacturers' advantage."[20] Moreover,
MITI has been urging further measures to strengthen the automotive
industry, including tax incentives and loan capital for mergers to
hasten rationalization and preventive measures against takeovers
by foreign firms.

What, then, have been the consequences of the maintenance
of national control over the Japanese automotive industry? In the
first place, it seems unlikely that the same degree of concentration
and rationalization of production could have occurred had the local
automotive industry been entirely dominated by subsidiaries of international companies. We already have seen how in Latin America
the tendency has been, once any locally owned producers have been
eliminated from the industry, for concentration to come to a halt
and for the market to remain fragmented between an excessive
number of firms. The Japanese automotive industry has avoided
such an outcome, and while this must partly be a consequence of
the energetic pursuit of rationalization within the industry by MITI,
it was made possible by the local ownership of all the firms in the
industry.

The second factor that derived from national control of the
automotive industry in Japan was the ability of the industry to make
the transition from growth based on the domestic market to an
export-oriented growth when the former began to slow down at the
end of the 1960s. In 1971, the first year in which new registrations
of vehicles in Japan decreased, growth of production was maintained
by an increase in exports of 63.7 percent. Exports to the United
States in 1971 almost doubled in volume compared to those of 1970,
and accounted for almost half the total. It is interesting in this
context to compare Japan's exports of 653,695 passenger cars to
the United States (mainly by Toyota and Nissan) in 1971 with the
total of less than 200,000 cars imported by the Big Three U.S.
producers from their affiliates overseas in the same year.[21] It is
difficult to believe that subsidiaries of U.S. companies would have
been permitted to make such major inroads into the domestic
market, not to mention the situation in third countries.

Another feature of the Japanese automotive industry that can
be partly attributed to its independence from foreign, especially
United States, domination, is the development of a product appropriate to local conditions. Virtually all the cars produced in Japan
have an engine capacity of less than 2,000 cc, with only 1 percent
of total production in 1969 being above this size. This is a conse-

quence of deliberate government policy giving preferential treatment
to cars of less than 2,000 cc. Since 1969, these have been subject
to a 15 percent commodity tax, whereas the tax on cars in the 2,000
to 3,000 cc class was 30 percent and that on luxury cars of over
3,000 cc, 50 percent. The government and the industry decided to
foster small car production since this was the sector with the best
prospects for exports.22 Again, it is difficult to see a country
where the major producers of cars were subsidiaries of General
Motors, Ford, or Chrysler being able to discriminate so heavily
against large cars.* In the same way, the development of small
cars and commercial vehicles with an engine capacity of less than
360 cc, a vehicle especially adapted to Japanese conditions, is
difficult to imagine in an industry composed of foreign subsidiaries.

THE SOVIET UNION AND EASTERN EUROPE

It is obvious that the form taken by the development of the
automotive industry in the socialist countries will be completely
different from both the dependent capitalist development found in the
Latin American countries and the independent capitalist development
of Japan. Unfortunately, there is no full-length study of the industry
in these countries available in English so that it has not been possible
to undertake a detailed investigation of the development of the industry.

A number of features of the automotive industry in Eastern
Europe and the USSR are well known. Perhaps the best known of
these is the priority given to commercial vehicles as opposed to
car production, a feature shared in common with the Japanese automotive industry. This is a direct consequence of government
decisions to allocate resources to truck production, which represents
production of investment goods, rather than to cars, which are a
consumer product. As Table 9.1 shows, heavy concentration on
commercial vehicles has only been pursued in the Soviet Union, the
other countries having proportions much closer to those of the
capitalist countries.

Car production has been concentrated on a few models in all
the countries under consideration, and the losses of economies of
scale due to market fragmentation have been avoided despite the
fact that government restrictions have kept total car output low.
In the USSR, five models were being produced in 1971 for a total

*It is interesting to contrast this with the really very limited
discrimination against large cars in the 1959 Argentinian legislation,
which was subsequently changed under U.S. pressure. See Chapter 3.

TABLE 9.1

Circulation of Cars and All Vehicles, 1970
(thousands of units)

	Cars	Total
USSR	1,560.0	5,635.0
Czechoslovakia	651.6	843.8
East Germany	980.0	1,200.0
Poland	479.4	771.7

Source: Motor Vehicle Manufacturers Association of the
United States, Inc., 1971 World Motor Vehicle Data (Detroit: 1972).

market of about 420,000 cars, an average output of 84,000. The
number produced varied from 20,000 for the Izhevsk to 180,000
for the Zhigula (the new car based on the Fiat 124).[23] The other
East European countries also produced a limited number of different
cars in order to obtain long production runs. Czechoslovakia produced almost 150,000 Skodas in 1971, while East Germany produced
about 90,000 Trabants and a few Wartburgs. In Poland, three models
are produced, the Fiat 125P, the Warzawa, and the Syrena, with a
total output of around 85,000. The Warzawa, however, is obsolete
and only produced in small quantities in the Fiat factory. Rumania,
when it began to produce cars at the end of the 1960s, chose to concentrate on one model, the Renault R-12.

Commercial vehicle production similarly has been concentrated
in a number of specialized establishments. In the Soviet Union, for
example, each factory concentrates on one model and its modifications. Since the factories are not in competition with each other,
there is no pressure to provide a whole range of models. Thus,
the Likachev works in Moscow specializes in medium trucks; the
GAZ works in Gorky, in light commercial vehicles and cars; the
Belaz works in Zhodino, in superheavy trucks; and the MAZ works
in Minsk, on medium and heavy trucks—to name only the most
important factories. This enables extremely large scales of production to be achieved; for example, the Likachev works is believed
to have a capacity of about 600 trucks a day. As one Soviet authority
points out, "Specialization and concentration are the characteristic
features of the automobile industry in the Soviet Union and form the
basis of mass production, which in turn is essential for the efficient
organization of production and for the maintenance of the production
process at a high technical level."[24] A similar pattern is followed
in Eastern Europe. In Czechoslovakia, for example, there are six

different commercial vehicle factories, each specializing in different
types or sizes of vehicles, while in Poland there are three main
commercial vehicle factories at Sarachowice (4-ton truck), Lublin
(light CVs and vans), and Jelez (8-ton truck).

The development of the automotive industry in the USSR and
Eastern Europe has relied heavily on technical assistance from the
major international automotive companies. The earliest development of the Russian automotive industry was in the period 1928-32
when new plants were set up in Moscow and Gorky and mass production organized in accordance with the most advanced techniques of
the day. In order to do this, U.S. experts, mainly from Ford,
provided technical assistance. More recently, in the late 1960s,
there has been a new spate of technical assistance contracts between
Eastern Europe and Western companies, mainly Fiat and Renault.
Fiat has set up plants in the Soviet Union, Poland, and Bulgaria;
Renault, in the Soviet Union, Czechoslovakia, Rumania, and Bulgaria.

The Rumanian contract with Renault is an interesting example
of the provisions of these technical assistance agreements.[25] Production was to be concentrated on one model, the R-12, although
initially CKD R-8s were imported and assembled locally as a means
of giving some training to the local work force. Local content was
set at 55 percent but it was intended to achieve 95 percent content
eventually. A number of subcontracts were signed transferring
the production of Estafette (the Renault van) gear boxes and front
and rear axles to Rumania, for export to France, in order to offset
the foreign exchange costs of parts imports. The procurement of
machinery was divided between Renault, which provided those
requiring special controls and a great deal of technical assistance
during assembly, and local suppliers, which provided machine tools
of a general nature. The control of the company remained in
Rumanian hands. In 1971, 20,000 cars were produced and it was
thought that the 1973 target of 50,000 cars with a 95 percent local
content would be achieved by 1974.

The development of the Yugoslav automotive industry has not
yet been mentioned in this section since present trends have more
in common with developments in underdeveloped capitalist economies
than with the other East European countries. Up to the mid-1960s,
the pattern was not significantly different, with production being
concentrated in four commercial vehicle producers and one car firm,
with two assembly plants producing a few cars. The Economic
Reform of the mid-1960s liberalized imports and aimed to make
profitability the prime concern of enterprises and establish the
convertibility of the dinar. As a result, imports rose rapidly to
account for 42 percent of the car market in 1969, falling subsequently
to 28 percent in 1971. There was also an increase in the number of

assemblers to four, each producing at a relatively small scale but
accounting for 33 percent of the total market by 1971.[26] The major
local firm (and the only producer to manufacture cars locally), ZCZ,
found its market share reduced to less than 40 percent. Following
measures in 1967 to permit foreign investment in Yugoslav enterprises, Fiat has invested $17 million in ZCZ and the company also
has received capital from the International Bank for Reconstruction
and Development and the International Finance Corporation to expand
its capacity. The opportunity to develop an independent automotive
industry has been passed over and the path of increased collaboration
with foreign companies is being followed.

The USSR and East European automotive industries do have
problems of their own. These take the form of outdated models and
old machinery, reflecting a lack of investment allocated to the sector,
particularly car production.[27] The significance of the experience
of the socialist countries for those of Latin America in this context
is twofold. The first aspect is the possibility of entering into technical agreements with the companies concerned without relinquishing
control over the local operations. The second point has been aptly
summed up by V. Pobedonostsev:

> This production system is due to the socialist nature of
> the Soviet economy. The development of the USSR auto-
> mobile industry is planned by competent government
> organizations, who, guided by the economic law of social-
> ism, will not permit the production of automobiles of the
> same tonnage and the same type at different factories.[28]

CONCLUSION

It appears from this chapter that the problems of the Latin
American automotive industry derive not so much from the inward-
oriented strategy of industrialization (which was shared in common
with Japan, the Soviet Union, and Eastern Europe) but from the
openness of the strategy in terms of its treatment of foreign capital,
which meant that the firms that benefited from the protectionist
measures were international companies and not national companies,
as in Japan, or state enterprises, as in the socialist countries.[29]
The failure to develop a rational productive structure, to develop
exports, or to give priority to commercial vehicle production over
cars can be traced back to the location of decision centers abroad
and the fact that the decisions taken are made with reference to a
larger global situation in which the individual Latin American country
is only one parameter. Furthermore, tariff protection and favorable

demand conditions in the early years of the development of the industry gave rise to high profits for foreign companies rather than providing a basis for internal accumulation as in Japan or the USSR. Put in a nutshell, these are all problems of dependent capitalist development.

NOTES

1. S. J. Parellada, "La Industria Automotriz en la Argentina," UNIDO (ID/WG 76/9), 1970, p. 174.

2. S. Macario, "Protectionism and Industrialization in Latin America," Economic Bulletin for Latin America 9 (1964): 61-101.

3. See Macario, ibid., for Chile and Mexico; and Parellada, op. cit., for Argentina.

4. See G. M. Bueno, "La Industria Siderúrgica y la Industria Automotriz," El Perfil de México en 1980, vol. 2 (Mexico City: Siglo XXI, 1971), p. 96.

5. See K. Rethwisch, "An Economic Analysis of the Mexican System of Developing an Automotive Industry and Some Proposed Alternatives" (Thesis, University of Maryland, 1969), Chap. 5.

6. Asociación Nacional de Fabricantes de Productos Auto-mótrices, El Presente y Futuro de la Industria Automotriz Mexicana (Mexico City: 1974), p. 38.

7. For an analysis of this movement and its origins, see C. V. Vaitsos, "The Changing Policies of Latin American Governments toward Economic Development and Direct Foreign Investment," paper presented at the Conference on Latin American-U.S. Economic Interactions, University of Texas at Austin, March 1973.

8. See J. Rubinstein, "El Reciente Régimen Jurídico Argentino de Nacionalidad de las Sociedades y Transferencia de Tecnología" (Paper presented at the FLACSO/ILDIS Conference, Santiago, 1971).

9. Ley No. 19135, Artículo 2 (author's translation).

10. D. Barkin, El Consumo y la Vía Chilena al Socialismo: Reflexiones en Torno a la Decisión Automotriz, mimeographed (1971), p. 2, on the basis of internal documents of the Comisión Automotriz.

11. Corporación de Fomento (CORFO), Licitación Pública Internacional, Industria Automotriz, Chile, 1971.

12. It has been suggested that such levels of output of cars are incompatible with the avowed income redistribution policies of the Unidad Popular government; see Barkin, op. cit., and S. Bitar and E. Moyano, "Redistribución del Consumo y Transicion al Socialismo," Cuadernos de la Realidad Mexicana, no. 11 (1972), pp. 25-44. We do not wish to enter into the debate over whether a socialist government in Chile should be developing an automotive industry at all.

13. It is interesting to contrast this approach with that advocated in UNIDO publications, which recommend giving top priority to choosing a model of car suitable for local conditions and only then considering the economic and financial terms on which this can be obtained. See UNIDO, The Motor Vehicle Industry (ID/78), 1972, pp. 57-70.

14. CORFO, Rapport du Comité d'Opérations Automotrices (Document presented to UNCTAD III, 1972).

15. S. Colvin, Algunos Antecedentes del Sector Automotriz en Chile: La Licitación Internacional y los Convenios Firmados con las Firmas Extranjeras, Departamento de Industrias, Facultad de Ciéncias Físicas y Matemáticas, Universidad de Chile, Publicación No. 75/05/C, 1973.

16. National Economic Development Office (NEDO), Japan: Its Motor Industry and Market (H.M.S.O., 1971), Appendix 16; and Toyota Motor Sales Co., 1974 The Motor Industry of Japan (Tokyo, 1974), p. 6.

17. NEDO, op. cit., p. 41.

18. S. Yamamoto, The Latest Development in Japanese Automobile Industry and Some Suggestions for Developing Countries, UNIDO (ID/WG 13/27), 1968, pp. 13-14.

19. An indication that prices of cars in Japan were considerably higher than in other developed countries in the 1950s is the fact that despite a reduction in price of more than 30 percent since the mid-1950s, the price per pound weight and per horsepower of Japanese cars tended to be higher than those of the other major producing countries in 1964. See I. Kravis and R. Lipsey, Price Competitiveness in World Trade (New York: National Bureau of Economic Research, 1971). At the end of 1956, the Austin A50, which sold at £514 in Britain, was being produced by Nissan in Japan and selling at around £1,000. This ratio of almost 2 is comparable to those at present found in Argentina with a similar local content.

20. NEDO, op. cit., p. 85.

21. Chrysler imported 55,000 Hillman Avengers and Mitsubishi Colts, General Motors, 85,000 Opels and Ford, 53,000 Capris from Germany. See Economist Intelligence Unit, "National Policies vs. International Economics," Multinational Business, no. 3 (1972), pp. 30-37.

22. See NEDO, op. cit., Chap. 7.

23. Economist Intelligence Unit, "The Russian Motor Vehicle Industry," Motor Business, no. 69 (1972): 30-45.

24. V. Pobedonostsev, The State and Development of the USSR Automotive Industry: Its Role and Significance in the National Economy, UNIDO (ID/WG 13/9), 1968, p. 16.

25. What follows is based on V. Anghel, Development of the Automobile Industry in Romania and Collaboration with Industry in Developed Countries, UNIDO (ID/WG 136/17), 1972.

26. Tomos 8,143, Unis 14,446, IMV 8,968, and Litostroj 6,302. P. Rakovic, Development of the Automotive Industry in Developing Countries in Cooperation with Industries in the Developed Countries, UNIDO (ID/WG 136/4), 1972, Table 3.

27. Insofar as this is a consequence of a deliberate decision to give priority to other sectors, then too much significance should not be attached to the lower productivity of the Soviet automotive industry relative to that of the advanced capitalist countries. Factors affecting the productivity of Soviet industry as a whole lie outside our scope, but see H. Ticktin, "Towards a Political Economy of the USSR," Critique 1 (1973): 20-41.

28. Pobedonostsev, op. cit., p. 15.

29. For this distinction, see F. Fajnzylber, "La Empresa Internacional en la Industrialización de América Latina" (Paper presented at FLACSO/ILDIS Conference, 1971), pp. 1-4.

10

CONCLUSIONS: DEPENDENT
INDUSTRIALIZATION AND
LATIN AMERICAN
DEVELOPMENT

This book has analyzed Latin American industrialization in the light of the experience of one particular industry. It has shown the way in which the development of the Latin American automotive industry is conditioned by developments in the international industry, of which the former is an integral part. Chapters 2 and 3 discussed the growth of concentration within the national automotive industries of the developed countries and the subsequent internationalization of the industry and the way in which the industry grew up, first as an assembly industry and then, from the mid-1950s onward, as a manufacturing industry in Latin America. Chapters 4 to 7 indicated the changes that occurred in the structure of the Argentinian, Chilean, and Mexican automotive industries, mainly during the 1960s, as a result of changing demand and supply conditions. These led to the elimination of the majority of the locally owned firms in the industry as a result of the financial and technological superiority of the foreign subsidiaries against which they were obliged to compete.

Nevertheless, despite this increase in concentration, the automotive industry in the Latin American countries studied had far more fragmented markets than those typically found in the developed countries. Moreover, since the industry had become almost entirely dominated by foreign subsidiaries, further concentration depended on developments in the international industry rather than on developments within the Latin American countries themselves. The consequences of this pattern of development were analyzed in Chapter 8 in terms of two interrelated factors, the structure of the industry and the role played by the multinational corporations.

It was seen in Chapters 2 and 3 that the structure of the Latin American automotive industry was partly a consequence of the nature of international competition in the industry, which led to a fragmentation of the market as a result of the entry of a number of foreign firms and the unwillingness or inability of host governments to limit their number. This has led to low volumes of output for each firm and hence high costs because of the failure to take advantage of scale economies. This and other factors, such as low capacity utilization, the restrictive practices of international firms, and the lack of price competition, have tended to lead to high prices, thus restricting the domestic market to the upper income groups and making exports uncompetitive.

At the same time, there has been a continued outflow of foreign exchange in the form of profits and royalty payments and to pay for imports of capital goods, even where, as in Argentina, high levels of domestic content have been attained, because of the domination of the industry by foreign firms. As well as continuing to impose considerable foreign exchange costs on the local economy, the industry has failed to make a significant contribution to employment creation as was once hoped.

Finally, in Chapter 9, the policies pursued by the Argentinian, Chilean, and Mexican governments were discussed and compared with those practiced in other countries, suggesting that the major defect of the policies employed for the promotion of the automotive industry was not an excessive inward orientation, but an excessive openness to foreign capital.

Although it has been pointed out, both in the introduction and within the text, that this is an industry study, and as such subject to certain limitations, it is not the case that the automotive industry is an isolated instance of a particular form of development in one or two countries, with no readily generalizable features that help understand the process of economic growth. It is not an aberration but rather a specific example of the relationship between Latin America and the world economy. As a result, it is possible to place the industry within a broader framework of dependent industrialization whose main features are discussed by way of conclusion.

THE PATTERN OF DEPENDENT INDUSTRIALIZATION

As discussed in the introduction, import-substituting industrialization in Latin America arose from the breakdown of the traditional pattern of development, or "desarrollo hacia afuera." It occurred at a time when the continent's links with the world economy were weakened, first as a result of the depression and then of the war. In the postwar period these links have been renewed and the pattern has been one of dependent industrialization characterized by considerable inflows of foreign investment and heavy reliance on imports of technology.

The industrialization of the now advanced countries took place under competitive conditions in the classic sense of freedom of entry and exit to and from industries. The Latin American countries have undergone the process under essentially monopolistic conditions, especially with their reintegration into the world economy in the postwar period.[1] By 1961, 57 firms in Argentina accounted for 22.6 percent of manufacturing output, while in Chile, in 1967, 0.6 percent of all firms accounted for 37.9 percent of industrial value added,[2] and in Mexico 0.83 percent of the firms controlled 64.28 percent of industrial production.

The reasons for this high level of concentration basically are twofold and will vary from industry to industry and country to country. First, as seen here, the prior existence of a highly oligopolistic structure at the international level tends to limit the possibilities of competition in the underdeveloped countries. What competition there is among these firms tends to occur in the advanced industrial centers where the bulk of their operations is located.* Second, there are technological factors that have been emphasized by Merhav,[3] deriving from the fact that technical progress in the advanced countries leads to larger and larger plants and that these scales are incompatible with having a number of firms competing in the underdeveloped economy, given the size of the local market. The narrowness of the market is itself a product of the low level of income and its unequal distribution. Finally, these factors are buttressed by government measures tending to create additional barriers to entry (and, incidentally, to exit where support is given to uncompetitive firms), such as import licensing and tariffs.[4]

Intimately associated with this concentration has been a high degree of penetration by foreign capital. The relationship between the two phenomena is by no means simple. As has just been suggested, the presence of foreign capital may in part explain concentration in particular industries.[5] On the other hand, it may be the existence of high levels of concentration and the consequent need for large amounts of capital in certain sectors that give a competitive advantage to foreign firms, leading them to invest locally. Finally, both concentration and foreign investment may be a consequence of a third factor, such as the technology used in particular industries. Whatever the exact nature of the relationship, the point is that both are linked and should be analyzed as complementary features.

---

*There is nothing immutable about this pattern and it is possible to imagine situations where the competition is particularly intense in the periphery.

In Argentina, for example, the participation of foreign firms
in highly concentrated industries is 33.5 percent (in terms of the
value of production) compared to 12 percent in industries of medium
concentration and only 1.8 percent in those with low concentration.[6]
In Chile during the 1960s, 55 out of 81 foreign investments made
under the Estatuto del Inversionista went to produce for monopolistic
or oligopolistic markets. Similarly, in Mexico, a high correlation
was found between foreign ownership and concentration.[7] Any analysis
of the industrial development of peripheral economies must give a
central place to the high degree of both concentration and foreign
participation in the manufacturing sector.

In order to analyze the consequences of the monopolistic nature
of the industrial structure, it is useful to compare two theoretical
cases, the competitive mechanism approximated by the experience
of the now developed countries during their industrialization, and
the oligopolistic mechanism, characteristic of the industrializing
Latin American countries particularly in the postwar period.[8]

In the competitive case, the benefits from increases in productivity are passed on to the consumer in lower prices, since the
temporary profits earned by the entrepreneur who introduces the
new innovation are eroded by competitors who follow suit. If the
new technique is not available to all firms, because, for example,
of technical discontinuities that make it accessible only to large
firms or because innovation is monopolized in some way, cost reductions will only partly be translated into price reductions (if at all).

The gains from increased productivity are then distributed
through higher profits or increased wages. This is the oligopolistic
mechanism. Katz has shown that in Argentina in the period 1935-43
there was a strong relationship between price movements and
changes in productivity, indicating that the situation approximated
the competitive case. In the postwar period, the correlation between
the two variables has declined, as has the elasticity of prices with
respect to productivity changes. In the period 1946-54, differential
changes in industry productivity were distributed partly in relative
price changes and partly in changes in factor payments, while in
the 1955-61 period price changes had lost all importance.[9] The
trend toward the operation of the oligopolistic mechanism in distributing the gains from technical progress correlates with the tendency
for concentration to increase with the reintegration of Argentina into
the world economy after World War II and particularly after the fall
of Perón in 1955.

Another feature of the oligopolistic, as opposed to the competitive, mechanism is the creation of barriers to entry and exit within
an industry. Thus, whereas in the competitive case supply and
demand are brought into long-run equilibrium through entries and

exits, this no longer operates under oligopoly. In this case the burden
of adjustment falls on fluctuations in capacity utilization.[10] This
means a low average level of utilization and considerable fluctuations
over the course of the cycle. In Argentina, for example, capacity
utilization was only 55 percent in the depression of 1963[11] and in
Chile it was estimated even lower at around 50 percent in the 1957
recession.[12]

The rate of accumulation of capital is also affected by the
market structure of the industrial sector, partly through the factors
discussed in the two preceding paragraphs. The existence of excess
capacity in the recession means that firms will not need to invest
when demand begins to expand again. In the developed countries,
the continued competition between oligopolies means that investment
is still important, especially in research and development in order
to discover new techniques and products. In the periphery, however,
competition is less acute and research and development insignificant
since new techniques can be imported at a lower cost, from the point
of view of the individual firm, than the alternative of developing its
own technology. The rate of investment is also limited by the narrowness of the market, which shall be discussed later.[13]

The rate of growth of industrial employment is a function of
both the rate of capital accumulation and the level of productivity.
Put another way, investment has a double effect of providing new
employment through increasing output and displacing labor through
the introduction of new techniques. The overall rate of growth of
employment depends on the balance between these two factors.

A characteristic of the development of the manufacturing
industry in Latin America has been its inability to absorb a sufficient
share of the growing labor force. The share of industrial employment
in nonagricultural employment declined continuously between 1925
and 1960, particularly after World War II.[14] This is accounted for
by two major factors: (1) the displacement of artisan employment
by factory employment where productivity is seven or eight times
greater; [15] (2) the relatively slow growth of factory employment
as a result of the low rate of accumulation and the highly capital-
intensive techniques being incorporated. The reinsertion of Argentina
in the world economy after the fall of Perón led to a significant
reduction in the level of industrial employment as a result of a
relatively low rate of growth combined with the labor-saving nature
of the new techniques introduced and the displacement of labor in
traditional sectors.[16] In the Chilean case the displacement of artisan
employment played an important part in explaining the slow growth
of the labor force in manufacturing.[17] The evidence also suggests
that, as in Argentina, the postwar period saw a new pattern with
increasing capital intensity and less employment creation.[18]

As was mentioned earlier, income distribution and the structure of demand are important factors explaining the pattern of growth of peripheral economies. The distribution of income is not, of course, an exogenous variable at the macroeconomic level. In Latin America, the highly unequal income distribution derives in part from the elastic supply of labor and the highly capital-intensive nature of industrial production that has led to a slow rate of growth of employment and the marginalization of considerable sections of the population. This means that the operation of the oligopolistic mechanism in the industrial sector tends to take the form of distribution of productivity gains via increases in profits rather than increases in wages, that is, productivity increases at a faster rate than real wages.[19] This is reflected in a reduction in the share of labor in the national income. In Chile, for example, the share of labor in manufacturing value added fell from 46.7 percent in 1950 to 36.5 percent in 1968, while in Argentina it fell from 41.3 percent in 1950 to 30.7 percent in 1960-61.[20]

The unequal income distribution conditions the pattern of demand in these countries.* It limits the possibilities of developing a mass market for nondurable consumer goods and leads to the increasing vertical utilization of existing market strata, that is, the high income groups, since it is they that provide the demand for the consumer durables produced by the high technology sectors. The lack of a mass market for these goods, however, means that their dynamic impulse is fairly short-lived. There is a period of rapid growth when local manufacture of the product is initiated, but once upper income groups are saturated, "trickling down" is not sufficient to sustain a strong positive growth rate.[21] The growth of demand for these products can only be maintained by a rapid growth of income for the upper income groups and an increasingly unequal distribution of income.[22] This appears to have been the pattern followed by Mexico in the 1950s and 1960s where the lowest 40 percent of the population was completely excluded from the general increase in national income,[23] and in Brazil, especially after the military coup.[24]

The development of a monopolistic sector within an economy also has an impact on the nonmonopolized sectors that still remain. In the monopolized sectors, factor returns exceed those in other industries.[25] The lack of employment opportunities in this sector leads workers to accept much lower remunerations in the competitive

_____

*Other factors, such as advertising and the extension of consumer credit, are also important in creating the existing pattern of demand, particularly in the case of foreign companies.

sectors, where firms are only able to compete through superexploitation of a relatively unorganized labor force.[26] On the other hand, the concentrated sectors are also privileged in terms of their access to capital.[27] Where the firms involved are foreign, their position is even more favorable.[28] As a result, the competitive sectors have difficulty in finding sources of credit and their expansion is further retarded.

The points suggested so far are a consequence of the monopolistic structure of the industrial sector and apply whether or not there is an important participation of foreign capital in local industry. This structure, however, is itself a consequence of the integration of the underdeveloped countries into the world economy.

Now the more specific consequences of the penetration of these economies by multinational corporations are discussed. The major aspect is the process of deepening dependence set in motion by an inflow of foreign capital. An initial inflow of foreign capital into an import-substituting industry in a peripheral economy at first improves that country's balance of payments, both on current account and on capital account. The subsequent growth of output and repatriation of profits by the foreign subsidiary leads to a reassertion of the original balance of payments problems that led to the encouragement of the initial investment.[29] The foreign subsidiary's profit rate is higher than the rate of growth of the manufacturing sector of the country in which it sets up.* These profits can then be reinvested locally or repatriated to the parent company. In the first case, the reinvestment of the whole of the profit earned will lead to a denationalization of local industry. In the second case, it will lead to a serious balance of payment outflow. In practice, profits are more likely to be distributed between reinvestment and repatriation, so that both problems will appear. The evolution of the pattern of demand discussed above will tend to lead to increasing repatriations and hence to balance of payments problems.[30]

The initial foreign investment has now run its course as a dynamic impulse to the economy, both in terms of a lack of trickle down to lower income groups to provide an expansion of the market and of relieving the initial balance of payments pressure that led to import substitution. As noted in the introduction, the situation is now even worse because the composition of imports has become more rigid since it is consumer goods that have been substituted, and export earnings also have to pay for the outflow of profits, interest, dividend, and royalty payments (see Chapter 1).

---

*This will be true for all but the most pessimistic assumptions concerning profitability and optimistic assumptions concerning growth.

There are two ways out of this dilemma, assuming that nationalization of foreign firms is impossible for political reasons. The
first, and perhaps the easiest, course is to attract foreign capital
into new industries, either through diversification by existing subsidiaries or new inflows of capital. This is attractive since it again
both relieves the balance of payments position and develops a new
leading sector for the economy. However, it only serves to postpone
the problems that will return in an even more acute form once the
dynamic impulse is exhausted. Moreover, the deterioration of the
foreign exchange position following each new inflow of foreign investment makes the initiation of a new cycle of investment more difficult,
since government guarantees of profit repatriations free of restrictions become less and less credible.

The second possible route is through the development of manufacturing exports.[31] In fact, the Latin American countries' exports
of manufactures are still relatively insignificant, at less than 8 percent of the region's total exports, despite the rapid growth rate of
16.7 percent per year between 1960 and 1969.[32] Such exports rarely
have been developed on a permanent basis in new product lines to
countries outside Latin America, and the area can only be considered
a marginal supplier. There is little diversification of these exports
and exports of traditional manufactures have shown little dynamism.[33]
A number of reasons account for the limited development of manufactured exports. It is at least in part a result of the contractual
limitations placed on local producers by foreign parents or technology
suppliers.[34] Foreign subsidiaries that could potentially make large
exports through the sales outlet of the parent company do not do so.[35]

Latin American manufactures also tend to be uncompetitive in
terms of their prices, although international comparisons, of course,
are sensitive to the exchange rate used. In general, the prices of
most goods in most Latin American countries are higher than in the
United States whether the free exchange rate or estimated parity
exchange rate is used.[36] In the text, the various factors responsible
for the high price of vehicles in a number of Latin American countries
have been discussed, and it is only through such studies that a complete picture of the underlying factors can be built up.

It is possible to arrive at some generalizations concerning
high costs and prices from what is known about the general pattern
of industrial development. High costs arise from the restrictive
practices of foreign companies, tying purchases of intermediates
and capital goods, overpricing inputs, and so on. They also arise
from the low volumes of production as a result of small fragmented
markets, which make it impossible to achieve efficient scales of
production, given modern technology, especially in industries such
as petrochemicals and basic chemicals, steelmaking, production of

semifinished copper, aluminum, and pulp and paper.[37] Another contributory cause is the tendency toward underutilization of existing capacity, characteristic of concentrated industries.

The lack of interfirm competition and the operation of the oligopolistic mechanism for distributing productivity gains mean that even when costs are cut, prices tend to remain high. Thus, it appears that the pattern of dependent industrialization, as well as creating a tendency toward the deepening of dependence, also places obstacles in the way of the escape through exports of manufactures.

In this chapter an overview has been attempted of the process of dependent industrialization of which the case of the automotive industry is a particular example. The evidence presented is suggestive rather than representing an empirical verification of a fully worked out model. Obviously, considerably more research is required in order to arrive at a full understanding of the nature of the relationship of Latin America to the world economy in the present period and of the consequences of this relationship for the internal productive structure and its development. Two lines of research would appear to be particularly fruitful in this respect, further studies of individual industries along the lines of this work* and further historical studies of the development of concentration in particular countries, its causes and consequences. We believe that in this work we have shown the importance of seeing the industrial development of peripheral countries in their international context and within a historical perspective.

NOTES

1. See E. Jorge, Industria y Concentración Económica (Buenos Aires: Siglo XXI, 1972), on the constant level of concentration in Argentina between 1935 and 1946; and J. Katz, Production Functions, Foreign Investment and Growth: A Study Based on the Argentine Manufacturing Sector (Amsterdam: North Holland Publishing, 1969), pp. 157-61, on the increase from 1946 to 1961, especially after the fall of Perón. On Chile, see R. Lagos, La Industria en Chile: Antecedentes Estructurales, Universidad de Chile, Instituto de Economía, Publicación 90, 1966, pp. 72-86; and S. Aranda and A. Martinez, "Estructura Económica: Algunas Características Fundamentales," in Centro de Estudios Socioeconómicos (CESO),

---

*Two studies being carried out for D. Phils. at the University of Sussex by Ruth Pearson on the cement industry and Peter West on the tire industry will be of interest in this context.

Chile, Hoy (Santiago: Siglo XXI, 1970) for the increase in concentration since 1937.

2. Katz, op. cit., p. 158; Aranda and Martinez, op. cit., Table 4; Ricardo Cinta G., "Burgesía Nacional y Desarrollo," in El Perfil de México en 1980, vol. 3 (Mexico City: Siglo XXI, 1972), p. 183.

3. M. Merhav, Technological Dependence, Monopoly and Growth (Oxford: Pergamon Press, 1969).

4. See L. J. White, Industrial Organization, Ownership Concentration, and Economic Development: A General Statement, Woodrow Wilson School, Princeton University Development Research Project DP 18, 1971, pp. 10-15.

5. See also O. Caputo and R. Pizarro, "Dependencia e Inversión Extranjera," in CESO, op. cit., pp. 196-201.

6. Consejo Nacional de Desarrollo (CONADE), La Concentración en la Industria Argentina en 1964 (Buenos Aires, 1969), Table 9.

7. For Chile, L. Pacheco, "La Inversión Extranjera y las Corporaciones Internacionales en el Desarrollo Industria Chilena," in Proceso a la Industrialización Chilena, CEPLAN (Santiago: Ediciones Nueva Universidad, 1972), Chap. 6. For Mexico, see F. Fajnzylber and T. Martinez Tarrago, Las Empresas Transnacionales, Expansión a Nivel Mundial y Proyección en la Industria Mexicana (Versión Preliminar)(Mexico, 1975), pp. 311-313.

8. The following analysis is based on P. Sylos-Labini, Oligopoly and Technical Progress (Cambridge, Mass.: Harvard University Press, 1962), Chap. VI.

9. Katz, op. cit., pp. 169-71.

10. See J. Steindl, Maturity and Stagnation in American Capitalism (Oxford: Blackwell, 1952).

11. P. Salama, Le proces de sous développement (Paris: Maspero, 1972).

12. Aranda and Martinez, op. cit., p. 98.

13. See ibid., pp. 84-86, for an analysis of the low rate of accumulation of the private sector in Chile.

14. See Economic Commission for Latin America (ECLA), The Process of Industrial Development in Latin America (E/CN. 12), 1966, p. 36.

15. Ibid., p. 40.

16. See Katz, op. cit., p. 106; and E. Cimillo, E. Gastiazoro, and E. Litschitz, "Acumulación y Centralización del Capital en la Industria Argentina (Paper presented to the Congreso de Economía Política, Buenos Aires, 1971), pp. 41-44.

17. R. Lagos, La Industria en Chile: Antecedentes Estructurales, Universidad de Chile, Instituto de Economía, Publicación 90, 1966, pp. 143-58.

18. Data presented by O. Muñoz, Crecimiento Industrial de Chile 1914-1964 (Universidad de Chile, Instituto de Economía y Planificación, Publicación 105, 1968), Table 5.1 and App. III 3, suggest such a change.

19. See Katz, op. cit., Table 6.2, for evidence of the much more rapid growth of productivity than wages in the period 1954-61.

20. Aranda and Martinez, op. cit., Table 10; and Katz, ibid., Table 2.1.

21. See D. Felix, Beyond Import Substitution: A Latin American Dilemma, Harvard University, Center for International Affairs, Economic Development Report 30, 1966, pp. 33-40, for evidence of the short duration as growth industries of dynamic industries in Argentina compared both to traditional industries and to industries in the United States. Muñoz suggests a similar pattern in Chilean industry. O. Muñoz, "Crecimiento Industrial, Estructura del Consumo y Distribución del Ingreso," in Proceso a la Industrialización Chilena, CEPLAN (Santiago: Ediciones Nueva Universidad, 1972), pp. 14-49.

22. D. L. Johnson, "Industry and Industrialists in Chile" (Ph.D. thesis, Stanford University, 1967), pp. 39-41.

23. C. Furtado, Economic Development of Latin America: A Survey from Colonial Times to the Cuban Revolution, trans. S. Macedo (Cambridge: Cambridge University Press, 1970), p. 64.

24. M. da C. Tavares y José Serra, "Más allá del Estancamiento: Una Discusion Sobre el Estilo de Desarrollo Reciente en Brasil," Revista Latinoamericana de Ciéncias Sociales, nos. 1-2 (1971): 2-38.

25. Sylos-Labini, op. cit., pp. 108-11.

26. See the analysis of the Argentinian case in Cimillo et al., op. cit., pp. 21-22; and of Mexico in Victor M. Durand Ponte, "México: Dependencia o Independencia en 1980," in El Perfil de México en 1980, vol. 3 (Mexico City: Siglo XXI, 1972), pp. 237-42.

27. On the concentration of credit in Chile, see Aranda and Martinez, op. cit., p. 73; on Mexico, see Durand Ponte, op. cit., pp. 242-44; on Argentina, see Feldman and Izcovich, "Estructura Financiera y Concentración Bancaria," Económica (January-April 1971): 43-73.

28. Seventy-five percent of bank credit in Peru and 50 percent in Mexico go to foreign firms. Information provided by C. Vaitsos, personal communication, 1973. See also Daniel Chudnovsky, Empresas Multinacionales y Ganancias Monopólicas (Buenos Aires: Siglo XXI, 1975) on the financial behavior of firms in Colombia.

29. This model is fully worked out in G. Lee, "An Assimilating Imperialism," Journal of Contemporary Asia, 1972.

30. This problem has been discussed in the Australian context by E. T. Penrose, "Foreign Investment and the Growth of the Firm," Economic Journal 66 (1956): 220-35.

31. See H. W. Arndt, "Overseas Borrowing—The New Model," Economic Record 33 (1957): 247-61.

32. ECLA, "Trade in Manufactures and Semi-Manufactures," Economic Bulletin for Latin America 27 (1972): 41-64.

33. See ibid. for these and other weaknesses.

34. United Nations Conference on Trade and Development (UNCTAD), Major Issues Arising from the Transfer of Technology to Developing Countries, UNCTAD, TD/B/AC 11/10 (1972), pp. 30-34.

35. F. Fajnzylber, Estrategia Industrial y Empresas Internacionales: Posición Relativa de América Latina y Brasil, ECLA, UN E/CN 121 12/ (1970), pp. 167-83.

36. ECLA, Process of Industrial Development, op. cit.

37. "Industrial Development in Latin America," Economic Bulletin for Latin America 14 (1969).

The concept of economies of scale in production has played an important part in Chapter 2. In this appendix, the key theoretical aspects are briefly analyzed and the various empirical estimates of scale economies in the automotive industry discussed and an attempt made to reconcile them.

The pure form of economies of scale is a static downward sloping long-run average cost curve. It is static because it applies to plants of different size at a given moment in time. The sources of decreasing costs have received considerable attention in the literature, the main ones being indivisibilities of initial fixed costs; economies of massed resources, for example, reducing the need for stocks; greater specialization of labor, economies of increased dimensions, for example, the 0.6 rule; and economies from specialization of plant.[1]

In terms of the argument of the text, it is of interest to know not only the level at which all scale economies are exhausted but also the slope of the long-run average cost curve at smaller volumes of output. In terms of Figure A.1, economies of scale are much more significant in industry I than in industry II, and it would be misleading to classify them in the same way because in both cases minimum costs are attained at an output Q'. Estimates of economies of scale, unfortunately, do not often give the shape of the cost curve over a large range of output. In practice, however, most studies distinguish between the minimum cost output and an output after which reductions in costs tend to be small.

FIGURE A.1

Economies of Scale with Different Cost Curves

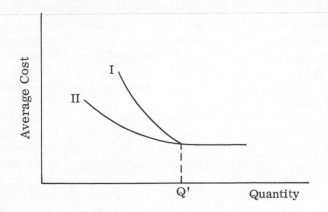

Source: Compiled by the author.

It is important also to note that the average cost curve is not only a technological relationship but also an economic one, since it can only be constructed on the basis of some set of factor prices. This may not be very important in considering economies of scale in various developed countries but it means that the relationships found in advanced countries cannot necessarily be held to apply in underdeveloped countries.

Economies of scale at the industry level have been measured by a number of different techniques. One approach is to use historical data of costs and output in order to construct unit cost curves. However, in an economy where technology, factor prices, and capacity utilization are all changing over time, the curves constructed in this way do not indicate economies of scale as defined above. At best, even if adjustments were made to take account of changes in factor prices and capacity utilization, the figures would indicate the combined effects of static economies of scale, dynamic economies (that is, learning by doing), and technical progress.

Similar objections arise if one attempts to use cross-section comparisons between firms with different levels of output. Again, cost differences may be the result of plants of different vintages, differences in capacity utilization, or different learning periods. It is unlikely that there will be sufficient plants, within an industry, to control for all these factors.

A third approach is to use some measure of the typical size of firm as an indicator of the economic scale of production, but again this says little about economies of scale at a given moment in time, nor is it necessarily the case that existing firms have exhausted all the economies of scale within an industry.

The fourth approach suffers in comparison to the others in that it is not based on actual cost and output figures. This involves estimates made by firms themselves or estimates from engineering and economic data of costs of production at different levels of output. It is a more satisfactory method than any of the others, however, since it does refer to the theoretical concept of scale economies, that is, changes in costs that accompany changes in output, other things remaining constant.[2] All the estimates discussed below are based on this method.

The manufacture of a motor vehicle is, as has often been said, an extremely complex operation. For a small car it involves the use of some 2,500 parts and a wide variety of raw materials, including steel, cast iron, rubber, wood, leather, glass, and textiles. The operation can be divided into four main processes, some or all of which may be performed by the terminal manufacturer depending on the degree of verticle integration of the industry and the particular firm concerned. The basic processes are assembly, machining, casting and forging, and pressing.

Casting involves pouring molten metal, usually iron, into a mold and allowing it to cool and solidify, while forging consists of pounding hot (but not molten) steel into shape. The most important castings used in car production are the engine block and cylinder heads, while forgings include the axle and crankshafts. Not all terminal manufacturers have their own foundry and forge, some preferring to buy castings and forgings from outside suppliers or even from other terminal manufacturers. Neither casting nor forging is usually sufficient to produce parts to the fine tolerances required for motor manufacture and, therefore, they must be machined, that is, milled, drilled, cut, bored, honed, and finished. Most of the internal metal parts of a car are formed by either casting or forging followed by machining. The exterior body parts are made by pressing. This involves the use of a large number of presses of various sizes to stamp out sheet metal to form body panels and smaller metal parts. To do this, a wide variety of dies must be used, which are different for different models.

The assembly process can be subdivided into a number of stages. Some components such as dynamos, carburetors, starter motors, and clutches are bought from outside the firm in their assembled form. Other parts, however, have to be put together to form subassemblies like engines, gear boxes, and bodies. The bodies have to pass through a paint shop to be painted and dried before the stage of final assembly when the body is dropped on the rear axle and springs and the various subassemblies and components are incorporated.

Numerous estimates have been made of the economies of scale in the automotive industry during the postwar period; therefore, no new research in this area was done. Table A.1 summarizes the findings of a number of these studies regarding the volumes of production at which a rather arbitrarily defined range of low average cost begins and at which economies of scale are exhausted, both in assembly and in fully integrated operations. The data indicate a range of estimates from 62,000 to 300,000 for assembly and 360,000 to 2,000,000 for integrated production as the level at which costs are minimized, and from 25,000 to 220,000 and 180,000 to 400,000, respectively, as the beginning of low cost production.

In order to go behind these figures and discover why they differ so considerably, as well as to find out which are the most accurate estimates, it is necessary to look at each of the four processes separately. The studies by White, Rhys, Pratten, Maxcy and Silberston, and Maxcy[3] are used for this purpose since they all give data on the minimum cost scale of production in each process. It should be remembered, however, that they refer to different dates and countries, so that some variations will naturally be expected.

TABLE A.1

Estimates of Economies of Scale in the Automotive Industry

Author	Year	Country	Beginning of Range of Low Average Cost		Full Utilization of Scale Economies	
			Assembly	Integrated	Assembly	Integrated
Bain[a]	1954	United States	60,000	300,000	180,000	600,000
Maxcy and Silberston[b]	1954	United Kingdom	60,000	400,000	100,000	1,000,000
Kaiser[c]	1955	United States		300,000	62,000	
Romney[d]	1958	United States		180- to 220,000		360- to 440,000
White[e]	1967	United States	100,000	200,000	200,000	400,000
Jurgensen and Berg[f]	1967	European Economic Community	25,000	200,000	50,000	500,000
Rhys[g]	1971	United Kingdom		200,000	200,000	2,000,000
Sicard[h]	1970	UDC	50,000		200,000	
Pratten[i]	1971	United Kingdom	220,000	250,000	300,000	1,000,000

Sources: a, b, c, d, and f quoted from H. Jurgensen and H. Berg, Konzentration und Wettbewert im Gemeinsamen Markt: Das Beispeil der Automobilindustrie (Vandenhoeck & Ruprecht, Gottingen, 1968).

  eL. J. White, The Automobile Industry since 1945 (Cambridge: Harvard University Press, 1971), p. 39.

  gD. G. Rhys, The Motor Industry (London: Butterworth, 1972), pp. 280–95.

  hC. Sicard, Les Relations Cout-volume dans l'industrie Automobile (UNIDO 1970), p. 4.

  iC. Pratten, Economies of Scale in Manufacturing Industry (Cambridge: Cambridge University Press, 1971), pp. 132–49.

All the authors are agreed that the minimum scale is relatively low in casting and forging. Maxcy and Silberston put it as low as 100,000 units per year, although the later studies suggest that it has doubled since the mid-1950s when they wrote. A similar trend appears to have occurred in assembly where both Maxcy and Silberston in Britain and Maxcy in Australia put the optimum around 100,000, while White and Rhys give estimates of 200,000 and Pratten even higher. The main factor underlying this increase has been the introduction of more automated tools, such as automatic welders, and the use of electronic controls. The latter has reduced the costs of producing a variety of models on a single assembly line, which, even when Maxcy and Silberston were writing, was "not the costly headache in assembly that it is in machining or pressing, although frequent changeover must reduce efficiency to some extent."[4] One British manufacturer estimated that putting a mix of models on a line reduced its capacity by 8 percent.[5]

The picture in the case of machining is not so clear. White, Pratten, and Maxcy put the optimum capacity between 250,000 and 300,000 a year. Rhys claims, however, that the optimum for engine blocks, gear boxes, and transmissions is around 1 million, but that British firms tend to use cheaper, more flexible equipment with a capacity between 250,000 and 350,000. This is difficult to reconcile with White's data for the United States, however. Finally, Maxcy and Silberston estimated that costs would fall to an output of 500,000, but since their publication, the flexibility of engine lines has increased and economies of scale have been reduced by equipment that permits the machining of engines with a varying number of cylinders and by the use of shell molding techniques that make for more accurate castings, thus reducing the machining required.[6]

All the studies concerned are agreed that the process in which scale economies are most important is pressing, and that it is this process that sets the optimum for integrated car production. Unfortunately, it is also for this stage that the various estimates differ most. As was pointed out above, there are two aspects to the stamping process as far as economies of scale are concerned. One is the optimum use of the presses and the other is the wear and tear of the dies used in the presses to stamp out parts. Only two of these studies distinguish between the maximum annual output of the presses and the length of life of the dies, but they are those of White and Rhys, which give the most divergent estimates for overall economies of scale.

Rhys indicates an optimum output for presses of 2 million, while White cites 2.5 million. Rhys estimates that the length of life of dies varies from 250,000 to 4 million units, depending on how deeply the steel has to be drawn. White gives an average length of life of only 400,000 for most dies. Dies, however, can be cycled to give fuller utilization of the expensive presses, so that an output of 2 million cars a year is not required to achieve the optimum scale for presses. The time lost in changing dies is relatively short, only a few hours, and has been reduced to as little as 30 minutes with some of the newer presses.[7] In the case of dies, lower annual volumes of output can be achieved through a longer life of model. The firm that spreads its tooling costs over two years is still at a disadvantage compared to a competitor that changes its dies every year because of the effect on the internal rate of return. It appears that the disadvantage is not great since the dies are not the most important part of a firm's investment. If one admits the possibility of cycling dies and amortizing some of them over a period of more than one year, then it would appear that White's estimate of 400,000 cars a year is not too low as an optimum for stamping operations.

If stamping sets the optimum for integrated operations, then an output of 400,000 would be associated with a duplication of both the assembly line and the machining operations. This points to the important fact that cost curves are not in fact smooth and continuous. Thus, in machining, costs fall to an output of around 250,000, above which two lines are required. Therefore, with a total output of 400,000 produced by two lines operating at 200,000 units each, costs may be slightly higher than at outputs between 200,000 and 250,000. At an output of 400,000, however, the problem is unlikely to be severe.

These calculations refer to the production of one basic model. If the production of a variety of models is considered, then the minimum scale will increase considerably. Pratten's calculations for a firm producing three basic bodies and five basic engines suggest that scale requirements increase almost proportionally with the increase in the number of models produced; that is, his figures seem to suggest that there is little saving from the use of common components in the different models.[8] This may underestimate the true extent of economies of scale for a large firm producing a number of models since large firms can spend more on innovation, obtain fuller utilization of new plant setup, reduce the costs of designing plants, and obtain lower prices from suppliers.

NOTES

1. See E. A. G. Robinson, The Structure of Competitive Industry, rev. ed. (Cambridge: Cambridge University Press, 1958), pp. 10-33; C. Pratten and R. Dean, The Economies of Large-Scale Production in British Industry: An Introductory Study (Cambridge:

270

At the University Press, 1965), pp. 11-20; A. Silberston, "Economies of Scale in Theory and Practice," Economic Journal 82 (1972): 369-91.

2. For a fuller discussion on these points, see R. Sutcliffe, Industry and Underdevelopment (Reading, Mass.: Addison-Wesley, 1971), pp. 198-216.

3. G. Maxcy, "The Motor Industry," in The Economics of Australian Industry ed. A. Hunter (Melbourne: Melbourne University Press, 1963), pp. 494-538.

4. G. Maxcy and A. Silberston, The Motor Industry (London: George Allen and Unwin, 1959), p. 79.

5. C. Pratten, Economies of Scale in Manufacturing Industry (Cambridge: At the University Press, 1971), p. 139.

6. Ibid., p. 138.

7. L. J. White, The Automobile Industry since 1945 (Cambridge: Harvard University Press, 1971), p. 21. Pratten, however, points out that changing dies increases wear and tear. See Pratten, op. cit., p. 135.

8. Pratten, op. cit., pp. 141-42.

TABLE B.1

Licensees and Subsidiaries of Major Automotive Manufacturers, 1970

	Alfa Romeo	AMC	BLMC	Citroen	Chrysler	Fiat	Ford	General Motors
Malta	x	x	x					
Portugal	x		x	x	x	x	x	x
Spain	x		x	x	x	x		
Greece					x			
Madagascar			x	x				
Algeria				x				
Morocco			x	x	x	x	x	x
Tunisia						x	x	
UAR						x		
Ghana								x
Guinea								x
Ivory Coast								
Liberia								
Nigeria			x		x		x	x
Senegal				x				
South Africa	x	x	x	x	x	x	x	x
Uganda			x					
Kenya						x		
Angola								
Iran		x	x	x	x	x		
Israel			x		x		x	
Turkey		x	x		x	x	x	

(continued)

275

(Table B.1 continued)

	Mercedes	Nissan	Peugeot	Renault	Toyota	Volkswagen	Volvo	Total
India			X		X	X		X
Pakistan			X		X	X	X	X
Malaysia	X		X		X	X	X	X
Philippines	X	X	X		X		X	X
Singapore			X				X	X
Thailand					X	X	X	
Korea						X	X	
Indonesia			X		X			X
Vietnam				X				
Taiwan								
Trinidad and Tobago			X					X
Dominican Republic								
Argentina		X		X	X	X	X	X
Brazil	X				X		X	X
Chile			X	X	X	X	X	X
Colombia					X			
Ecuador			X					
Peru		X	X		X	X	X	X
Uruguay	X	X	X		X	X	X	X
Venezuela		X			X	X	X	X
Costa Rica		X	X		X	X		X
El Salvador								
Bolivia								
Mexico		X			X		X	X
Paraguay	X					X		

276

Country	1	2	3	4	5	6	7	
Malta	x							3
Portugal	x	x	x	x	x	x	x	14
Spain				x		x		8
Greece								1
Madagascar	x		x	x				5
Algeria	x			x				2
Morocco				x				8
Tunisia				x				3
UAR	x	x		x	x	x		3
Ghana	x							5
Guinea								1
Ivory Coast				x				1
Liberia								
Nigeria	x		x					6
Senegal								1
South Africa	x	x	x	x	x	x		14
Uganda	x							2
Kenya	x							2
Angola	x					x		2
Iran	x							7
Israel							x	3
Turkey	x			x		x		8
India	x	x						6
Pakistan								5

(continued)

277

(Table B.1 continued)

	Mercedes	Nissan	Peugeot	Renault	Toyota	Volkswagen	Volvo	Total
Malaysia	x		x	x		x		10
Philippines	x	x	x	x	x	x		12
Singapore	x	x		x	x	x		8
Thailand	x	x			x			6
Korea					x			3
Indonesia						x		4
Vietnam								1
Taiwan	x	x						2
Trinidad and Tobago								2
Dominican Republic					x			1
Argentina	x		x	x				9
Brazil	x			x	x	x		7
Chile		x	x	x				9
Colombia				x				2
Ecuador	x							2
Peru		x	x	x	x	x	x	12
Uruguay	x		x	x	x	x		12
Venezuela	x	x		x	x	x		10
Costa Rica		x		x	x	x		9
El Salvador								
Bolivia								
Mexico		x		x		x		7
Paraguay		x				x		4

278

TABLE B.2

Production of Vehicles in Latin America,
1955–73
(thousands of units)

Year	Cars	Commercial Vehicles	Total
1955	29.4	31.5	60.9
1956	23.1	43.6	66.7
1957	32.4	69.8	102.2
1958	46.1	98.1	144.2
1959	68.3	128.7	197.0
1960	117.3	171.9	289.2
1961	183.9	175.8	359.7
1962	219.4	186.3	405.7
1963	233.2	155.3	388.5
1964	309.8	187.6	497.4
1965	352.7	194.1	546.8
1966	390.6	209.6	600.2
1967	411.7	202.3	614.0
1968	451.2	240.6	691.8
1969	585.2	267.0	852.2
1970*	635.9	316.5	952.4
1971*	790.8	332.4	1,123.2
1972*	890.1	354.6	1,244.8
1973*	994.0	484.2	1,478.2

*Excluding Uruguay.

Sources: For 1955–69, Economic Commission for Latin America (ECLA), Perspectivas y Modalidades de Integración Regional de la Industria Automotriz en América Latina, ECLA/DI/DRAFT/92, División de Desarrollo Industrial, 1973, Table I.11; for 1970–73, Asociación de Fábricas de Automotores (ADEFA), Industria Automotriz Argentina (Buenos Aires: ADEFA, 1975).

TABLE B.3

Vehicles in Circulation in Latin America,
1955–72
(thousands of units)

Year	Cars	Commercial Vehicles	Total
1955	1,476.3	1,251.3	2,727.6
1956	1,548.7	1,304.0	2,852.7
1957	1,671.5	1,419.0	3,090.5
1958	1,777.4	1,500.8	3,278.2
1959	1,991.1	1,677.0	3,668.1
1960	2,186.5	1,824.3	4,010.8
1961	2,457.3	1,942.2	4,399.5
1962	2,677.3	2,088.3	4,765.6
1963	3,001.0	2,218.9	5,219.9
1964	3,264.5	2,355.7	5,620.2
1965	3,744.1	2,490.5	6,234.6
1966	4,205.4	2,656.3	6,861.7
1967*	4,669.0	2,807.0	7,476.0*
1968*	5,187.3	3,044.4	8,231.7*
1969	5,852.9	3,291.4	9,144.3
1970	6,595.1	3,612.5	10,207.6
1971	7,390.6	3,842.9	11,233.5
1972	8,252.7	4,201.2	12,453.9

*Includes estimates for some countries.

Sources: For 1955–69, Economic Commission for Latin America (ECLA), Perspectivas y Modalidades de Integración Regional de la Industria Automotriz en América Latina, ECLA/DI/ DRAFT/92, División de Desarrollo Industrial, 1973, Table I.11; for 1970–72, Asociación de Fábricas de Automotores (ADEFA), Industria Automotriz Argentina (Buenos Aires: ADEFA, 1975).

TABLE B.4

Imports of Vehicles to Latin America,
1955–69
(thousands of units)

Year	Cars	Commercial Vehicles	Total
1955	68.4	66.4	134.8
1956	66.8	70.9	137.7
1957	73.8	134.0	207.8
1958	87.1	117.2	204.3
1959	92.9	122.9	215.8
1960	85.4	67.1	152.5
1961	72.9	55.1	128.0
1962	52.6	44.6	97.2
1963	54.5	36.5	91.0
1964	63.4	35.7	99.1
1965	63.8	40.6	104.4
1966	71.6	47.2	118.8
1967	62.8	44.8	107.6
1968	54.8	38.0	92.8
1969	55.2	40.1	95.3

Source: Economic Commission for Latin America (ECLA),
Perspectivas y Modalidades de Integración Regional de la Industria
Automotriz en América Latina, ECLA/DI/DRAFT/92, División
de Desarrollo Industrial, 1973, Table I.11.

TABLE B.5

Gross Domestic Product per Capita and Cars
per 1,000 Inhabitants in 26 Countries,
1958 and 1969

Country	GDP per Capita (dollars)		Cars per 1,000	
	1958	1969	1958	1969
Costa Rica	387	452	11.1	14.7
Ecuador	178	232	1.8	4.0
El Salvador	220	262	7.2	8.2
Nicaragua	258	364	7.0	12.8
Puerto Rico	595	1,622	44.0	185.5
Ceylon	125	148	7.3	6.9
Taiwan	108	292	0.7	2.9
Japan	314	1,510	2.9	67.8
Philippines	198	322	3.0	7.3
Singapore	435	779	37.5	67.2
Iraq	209	311	4.6	6.1
Israel	708	1,484	10.9	44.3
Belgium	1,030	2,079	70.0	199.1
France	1,113	2,402	100.7	231.9
West Germany	931	2,178	57.4	207.8
Italy	528	1,369	28.4	169.8
Netherlands	767	1,974	37.5	171.2
Austria	662	1,436	40.9	151.4
Denmark	1,090	2,417	68.6	208.5
Norway	1,035	2,277	48.9	181.7
Sweden	1,342	2,713	131.0	275.0
Switzerland	1,293	1,647	77.4	206.0
Finland	815	1,737	31.9	136.8
Ireland	477	961	52.0	121.2
Spain	322	808	6.3	60.7
New Zealand	1,290	1,816	210.8	308.2

Source: United Nations, Statistical Yearbooks, 1965 and 1970.

TABLE B.6

Demand for Cars and Commercial Vehicles
in Argentina, 1960-74

	Cars		
Year	Sales from Local Production	Imports	Total
1960	39,844	3,251	43,095
1961	78,911	2,876	81,787
1962	86,084	2,145	88,229
1963	76,352	863	77,215
1964	114,921	544	115,465
1965	134,746	503	135,249
1966	130,256	462	130,718
1967	130,485	460	130,945
1968	132,792	455	133,247
1969	148,746	382	149,131
1970	167,605	211	167,816
1971	193,387	253	193,640
1972	198,403	344	198,747
1973	219,305	128	219,433
1974	204,379	n.a.	
	Commercial Vehicles		
1960	47,879	1,856	49,735
1961	56,015	2,071	58,086
1962	38,363	3,887	42,250
1963	29,814	823	30,637
1964	52,617	742	53,359
1965	56,039	604	56,643
1966	47,118	999	48,117
1967	47,015	1,442	48,457
1968	51,681	630	52,311
1969	61,349	488	61,837
1970	54,840	239	55,079
1971	59,735	388	60,123
1972	63,393	56	63,449
1973	65,995	90	66,085
1974	66,859	n.a.	

Sources: Fiat (unpublished data) and Asociación de Fábricas
de Automotores (ADEFA), 1974 Industria Automotriz Argentina
(Buenos Aires: ADEFA, 1975).

TABLE B.7

Vehicles in Circulation, Argentina, 1951–74

	Cars	Percent Increase	Commercial Vehicles	Percent Increase
1951	329,424		244,878	
1952	336,086	2.0	250,946	2.5
1953	329,272	-2.0	254,640	1.5
1954	312,098	-5.2	251,990	-1.1
1955	336,228	7.7	265,453	5.3
1956	346,895	3.2	277,237	4.4
1957	364,458	5.1	306,524	10.6
1958	389,624	6.9	327,689	6.9
1959	430,754	12.6	357,788	9.1
1960	473,517	9.9	392,019	9.5
1961	534,940	12.9	437,819	11.6
1962	624,328	16.7	485,601	10.9
1963	696,848	11.6	519,291	6.9
1964	805,694	15.6	572,502	10.2
1965	914,578	17.5	573,370	—
1966	1,030,698	12.7	621,121	8.3
1967	1,138,636	10.5	661,115	6.4
1968	1,240,521	8.9	667,718	1.0
1969	1,350,662	8.9	705,600	5.7
1970	1,488,782	10.2	736,202	4.3
1971	1,679,779	12.8	832,091	13.0
1972	1,852,408	10.3	887,641	6.7
1973	2,016,140	8.8	926,814	4.4
1974	2,160,035	7.1	965,868	4.2

Sources: Asociación de Fábricas de Automotores (ADEFA), 1974 Industria Automotriz Argentina (Buenos Aires: ADEFA, 1975); own elaboration.

TABLE B.8

Index of Vehicle Prices, Argentina,
1960-74

Year	Cars	Commercial Vehicles	Total
1960	100.0	100.0	100.0
1961	98.6	98.8	96.0
1962	86.3	88.1	87.1
1963	80.8	78.8	80.1
1964	74.5	73.2	74.0
1965	72.8	74.4	73.4
1966	73.5	79.0	74.9
1967	72.8	79.3	74.7
1968	69.2	80.7	72.9
1969	63.4	75.3	67.3
1970	55.7	66.8	58.7
1971	48.5	58.5	51.2
1972	41.7	52.6	44.9
1973	41.8	53.3	44.8
1974	45.0	57.4	48.5

Source: Asociación de Fábricas de Automotores (ADEFA),
1974 Industria Automotriz Argentina (Buenos Aires: ADEFA, 1975).

TABLE B.9

Production and Imports of Motor Vehicles, Chile, 1960–74

Year	Production			Imports		
	Cars	Commercial Vehicles	Total	Cars	Commercial Vehicles	Total
1960	1,854	463	2,317	4,273	11,609	15,882
1961	2,491	1,448	3,939	3,866	13,628	17,494
1962	5,170	1,445	6,615	2,658	6,434	9,092
1963	6,089	1,850	7,939	2,059	2,670	4,729
1964	6,355	1,442	7,797	8	1,947	1,955
1965	6,171	2,399	8,570	1,833	1,355	3,188
1966	4,434	2,662	7,096	2,320	6,494	8,814
1967	9,552	3,605	13,157	1,580	7,011	8,591
1968	12,756	5,286	18,042	3,843	6,299	10,142
1969	17,105	4,964	22,069	2,500	5,000	7,500
1970	20,684	3,907	24,591	n.a.	n.a.	n.a.
1971	21,250	2,220	23,470	2,250	2,704	4,954
1972	23,470	2,864	26,316	3,478	3,337	6,815
1973	15,794	1,221	17,015	3,702	1,044	4,746

Sources: Comisión Automotriz for production (unpublished data); and Asociación Chilena de Importadores de Automóbiles (ACCIA)(unpublished data) for imports.

TABLE B.10

Vehicles in Circulation, Chile, 1955–72

Year	Units	Commercial Vehicles	Total
1955	48,263	49,906	98,169
1956	52,306	52,302	104,608
1957	53,913	59,247	113,160
1958	53,772	61,731	115,503
1959	56,163	67,464	123,627
1960	57,578	68,753	126,331
1961	58,804	76,230	135,034
1962	72,573	95,361	167,934
1963	83,454	96,748	180,202
1964	89,098	98,869	187,967
1965	97,690	105,380	203,070
1966	108,248	111,488	219,736
1967	115,526	117,310	232,836
1968	130,225	124,335	254,560
1969	149,853	135,648	285,501
1970	176,066	151,817	327,883
1971	193,914	169,240	363,154
1972	216,091	160,446	376,537

Sources: Comisión Automotriz (unpublished data); and
Asociación Chilena de Importadores de Automobiles (ACCIA)(unpublished data).

TABLE B.11

Demand for Cars in Mexico, 1950–73

	Price Index of Vehicles and Accessories[a]	General Price Index[a]	Apparent Consumption of Cars[b]	Cars in Circulation[c]
1950	72.3	72.5	20,013	173,080
1951	79.4	89.9	44,503	209,270
1952	82.0	93.2	34,162	236,975
1953	82.3	91.4	40,058	253,354
1954	100.0	100.0	32,484	273,697
1955	115.6	113.6	35,464	308,097
1956	122.6	118.9	32,109	320,429
1957	131.9	124.0	37,017	365,796
1958	141.3	129.5	38,098	378,886
1959	149.2	131.0	50,230	437,657
1960	150.6	137.5	63,669	483,101
1961	151.0	138.8	56,646	520,691
1962	153.4	141.3	55,265	548,151
1963	154.4	142.1	67,753	617,690
1964	158.3	148.1	85,004	687,787
1965	158.7	150.9	89,829	771,118
1966	167.7	152.8	104,087	812,415

288

Year				
1967	168.3	157.2	107,736	917,374
1968	168.3	160.2	121,951	999,910
1969	168.4	164.3	136,955	1,133,084
1970	168.7	174.1	159,836	1,233,824
1971	168.6	180.6	176,054	1,338,404
1972	169.1	185.7	185,955	1,520,144
1973	174.1	214.9	210,631	1,766,504*

*Estimate.

Sources: [a]Banco de México, S.A., Informe Anual 1970 (Mexico City: 1971), Table 12; Banco de México, S.A., Informe Anual 1974 (Mexico City: 1975), Table 15.

[b]For 1950–54, Nacional Financiera, Informe Anual 1966 (Mexico City: 1967), Table 42; for 1955–65, ECLA, The Demand for Motor Vehicles in Latin America (UNIDO, ID/WG, 76/1, 1970); for 1966–73, AMIA, La Industria Automotriz de Mexico en Cifras, 1973 (Mexico City, 1974), p. 62.

[c]For 1950–70, Secretaría de Industria y Comercio (SIC), Dirección General de Estadística (DGE), Anuario Estadístico de los Estados Unidos Mexicanos, 1970–71 (Mexico City: 1973), Table 12.21. SIC, DGE, Anuario Estadistico de los Estados Unidos Mexicanos 1964–65 (Mexico City: 1967), Table 12.18. SIC, DGE, Anuario Estadistico de los Estados Unidos Mexicanos 1958–59 (Mexico City: 1960), Table 301.

For 1971–73, AMIA, La Industria Automotriz de México en Cifras, 1973 (Mexico City: 1974), p. 15.

TABLE B.12

Growth of Vehicle Production and Gross Fixed Investment, Argentina, 1959–74

	Car Production	Commercial Vehicle Production	Growth Rates (percent)			Ratio Commercial Vehicles/ Investment
			Commercial Vehicles	Invest- ment		
1959	18,290	14,662	—	—		—
1960	40,144	49,194	235.5	51.1		4.6
1961	78,274	57,914	17.7	16.6		1.1
1962	90,648	39,232	-32.3	-9.0		3.6
1963	75,338	29,561	-24.7	-15.3		1.6
1964	114,617	51,866	75.5	11.0		6.9
1965	133,734	60,802	17.2	4.4		3.9
1966	133,812	45,641	-24.9	3.3		—
1967	130,297	45,021	-1.4	5.0		—
1968	127,965	53,011	17.7	12.4		1.4
1969	153,047	65,543	23.6	15.8		1.5
1970	167,000	52,599	-19.7	7.3		—
1971	193,105	60,132	14.3	7.0		2.0
1972	200,885	67,708	12.6	5.5		2.3
1973	219,439	74,303	9.7	-2.1		+
1974	212,088	74,224	-1.1	n.a.		n.a.

+ Increase in numerator accompanying decrease in denominator.
- Decrease in numerator accompanying increase in denominator.

Sources: ADEFA; BCRA data as quoted in Fundación de Investigaciones Económicas Latinoamericanas, Indicadores de Argentina (Buenos Aires) various issues; own elaboration.

TABLE B.13

Market Shares by Firm in the Argentinian Automotive Industry, 1960–73

	1960	1961	1962	1963	1964	1965
Chrysler	4.8	5.4	7.7	7.9	6.3	8.3
Fiat	4.8	8.3	10.9	17.7	14.1	14.8
Ford	13.2	9.9	9.1	8.7	16.1	15.6
General Motors	12.4	9.9	9.3	8.7	11.6	13.0
Industrias Kaiser Argentina	37.2	31.0	30.8	26.4	30.1	29.1
Mercedes–Benz	2.9	2.7	1.8	1.6	1.3	1.6
Siam di Tella	4.6	10.3	5.5	8.1	7.1	6.7
Autoar	1.6	1.8	1.3	0.2	–	–
Cisitalia	–	0.2	0.3	–	–	–
Citroen	1.1	3.1	4.2	3.2	4.2	2.4
Dinborg	0.7	1.2	0.4	–	–	–
DINFIA (IME)[a]	4.1	2.4	2.9	4.0	2.3	1.7
Fábrica de Automotores Utilitarios	0.2	0.1	0.1	0.1	–	–
Goliath Hansa	0.5	0.8	–	–	–	–
IAFA	2.1	3.7	6.8	8.0	1.6	3.4
Industria Automotriz Santa Fe (SAFRAR)[b]	1.0	2.2	3.1	3.3	3.6	2.8
ITA	*	*	–	–	–	–
Isard	1.7	2.9	3.5	2.2	1.4	0.3
Los Cedros[c]	2.7	0.9	0.8	–	–	–
Metalmecánica	3.8	3.3	1.5	0.2	0.1	0.2
Onfre Marimon	*	–	–	–	–	–
Panambi	0.3	–	–	–	–	–
Deca	–	–	–	–	–	–

(continued)

	1966	1967	1968	1969	1970	1971	1972	1973
Chrysler	8.0	7.3	6.8	8.2	6.4	6.7	10.5	9.4
Fiat	20.2	23.3	22.8	22.6	23.1	24.1	23.7	22.7
Ford	17.0	16.3	15.0	16.5	14.0	17.6	18.8	21.2
General Motors	12.0	12.6	12.4	13.9	14.9	12.6	10.1	10.1
Industrias Kaiser Argentina	22.3	21.2	21.0	15.7	14.8	15.3	15.1	15.7
Mercedes-Benz	1.3	1.8	2.3	2.6	3.3	3.2	3.2	2.6
Siam di Tella	5.3	0.9	–	–	–	–	–	–
Autoar	–	–	–	–	–	–	–	–
Cisitalia	–	–	–	–	–	–	–	–
Citroen	3.5	5.2	6.6	7.0	8.3	6.2	6.8	6.0
Dinborg	–	–	–	–	–	–	–	–
DINFIA (IME)a	1.5	2.1	2.8	3.5	3.2	2.8	2.7	2.2
Fábrica de Automotores Utilitarios	–	–	–	–	–	–	–	–
Goliath Hansa	–	–	–	–	–	–	–	–
IAFA	6.1	7.6	9.6	9.4	11.8	11.3	9.0	9.9
Industria Automotriz Santa Fe (SAFRAR)b	2.6	1.6	0.6	0.5	–	–	–	–
ITA	–	–	–	–	–	–	–	–
Isard	–	–	–	–	–	–	–	–
Los Cedrosc	–	–	–	–	–	–	–	–
Metalmecánica	*	–	–	–	–	–	–	–
Onfre Marimon	–	–	–	–	–	–	–	–
Panambi	–	–	–	–	–	0.2	–	–
Deca	–	–	–	*	0.1	0.2	0.1	0.1

*Negligible.
aBecame IME in 1966. bBecame SAFRAR in 1966. cMerged with Isard in 1963.

Sources: Asociación de Fábricas de Automotores (ADEFA), Informe Estadístico, no. 577 (May 31, 1974), p. 2, and own elaboration. Calculated as shares of the volume of output.

TABLE B.14

Market Shares by Firm in the Chilean Automotive Industry, 1962–73

	1962	1963	1964	1965	1966	1967	1968	1969	1970	1971	1972	1973
Ford	10.2	–	–	–	13.2	22.7	14.5	21.3	20.0	0.1	–	–
Fiat	1.2	16.2	6.6	9.2	24.1	8.4	16.3	20.0	18.1	33.1	59.5	47.8
San Cristobal	–	2.1	4.2	3.0	5.6	7.7	12.4	15.6	13.4	17.5	14.1	19.2
General Motors	9.6	12.0	13.7	12.8	7.6	15.2	15.8	11.5	20.4	13.4	–	–
Citroen	21.4	14.3	12.8	10.4	9.0	7.7	8.9	9.3	8.1	18.8	12.2	18.9
Nun y German	6.5	8.6	11.5	8.0	10.7	16.7	9.6	6.5	6.1	1.0	3.5	0.3
Nissan	1.8	–	7.8	8.0	–	–	2.9	4.6	3.7	7.5	2.8	3.3
British Leyland	3.1	8.1	6.3	5.6	–	2.1	4.1	4.6	5.8	8.2	7.6	10.5
Indauto	–	–	2.9	–	4.2	–	–	3.6	4.2	–	–	–
Tecna	1.1	6.5	3.2	4.1	2.4	5.0	0.2	2.4	–	–	–	–
Imcoda	–	0.4	0.8	3.5	0.4	0.7	0.2	0.6	0.4	0.3	0.2	–
Chilemotores	12.0	18.1	11.1	11.2	22.2	12.5	10.7	–	–	–	–	–
Federic	6.9	3.4	4.1	4.6	–	0.5	4.2	–	–	–	–	–
Integrauto	–	–	0.9	0.8	–	0.8	–	–	–	–	–	–
Volvo	3.4	5.4	4.3	10.1	–	–	–	–	–	–	–	–
Socovem	8.2	–	4.2	3.0	–	–	–	–	–	–	–	–
Anglo–am	2.0	–	2.4	2.6	–	–	–	–	–	–	–	–
Wal	–	–	1.7	1.7	–	–	–	–	–	–	–	–
Fisk	2.7	1.6	1.5	1.2	–	–	–	–	–	–	–	–
Divema	0.9	3.3	–	0.2	–	–	–	–	–	–	–	–
Anca Motors	3.8	–	–	–	–	–	–	–	–	–	–	–
Anglo Chilena	3.6	–	–	–	–	–	–	–	–	–	–	–
Cuelfard	1.6	–	–	–	–	–	–	–	–	–	–	–

Dashes indicate no production.

Sources: 1962–69, Gamma Ingenieros Estudio de la Industria Automotriz Chilena (UNIDO ID/WG 76/6, 1970), Table 30; 1970–73, CORFO, División Industria Automotriz (unpublished data). Calculated by multiplying output volumes by average prices.

TABLE B.15

Market Shares by Firm in the Mexican Automotive Industry, 1963–73

	1963	1964	1965	1966	1967	1968	1969	1970	1971	1972	1973
Automex	21.0	21.5	28.9	23.0	23.3	20.0	21.5	20.9	17.2	17.4	18.8
Ford	24.4	26.5	22.0	24.0	20.6	20.9	20.8	20.0	19.8	18.8	17.1
General Motors	22.2	23.1	17.2	20.0	19.2	19.7	16.6	14.2	14.7	14.0	13.4
Nissan	2.5	3.0	1.1	1.2	5.3	5.6	7.8	8.4	8.6	9.4	9.0
VAM	4.8	5.4	6.3	7.0	6.7	7.2	6.7	7.1	6.8	6.5	6.7
Volkswagen	8.2	9.0	13.4	15.2	15.2	15.3	15.6	19.1	23.2	24.6	27.3
DINA	9.2	6.2	6.7	7.9	9.4	8.9	10.0	9.7	9.3	8.9	7.3
International	4.2	3.3	3.2	1.5	0.3	0.3	0.3	0.4	0.4	0.4	0.3
Trailers de Monterrey	–	0.1	*	0.2	0.2	0.2	0.2	0.1	*	*	*
Representaciones Delta	2.3	1.9	1.0	–	–	–	0.5	–	–	–	–
FANASA	–	–	–	–	–	1.0	–	–	–	–	–
Other	1.2	–	–	–	–	–	–	–	–	–	–

*Negligible.

Sources: AMIA Informe Estadistica, no. 73 (January 15, 1972), pp. 1–3; Informe Estadistica, no. 102 (June 15, 1974), pp. 2–4; own elaboration. Calculated as shares of the volume of output.

294

RHYS OWEN JENKINS is a lecturer in the School of Development Studies, University of East Anglia, Norwich, England. At present he is a visiting researcher at the Centro de Investigacion y Docencia Economicas, Mexico, working on multinational corporations and exports of manufactures.

Dr. Jenkins has written articles on the automotive industry in Latin America and the European Economic Community and has worked as a consultant on the transfer of technology for UNCTAD.

Dr. Jenkins holds an M.A. from the University of Cambridge and a D. Phil. from the University of Sussex.

*THE MULTINATIONAL CORPORATION AND
SOCIAL CHANGE
> edited by David E. Apter
> Louis Wolf Goodman

THE NATION-STATE AND TRANSNATIONAL
CORPORATIONS IN CONFLICT: With Special
Reference to Latin America
> edited by Jon P. Gunnemann

MULTINATIONAL PRODUCT STRATEGY: A
Typology for Analysis of Worldwide Product
Innovation and Diffusion
> Georges Leroy

INTERNATIONAL LABOR AND THE MULTI-
NATIONAL ENTERPRISE
> edited by Duane Kujawa

ECONOMIC NATIONALISM IN LATIN AMERICA:
The Quest for Economic Independence
> Shoshana B. Tancer

NATIONAL CONTROL OF FOREIGN BUSINESS ENTRY:
A Survey of Fifteen Countries
> Richard D. Robinson

INTERNATIONAL REGULATION OF MULTI-
NATIONAL CORPORATIONS
> Don Wallace, Jr.

CHRYSLER UK: A Corporation in Transition
> Stephen Young
> Neil Hood

*Also available in paperback as a PSS Student Edition